# London Writing of the 1930s

**Midcentury Modern Writers**
Edited by Professor Maud Ellmann, The University of Chicago

This series contributes to the on-going expansion of Modernist Studies by redirecting attention to midcentury writing (c. 1928–1960). Some of the finest writing of this period resists the taxonomies of academic criticism, especially the so-called 'great divide' between high-brow and popular literature. This series aims to enrich the canon of modernist studies by restoring unjustly neglected writers, groups of writers and forms of writing to the prominence that they deserve.

**Published titles**
*Ivy Compton-Burnett*
Barbara Hardy

*London Writing of the 1930s*
Anna Cottrell

Please find the series website at: www.edinburghuniversitypress. com/series/mcmw

# London Writing of the 1930s

Anna Cottrell

EDINBURGH
University Press

Edinburgh University Press is one of the leading university presses in the UK. We publish academic books and journals in our selected subject areas across the humanities and social sciences, combining cutting-edge scholarship with high editorial and production values to produce academic works of lasting importance. For more information visit our website: edinburghuniversitypress.com

Edinburgh University Press Ltd
The Tun – Holyrood Road,
12(2f) Jackson's Entry,
Edinburgh EH8 8PJ

Typeset in 10.5/13 Adobe Sabon by
IDSUK (DataConnection) Ltd, and
printed and bound in the United States of America

A CIP record for this book is available from the British Library

ISBN 978 1 4744 2564 3 (hardback)
ISBN 978 1 4744 2566 7 (webready PDF)
ISBN 978 1 4744 2565 0 (paperback)
ISBN 978 1 4744 2567 4 (epub)

# Contents

# Acknowledgements

I have written this book with the help and advice of many people and organisations. I particularly would like to thank:

The Harry Ransom Center and the UCL archives for providing me with access to the Patrick Hamilton and George Orwell archival materials; the National Art Library at the Victoria & Albert Museum and the British Library for making researching rare and out-of-print material possible; John-Paul Kernot of the Bill Brandt Archive, James Sandwith, Natasha Cambridge at London Transport Museum, and Brigitte Moral for help with photographs; Jackie Jones and Adela Rauchova at EUP, for a smooth and stress-free process. For reading and commenting on the manuscript in its various incarnations, I am grateful to: Maud Ellmann, Jan Montefiore, Greg Dart, and Michael Sayeau. Special thanks go to Kasia Boddy, who has been there from the beginning. I'd also like to thank Alicia Rix and Urvashi Vashist for conversations about life, literature and writing. Last but not least, a big thanks goes to my husband, Philip Cottrell, for his care and support.

Parts of Chapters 1 and 4 of this book have appeared, in a different form, in *Critical Quarterly* and *Literature & History*.

# Series Editor's Preface

Midcentury Modern Writers opens new vistas in modernist studies by restoring undervalued writers, genres, and literary movements to the twentieth-century literary canon. The reasons for
this critical neglect are manifold, but they include a tenacious
bias in favour of male writers associated with the European
metropolis, especially London and Paris. Even Virginia Woolf
was begrudged a place in the pantheon of 'High Modernism'
until the resurgence of feminism in the 1970s. Meanwhile, other
distinguished women writers of the midcentury, along with their
male contemporaries, have receded from view, overshadowed
by towering figures like Joyce and Eliot.

The purpose of this series is not to topple these figures but to
enrich our sense of the contestation between forms and genres
in the midcentury period, roughly from 1928 (when British
women were finally granted the vote on equal terms with men)
to the 1960s. The traditional modernist canon, comprising a
small band of experimental pioneers, obscures not only the creative wealth and variety of these five decades but even those
features that distinguish modernists from their literary rivals.
A fresh view of the period, undistorted by the fetishisation of
modernism, reveals that the mainstream is often difficult to distinguish from its tributaries; tradition and experiment overlap
in ways that disrupt conventional critical taxonomies and hierarchies. Likewise, highbrow and popular literary forms galvan-
ise each other, despite the so-called 'great divide' that critics
have imposed between them.

Midcentury Modern Writers includes both single-author
studies and wide-ranging thematic and generic surveys of the

period. The authors of these original studies have been selected from established and emergent voices in Anglophone literary studies on the basis of their expertise, inventiveness, and clarity, in the expectation that this series will open up new avenues of investigation for students and their teachers, as well as for specialists in the field. Ultimately, this series strives to change the way we read, teach, and study modern writing in English.

General Editor
Maud Ellmann

# Introduction

This book is about 1930s writing and photographs of London; in particular, it is about the ways in which the decade's writers and image-makers represented the spaces of leisure and home that came to define the capital during the decade. Central London in the 1930s boasted an inclusive and exuberant leisure culture that became central to the period's notions of what it meant to be a Londoner and of how this London identity was shaping modern life. London was by no means the only prominent setting in the 1930s, but it was the one that most closely aligned with some of its most urgent preoccupations – namely class, mass democracy, the changing modes of sociability, and gender.

The central areas of West London are deliberately given priority as settings in the chapters that follow. The women and men whose leisure hours were spent out in the West End and the nearby areas of Soho and Fitzrovia became synonymous in the cultural imagination of the decade with the places they visited or occupied, such as the cinema, the teashop, the café bar and the bedsit. These leisure pursuits were sometimes equated with uncomplicated escapism. Yet, as the readings in this book will demonstrate, this was not the only, or even the dominant, interpretation of such milieus in the period's literature. Instead, insecurity and anxiety colour many literary versions of teashop encounters and nights out at the cinema.

The geographical focus of this book is firmly on central London. It is true that by the mid-1930s suburban Londoners could enjoy metropolitan pleasures such as the cinema and the café locally, significantly reducing the crowds out in the

West End. This study's last chapter does explore the relationship between central London and the suburbs, focusing on representations of domestic spaces. However, a full consideration of the 1930s suburban milieu is beyond the scope of this book. Local and suburban London and its representations have been the subject of several studies of London literature and culture,[1] and the routines of commuting are central to those analyses. I, on the other hand, am interested in the compact culture of central West London where everything is easily reached either on foot or by bus.

On the one hand, the choice of the central West London was prompted by the need to address the numerous parallels between 1930s writing of the West End and the East End fictions of the later nineteenth century. Throughout the book, I look at examples of appropriations by 1930s London writers of nineteenth-century East End fiction and its adaptation to the narratives of West End leisure. On the other hand, the literature of the West End was chosen because it was London's most cosmopolitan area at the time; only in the West End was it possible to write about London as though it were New York; only a Soho café could create a convincing illusion of Paris or Rome in London.[2]

The foreignness of the West End and surrounding areas of London easily translated into cultural anxiety – about Americanisation, mechanisation and feminisation. Not only did the new spaces of leisure, cafés and cinemas aspire to American modernity or French chic, but they were also designed first and foremost for women. T. S. Eliot and Aldous Huxley lamented the pervasiveness of the new 'synthetic' forms of leisure, juxtaposing them with the organic and authentic working-class forms of leisure on the one hand,[3] and with the serious cultural institutions such as the theatre on the other. One of the aims of this book is to examine the gap that existed between the persistent critique of London's spaces of leisure as palaces of vulgar daydreaming and distraction, and the nuanced versions of the same spaces in the literature, art and photographs of the period that present them as sites of self-knowledge and bitter realism.

The effects of modern leisure upon urban minds was extensively theorised throughout the first half of the twentieth century. Distraction became a universal term of disparagement for the presumed inability of the masses to concentrate on anything, especially on serious art. T. S. Eliot's tautological 'distracted from distraction by distraction'[4] in *Four Quartets* is often referred to as exemplary of the presumptions about 'the masses' held by many members of the cultural elite.[5] Much of this thinking about distraction chimed with earlier theories of urban life that emphasised 'sensory overstimulation' – Georg Simmel's 'The Metropolis and Mental Life' (1903) was the most prominent among several others.[6] During the 1930s, however, these theories of overstimulation and oversaturation within the urban field coexisted with different, though no more sympathetic, explanations of typical city-dwellers and their cultural preferences.

The typical Londoner was now frequently represented not as distracted, but as dreamily and passively staring at the artificial luxury designed specifically, it would seem, to imperil his or her ability to think. The idea of the darting, distracted look was replaced with the notion of the thoughtless gaze. Like the distracted look, this thoughtlessness was associated primarily with women, and with the feminisation of culture. The decade's numerous tirades against urban mass culture seem to inevitably rely upon images of idle women – 'glamour girls in seven-&-elevenpenny stockings drinking cocktails on swansdown sofas' in Louis MacNeice's 'Blacklegs',[7] or the gorgeous Hermione in George Orwell's *Keep the Aspidistra Flying* – always 'asleep or half asleep in one of the monstrous armchairs in front of the fire'.[8] At its least sympathetic, the 1930s image of a modern woman involves her dumbly staring in front of herself; whether drunk on cocktails or on films, she observes the surrounding world with a mindless amiability. For some of the period's writers, there no longer appeared to be a difference between this sort of looking and the spaces within which it occurred – Orwell did not always think it necessary to make the distinction between inherent feminine passivity and the influence of the modern artificially created environments. In his article

'Pleasure Spots', published in 1946 but fully relevant to the 1930s, he recycled the famous metaphor of 'the womb' from 'Inside the Whale' (1940), this time applying it to every leisure space from a modern ocean liner to a teashop, places where 'light and temperature are always artificially regulated'.[9]

It should be noted that the spaces discussed in this book were not new in the 1930s – teashops had been around since the 1870s, cinemas since the early 1900s, boarding houses since the mid-nineteenth century, and leisurely streetwalking around the West End had begun with the coming of street lighting in the early 1800s. All of the *mise en scènes* discussed in the chapters that follow had a rich prehistory by the 1930s. However, by the 1930s the novelty of these spaces had been exhausted, and rather than emphasising the opportunities they offered for relaxation and anonymity, they now functioned as settings in which anonymity could only underline a character's sense of isolation.

The same activities that had previously symbolised women's liberation from the constraints of domesticity now demonstrated the opposite – just how little liberty women really had. If 1920s fiction at least occasionally evoked the image of the carefree and rebellious Flapper, young and enjoying city life to the full, 1930s writing made a distinct preference for a different type – a shabby, often ageing woman with a frightened face sitting alone in a café or cinema, on her own through anything but choice.[10]

One of the reasons for the growing prominence of this image of femininity during the decade was its constant identification with thoughtless perception. One might suggest that the novels of Storm Jameson and Patrick Hamilton that put at their centre inarticulate lower-middle-class characters formed a response of sorts to stereotypes of such Londoners cemented in the 1920s. T. S. Eliot's *The Waste Land* (1922) was one text that presented the lower-middle-class look as the opposite of deep contemplation. Thus in the 'The Fire Sermon' section of the poem, the typist sees off her 'young man carbuncular' – 'her brain allows one half-formed thought to pass: / "Well now that's done: and I'm glad it's over."'[11] In an early draft of the poem, Eliot elaborated further on the inner inarticulacy of Londoners, that 'swarming life' characterised by '[k]nowing "neither how to think, nor how to feel"', and '[l]ives only in the awareness of the observing eye'.[12]

For those writing after (and often against) Eliot, the nature and value of lower-middle-class perceptions of London was an important aesthetic and political issue. As Amy Clukey puts it, these are characters to whom the 'deep interiority' that mediates a sensitive observer's interaction with the city is unavailable.[13] In Eliot's version, the tawdry encounter in a London bed-sitting room happens essentially *because* the couple are only semi-aware of the squalor of their lives. *London Writing of the 1930s* focuses on versions of Londoners who were just like Eliot's shop girl, but that, unlike Eliot's, insisted that they were astute in ways that were not cancelled out by their inability to articulate their predicament fully. As will become clear, the skill in rendering subjectivities in this way, via meticulously observed external detail, was systematically dismissed as inferior and amateurish during this period, but it is this very skill that makes for the period's most original writing.

Subdividing interwar literature into decades has not always done its 1930s component favours. At the height of the popularity of 'the Thirties' in the 1980s and 1990s, there was a tendency to focus narrowly on the political orientations of the decade's prominent literary figures, and to suggest that, while the 1920s were mainly about form, the radical 1930s prioritised content, which was sometimes read as an extension of the politics.[14] From the mid-1990s onwards, studies of the period that focused on its lesser-known or neglected writers, most of them women, opened up discussions of the period that moved beyond what Maroula Joannou identified as the 'artificial' 'demarcation between traditional and experimental modes of writing'.[15] More recent overviews of the literary 1930s have incorporated the decade's writing into a wider discussion of modernism after the 1920s, or late modernism, or midcentury modernism, often adopting wider temporal frames of 1918–39, or even 1918–1950. This has been a productive practice, which has helped to dispel the myth of the anti-modernist, reactionist

1930s, or the so-called 'realist turn', a term that has unhelpfully perpetuated a reductive version of realism as traditionalist or somehow opposed to psychological insight.

Bearing these important challenges to the limitations of narrow periodisation in mind, I would argue that zooming in closely on the decade still has it uses. What these uses might be is hinted at intriguingly in Chris Baldick's recent study of the literature of the 1920s. Baldick argues that there is a perceptible difference between the two decades, which he locates in the prominence of 'the documentary impulse to seek out and record the unique sights and sounds of the present day': it was 'as underdeveloped in the Twenties as it was overdeveloped in the Thirties'.[16] I would argue that those sights and sounds were urban – the turn towards the recording of them is a turning, from the late 1920s onwards, towards London as a dominant setting, towards non-intellectual modes of experiencing the city, and towards models for representing such urban experience that were non-literary.

Such turns made sense during the decade that saw many of its literary practitioners express profound dissatisfaction with what and whom novels tended to be about, and with the people who typically wrote them. That fiction – and the novel in particular – needed revitalising, was argued vocally by, among others, the rising star of the London radical literary scene Storm Jameson. In her essay 'Documents' (1937), written for the radical Left-wing journal *Fact*, she offered solutions to the absence in England of true 'socialist literature' – that is, according to Jameson, a literature that would expose the conditions of non-middle-class lives in ways that would compete with the most sophisticated literary fiction. Jameson's most ingenious proposal calls for a literature that would be 'equivalent' to documentary film. 'As the photographer does', she suggests, so the writer must 'keep himself out of the picture while working ceaselessly to present the fact from a striking (poignant, ironic, penetrating, significant) angle. The narrative must be sharp, compressed, concrete. The emotion should spring directly from the fact.'[17] Jameson's search for new forms within the innovations in the visual arts is partly dictated by her disappointment in the literary models already available: either too egotistical (Modernism), or too melodramatic (Naturalism). This was not a unique or new perspective: the call for a literature that would rely on observation rather than overbearing authorial explication had been advocated by many since the mid-nineteenth century, not least by Emile Zola, who in his own manifesto for a new fiction, 'Le Roman experimental' (1861), advocated that the writer become an 'observer' who 'puts down purely and simply the phenomena he has before his eyes . . . He ought to be the photographer of phenomena.'[18] Jameson's round condemnation of the Naturalists' 'tupenny-ha'penny dramas' came several years after the publication of her own thoroughly Zolaesque novel *A Day Off* (1933). Zola is the often-rejected but constant presence in the fictions of several London writers whose work is central to this book, and Jameson typifies the habitual embarrassment this writer's influence seems to have provoked in the generation of writers who tried to make it in London from the late 1920s onwards. Yet her references to photography and documentary film are more than an unreconstructed borrowing or paraphrasing of Zola; for Zola, comparing the writer to the photographer was purely metaphoric – for Jameson, this comparison acquires a new force. Galvanising Jameson's manifesto for a new literature is a fundamental doubt that literature really is superior to the non-verbal arts, and the hope that, even if the writer must still work with words, rather than camera angles, the novel may learn to *think* differently, in terms of its subject's experiences, rather than within the closed circuit of the writer's mind. In a 1929 lecture, 'The Georgian Novel and Mr Robinson', she had made her point even more clearly, praising Ford Madox Ford's tetralogy *Parade's End* (1924–8) as a series of novels in which we see '*by means of*' the character.[19]

There is another, and equally important, aspect of Jameson's essay that makes it thoroughly representative of the period's preoccupations and anxieties: she advocates a self-conscious and forceful distancing of the new literary mode she advocates from journalism. 'No writer is satisfied to write journalism, nor is this what is wanted', she asserts.[20] Journalism's objectivity is crude – and, to extend Jameson's visual metaphors, blind. Jameson takes a particular issue with 'ghastly' journalistic reports of poverty, which, according to 'Documents', dehumanise their subjects by depriving us of vital sensory realities of their social condition: 'We do not *see* the woman stripping the filthy, bug-ridden wall-paper from the thin wall of her attic.'[21] Photography and documentary film, then, serve up the facts in a way that enables such crucial seeing, and that allows facts to become literary without losing any of their objective force. For Jameson, as for many in the 1930s, photography still carried connotations of a detached, unassailable objectivity, an association she balances uneasily with the need for aesthetic agency or 'angles' – the subjective component that elevates art above the confidently dismissed 'mere journalism'.

Many of the writers this book considers started out as 'mere journalists' – and many, in fact, had to continue supplementing their income with journalism long after their literary careers were launched. Betty Miller and Norah Hoult both wrote for newspapers, with Hoult reviewing theatre productions and fiction for a number of Irish and British periodicals through-out the 1930s; Betty Miller studied journalism at University College London, and George Orwell wrote reviews and essays throughout his career. There were several reasons, beyond writers' financial needs, why the lines between literary and journalistic practices were so often blurred during this decade. The growing political commitment of many writers, especially from the mid-1930s onwards, was one;[22] the other was the fact that fiction and journalism often turned to the same subject matter – daily life in the modern city. At this time, the lower middle class and their milieus became synonymous with modern London – and, by extension, with the newly encroaching representational modes: the journalism that now constantly availed itself of images, and the countless novels that made London its settings and, as it seemed to the more sceptical, barely rose above the journalism in quality. It is worth looking into such insults in more depth: they referred in intriguing ways to several aspects of the period's representations of the urban that do indeed share preoccupations with photographic and journalistic practices, even if the conclusion of such critical exploration was often that such intermingling of modes could only signal a fundamental misunderstanding of the purposes and rules of literary art.

## Descriptive Fictions

In a review of 'new novels' for the *New Statesman* in 1937, V. S. Pritchett wrote of George Buchanan's London-set novel *Rose Forbes* that 'a lot of it is very adroit camera work, an album of small, clear pictures . . . and the pictures are the unremarkable ones that a very ordinary woman would have taken'.[23] That taking photographs here is equated with an unremarkable, de-individualised, female observer whose only distinguishing feature is that she is not just ordinary, but 'very' ordinary, attests to just how mundane an activity picture-taking had become by the late 1930s. Rapid technological innovation in the construction of photographic equipment during the first decades of the twentieth century made basic handheld cameras easy to use and affordable for most after the First World War. The popular Kodak handheld 'Brownie' cameras, for instance, became so cheap after 1918 that nearly anyone could afford one.[24] This wide availability of increasingly sophisticated cameras finally democratised the process Michael North has described as 'the habit of seeing photographically'. According to North, 'certain oddities of the camera, especially its tendency to frame particular points of view and to isolate one moment from another, have become second nature for human observers as well'.[25] This transformation of ordinary vision in turn triggered a shift in the notions of the processes involved in representation: 'If mere seeing can be thought of as in part representational, then the slightest act of attention is sufficient to make the artfulness of the ordinary apparent.'[26]

Predictably, the nearly universal access to such effortless artfulness worried those who perceived a correlation between an increase in the number of amateur photographers and that of upstart writers. That the novel was now somehow about seeing rather than knowing became a critical commonplace; novels seemed to be written increasingly by people who habitually relied on the conveniences of photographic framing – and on the similarly careless and amateurish habits of noting or jotting things down, *à la* a modern reporter. To the critics unsympathetic to the proliferation of London-set fiction during this period, fiction increasingly seemed like something anyone 'with eyes, ears, and pens and not much else' could write.[27]

Among those disappointed by the combination of deftness in recording London's ubiquitous settings with the choice of unremarkable characters was George Orwell. In the role of a reviewer for *New English Weekly*, Orwell elaborated on what he perceived to be a causal link between urban subject matter and a lack of literary merit in a damningly lukewarm assessment of Patrick Hamilton's trilogy *Twenty Thousand Streets under the Sky* (1935):

> He has set out, sincerely enough, to write a novel about 'real life', but with the Priestleyan assumption that 'real life' means lower-middle-class life in a large town and that if you pack into your novel, say, fifty-three descriptions of tea in a Lyons Corner House, you have done the trick.[28]

The choice of characters appears to be the main cause of this slipping into boring descriptiveness; presumably, a novel like one of Hamilton's is oversaturated with descriptions of teashops because the characters are too uninteresting, too lower middle class and too unreflective to warrant a sustained psychological examination. Eight hundred pages have been wasted, in Orwell's view, on 'the not very complicated relations between a literary young man bartender, a goodhearted barmaid who loves the bartender in vain, and a worthless little prostitute who does the bartender out of his money'.[29] The contempt here is directed not so much at the London settings Hamilton had chosen – Orwell himself would offer descriptions of pubs and teashops in *Keep the Aspidistra Flying* (1936) – but at the characters that inhabit them. One might as well cram a novel with descriptions of teashops when the human material is so thin.

Descriptive writing had attracted fierce criticism long before Orwell and Priestley complained about London novels in the 1930s; as early as 1858 R. H. Hutton claimed that women in particular opt for the realist literary form due to the 'main deficiency of feminine genius', which 'can observe, "recombine", "delineate", but cannot analyse or reason'.[30] Foreignness was an equally popular reason given for a writer's – or painter's – preference for formless description over coherence or 'synthesis'.[31] By the time Georg Lukács was lambasting what he termed 'formalism' – that is, Naturalism and Modernism[32] – as empty description, he had only his Marxist persuasion to add to the already long tradition of critiquing authors who offered too much or the wrong kind of description. In an essay titled 'Narrate or Describe?' (1936), Lukács argued for a distinction between the (good) realist detail provided by Tolstoy and Balzac, and the (bad) 'tableaux' of Zola and Flaubert. Lukács took issue especially with the tendency of Naturalist prose to focus excessively on passive observation rather than action. While in Balzac and Tolstoy 'we experience events which are inherently significant because of the direct involvement of the characters', in Zola and Flaubert, he argues, 'the characters are merely spectators' of 'tableaux', which in turn position readers as mere 'observers'.[33] The novelist's job, according to Lukács, was to subordinate external detail to the action of the plot – and, by extension, to the complex social and ideological fabric into which the novel's multiple lives are intricately woven. Tolstoy and Balzac pass the test, but no one writing in the twentieth century.

Lukács's criticism of descriptive detail was particularly forceful, but by no means unique to the period. In the same year that saw the publication of 'Narrate or Describe?', the critic and novelist Philip Henderson dismissed John Dos Passos's *Manhattan Transfer* (1924) and its 'detailed realism' while praising John Sommerfield's *May Day* (1936) for 'mak[ing] a synthesis of the apparently chaotic life of London by relating its many-sidedness to the unifying principle of the class struggle'.[34] Synthesis was routinely extolled as a virtue, while collecting fragments denounced as apolitical and lazy. Raymond Mortimer, reviewing *Livingstones* (1933), a London-set novel by a minor 1930s author Derrick Leon, disapproved of its tendency to settle for the '*tranche de vie*', while conceding that it 'does just rise above photography' because 'of its critical implications about present society'.[35]

The novels that form the primary focus of this book tend to prefer slices of life over sweeping panoramas, and accumulations of detail over narrative omniscience and the social 'synthesis' that is its *modus operandi*. Despite the numerous reassessments of 1930s fiction in recent decades, the meanings assigned to the details of urban life are still predominantly sociological. Although in many other areas of literary scholarship the distinctions between realism and the avant-garde, outwardness and inwardness, are no longer seen as absolute,[36] where the urban novel is concerned, the convenient divisions have endured. In recent studies, the interwar London novel has been discussed in relation to very specific contexts of the period's political developments – the threat of fascism, the commitment of many British intellectuals to socialism, and London's role as the meeting point of these tensions. In a recent collection of essays on twentieth-century literary London, Chiara Briganti writes that, in Storm Jameson's trilogy *The Mirror in Darkness*, the setting 'is increasingly the London of the clash of classes that culminates in the collapse of the General Strike' and in which the protagonist Hervey's 'voice is ultimately drowned out by those of a vast number of characters'.[37] And Phyllis Lassner argues that, in Jameson's fiction, 'it is the accretion of historical events from the war through the General Strike and Great Depression that overwhelms the fantasied or Freudian privileges of a private self'.[38]

Typically, such readings of metropolitan fiction rely on panoramic set pieces within the novels that also contain small-scale scenes of quotidian experience. Both are equally important, but this is rarely acknowledged in critical readings of London fiction. Recently, Leo Mellor has written that twentieth-century writers found 'ways of successfully experiencing and representing versions of London' in 'grasping essences, details, codes – or shuddering in awe of its totality'.[39] I would argue that the two modes are best read as co-dependent, especially in the work of 1930s authors who aimed at relating the personal experiences of Londoners to the larger social developments in the city. It may be useful to extend Pritchett's metaphor of a typical London novel as 'an album of small and clear pictures': such an album includes both close-up scenes of leisure and panoramic views of the vast movements of city-dwellers at a time of social and economic upheaval. The individual and the collective are both given space in London fiction of the period, but the order of importance that privileges the collective and the panoramic has been imposed artificially.

Lukács's map of European fiction proves useful in tracing the literary lineage of this kind of fiction: the 'photographic' London novel, like the French Naturalism of the 1880s, grew out of a belief that meticulous observation *could* amount to psychological insight, especially where marginalised or precarious lives were concerned. And like their Naturalist predecessors, the tales such novels told were often unhappy and anxious ones, about city lives that were circuitous and that rarely added up to anything but the sum of so many nights and days spent moving on from one London interior to the next.

## London Naturalism

London writing of the 1930s abounds in tales of sordidness and decline, and in scenes of debased courtship and mechanical 'romance' – in ugly arguments, abortions and graphic portrayals of physical and emotional breakdown. Authors such as Patrick Hamilton, Storm Jameson and Jean Rhys pursued a different strand of urban literature from the one that celebrated the pleasures of leisurely streetwalking, or the liberating possibilities of living on one's own. Instead, they turned towards tales of city life that emphasise stasis, impasse and social and sexual ruin. And the character that became the embodiment of this aesthetic was the struggling shop girl or film extra, the ageing dance hostess and the unmoored suburban housewife beginning a new life in London following a divorce or the death of her husband.

David Baguley, in his study of Naturalist fiction, introduces an important qualification to the classic definition of Naturalism as a genre dominated by tales of decline and death. Baguley identifies another strain of Naturalism, which is characterised by a 'circular scheme . . . a series of aborted adventures, of events that never really take place', and conveys 'a view of human life that is problematic, characterised by inertia, lassitude, dejection, disgust or resignation'.[40] He particularly stresses the prominence of 'sordid' dramas of 'routine sexuality': 'Love remains the supreme illusion that Naturalist literature submits to its "cruel analysis", reducing it to physiological urgings and obstetric consequences, dwelling upon the vast gulf of selfishness and deception that separates lovers.'[41] One way to read the novels I discuss is as profoundly anti-romantic variations on the motif of the chance meeting in a big city. Narratives of romance spontaneously generated by the contingent nature of the city are replaced by tales of mechanical and exploitative emulations of love. For an era supposedly steeped in Hollywood dreams of sugar-coated romance, the 1930s produced a great number of novels in which heterosexual love is stripped of all glamour. Unwanted pregnancies and callous desertions abound, as do reductions of love to prostitution in all but name; in Storm Jameson's *A Day Off*, for instance, the protagonist's last affair begins, tellingly, with a crude offer of a salary of sorts – 'would two pounds a week mean anything to you?'[42] – while Jean Rhys's protagonists are routinely paid off by bored men wishing to disentangle themselves.

It matters to writers of the period where these unromantic encounters happen – the sickening deals between unloving couples are often struck in places that were previously associated with the spontaneity and healing anonymity of city life. Such spaces as the café or cinema were supposed to temporarily distract their patrons from the dullness of routines of home and work, but, in practice, tedious routines and inflexible hierarchies prospered within them. For every description of a single woman enjoying her time off over a cup of tea, there is always, in the period's fiction, one that involves a woman like her being looked over uncharitably by other women or waiters, and who has purchased the cup of tea with her last money. Social and sexual humiliations, not independence and relaxation, dominate accounts of urban sociability during the decade. The typical victim of such misfortunes was a woman with social pretensions and standards, but without any means to long-term economic stability. British fiction of the 1930s very rarely subjected working-class women to the cruel fates that routinely befall shop girls or secretaries. The late-Victorian tales by George Moore, Margaret Harkness or George Gissing that focussed on working-class women ruined by illicit sexual contact with wealthier men came to be replaced with plotlines involving heroines who are no longer subject to the rigid norms of sexual propriety pre-1918, but who have everything to lose in the game of social aspiration. Their movements around the city are far more uncertain than those of their Victorian and Edwardian working-class counterparts who at least possess a sense of belonging to a particular street or part of London. For instance, the period's Soho fictions, discussed in Chapter 2, tend to draw a sharp distinction between the rooted working-class inhabitants and their anxious, peripatetic, socially ambitious counterparts. The working-class characters in the period's London fiction have clear maps of the city, which include areas where they do not go or even despise; in John Sommerfield's *May Day*, the workers' revolution is envisaged as the smashing of windows of the pretty stuccoed houses that his characters know they may never own; by contrast, a petit-bourgeois character from the period is dreamy enough to cling to the fantasy that she may one day, somehow, end up living in one. The lower middle class exist in such dangerously dreamy states in fictions by, among others, Patrick Hamilton, Jean Rhys, Betty Miller and Storm Jameson. The lives they describe are lived on an imaginary cusp of a big change – Hamilton's hapless barmaid Ella in *Twenty Thousand Streets under the Sky* (1935) expects an inheritance, which falls through; Rhys's characters linger outside expensive clothing shops thinking how the right dress might turn around their uncertain lives; and Jameson's numerous 1930s alter egos hope in vain to leave their inauspicious beginnings behind and become writers.

This urban type often found herself on the receiving end of harsh criticism, both in literary representations and cultural commentary; she was routinely accused of being distracted, passive and smug. Her cultural and social pretensions irritated, among others, the usually more tolerant Louis MacNeice, who in a 1938 essay on modern theatre described a matinee West End theatre audience as consisting mainly of lower-middle-class women – 'suburb-dwellers, spinsters, schoolteachers, women secretaries, proprietresses of teashops'. The assumption is that these women go without any real understanding of the high art form they are consuming – '[t]he same instinct leads them which makes many hospital nurses spend all their savings on cosmetics, cigarettes and expensive underclothes'.[43] It is difficult to tell what MacNeice finds more irksome: these women's passive consumerism, or the fact that they are careless with their disposable incomes. One does wonder how many hospital nurses MacNeice had known in order to be able to generalise with such confidence about their tastes in underwear, but the denunciation of the city-dwellers who had desires and interests above their social status is both entirely typical of the period and has a long cultural history going back as far as the early nineteenth century.

The earliest predecessors of this much-maligned figure are, in fact, male. The clerks, suburbanites and Cockneys that entered the fiction and cultural criticism of the 1810s–1820s were subject to much the same ridicule as the lower-middle-class woman of the later nineteenth century. As Greg Dart explains, 'the figure of the Cockney begins to accrue new freight and meaning in the 1810s, fast becoming a symbol for all that was wrong with modern life, not least in his promiscuous straddling of city and suburb, old and new, vulgar and genteel'.[44] The modern woman of the 1930s shares with these earlier figures the unsettling quality of straddling high and low cultures, as well as the perennial accusations of vulgarity. As Geoffrey Crossick points out, the clerk 'was always seen as comically self-important';[45] his pretentiousness and mercantile interest were pointed out as early as the 1860s, uniting descriptions of men in such professions as office work, shopkeeping and journalism. George

Gissing's scathing reference to the 'quarter-educated mob'[46] in 1892 was peculiarly aggressive, but not unrepresentative of the cultural consensus about this figure with expectations, but without the cultural and social pedigree to really hope to bring those expectations to fruition.

This figure acquired a European-wide prominence by the middle of the nineteenth century. In a study of Zola, Susan Harrow links the emergence of the financially precarious, socially ambitious and psychologically unhinged urbanite to the 'process of modernization' that shook Paris in the mid-nineteenth century.[47] Harrow points towards the 'parallel' processes of the Haussmannisation of Paris and the development of the 'entropic' narratives of Zola; the Café Riche episode in Zola's *La Curée* (1871) is shown to be exemplary of these processes. It signals the beginning of Renée Saccard's decline; she is intoxicated by Paris, as it were, and falls into a 'blankly receptive' state, absorbed in an 'empty viewing' of the city around her.[48]

Nineteen-thirties versions of urban women frequently point to similar states of blank receptivity, a mode of perceptual alertness that masks a deep sense of humiliation and constant economic worries, and a knowledge, only partially softened by the access to leisure, that this unmoored and uncertain state was permanent. It would not be accurate, however, to suggest that in London this insecurity was the product of a fundamental societal shift of the kind in which Zola's Parisian had been caught, or that the 1930s were 'transitional', in this respect, any more than any other decade of the first half of the twentieth century. Working women's lives were no harsher in the 1930s than they had been in the 1910s. The unhinged heroine blankly surveying the city around her is already there in Katherine Mansfield's short story 'Pictures' (1917), about a singer who comes down in the world and, finally, allows herself to be picked up by a sleazy man in a Piccadilly café. She also is there in Henry James's 'In the Cage' (1898), in which a dreamy telegraphist lives through a crisis of class-based shame and ambition, experienced as an unrequited infatuation with a wealthy Mayfair resident. There was also, in Mansfield again, the tired hat shop assistant Rosabel, whose miserable evening after work, spent in a tiny bed-sitting room, is brightened by daydreams of a wealthy marriage.[49]

These examples, however, do not amount to a coherent literary trend; it was in the 1930s that this character type came to dominate urban fiction in a way that had not been the case during the previous decades. London literature before 1925 was predominantly concerned with middle-class women and their changing relationship to the city. Nor do 1920s Bright Young Things have much in common with the kind of Londoner this book examines. In this sense, Waugh's *Vile Bodies*, although published in 1930, is a novel of the 1920s; the wild nocturnal pursuits of his characters have little in common with the anxious and often dreary nights out discussed here.

There were several reasons for the sudden rise in the popularity of the lower-middle-class Londoner of small means as a character type, and I would argue that unearthing these reasons requires an approach that takes into account the material history of London on the one hand, and the literary tastes of the writers who made London their setting on the other. The visual and spatial organisation of central London changed rapidly during and immediately after the First World War, as did the appearance of women out in the city's streets. By the late 1920s, there was no longer anything unusual or transgressive about this increased visibility of women in central London, and accounts of women's presence in the West End and Soho increasingly emphasised the city's harsh effects on their minds and bodies, rather than the liberating possibilities of streetwalking or shopping.

References to cracked make-up, swollen veins, glassy eyes and twitching jaws become significantly common – all bodily manifestations of the stresses of city living that were not concealed but made more apparent by the settings in which the lower-middle-class woman was most frequently seen. The motif that recurs again and again in the fiction of the period is of women wishing to hide – in their bedsits or in the darkness of the cinema; feminine visibility is no longer a sign of liberation. Even in scenes that involve dancing (in Soho and West End nightclubs) the emphasis is often on the unnaturalness and stiffness of the activity.

Women in 1930s novels are folded into a Zolaesque aesthetic not because they are undergoing an unprecedented, seismic shift in social attitudes, but because London's spatial arrangements during this time mercilessly expose all the challenges and strains that were part of urban living for people struggling to retain a sense of dignity on very small, often irregular incomes. London's indoor settings, particularly those that were brightly lit, presented these daily struggles and humiliations in newly obvious, lurid ways.

If, as David Baguley suggested, Naturalism is a literature of 'pessimism' 'founded on observation',[50] an aesthetic mode as much as a genre, then I would argue that what happened in 1930s British fiction of London was a turn towards this mode, which had its underpinnings in ways of seeing as much as in historical realities. It is worth remembering at this point that Naturalism emerged partly from intense engagements with the aesthetics of Impressionist painting – and that Naturalism may be closer in its aesthetic aims to Surrealism, abstract art and even Aestheticism, rather than Realism.[51]

The category of the impression and the adjacent concept of the effectively used detail mattered to the French Naturalists, especially to Zola who produced a body of writing on painting. In his endorsement of Edouard Manet's *Olympia* (1863), Zola praised Manet's innovative, anti-realist use of detail: 'Observe the head of the young girl; her lips are two fine pink lines, her eyes are no more than a few black brush strokes. Then, note her bouquet [. . . ]: swathes of pink, of blue, of green. Everything is simplified.'[52] We encounter this type of imaginative detail, which functions beyond the demands of realism, in Zola's fiction. In *L'Assommoir* (1877), the scene where the beleaguered Gervaise Coupeau is forced to prostitute herself for her dinner in the boulevards of Paris is punctured with intense visual detail that, instead of contributing to the verisimilitude of the scene, renders it unreal, as though the participants were no longer human, but objects in a setting. Gervaise is soliciting the streets shoulder to shoulder with multitudes of other women, so many, it seems, that she forgets that they are in any way like herself. We are presented with a tableau, devoid of dialogue and movement. The bawdy Parisian thoroughfare is plunged into a silent semi-darkness: 'They'd stay there for minutes at a time, never stirring, as patient and upright as the meagre little plane trees.'[53]

Gervaise's growing fatigue and hunger effect strange changes in her vision – within a few hours her observations become more and more stylised, no longer registering any human presence, but, rather, uncertain shapes, like the 'dark shifting smudge' of a man she tries to accost, and bizarre accents of colour, such as a grotesque woman in 'a yellow scarf'.[54] The simile 'like plane trees' morphs into a stark metaphor: it is now 'as if the outer boulevards had been planted with women'.[55] And as the perennial, destructive darkness of the Parisian night grows deeper, Gervaise's impressions become more and more fragmented:

> They'd pass into the sudden light of a lamp-post, where their wan, mask-like features would loom into clear view, then they'd vanish once more, reclaimed by the darkness, the white edge of a petticoat swinging as they slipped back into the disturbing, enticing shadows of the pavement.[56]

To whom does this overtly aesthetic visual construction belong, about whose looking are we reading? For David Trotter, for instance, Zola's painterly descriptions, such as Octave Mouret's glance at a pile of linen through an open door in *Pot-Bouille* (1882), 'is there for us, not for him [Mouret]'.[57] Yves Chevrel, on the other hand, in his attempt to establish a 'poetics' of Naturalism, identifies 'one of the major aims of Naturalist novelists' as 'giving the common people access to literary expression'.[58] According to Chevrel's interpretation of Naturalist aesthetic, a visual moment such as the one in *Pot-Bouille* belongs to the character first, the reader second.

Is the elaborate play with colour and detail in the passage from *L'Assommoir* quoted above for our eyes only? Does Gervaise's state of extreme physical and mental distress render her indeed unable to think or feel, as she certainly is towards the end of the scene, walking blindly and desperately through the snow? I would argue that the passage in particular, and Zola's work in general, can only have relevance for twentieth-century writing if this is not the case, if it is Gervaise who sees women as tree-like shapes and notices the edge of the white petticoat absorbed into the darkness of the Parisian night. Her experience is both an extreme and debasing one, and one that uncovers, in a perverse paradox, an imaginative and highly sophisticated aspect of her interiority. The scene both signals the beginning of Gervaise's final decline and re-humanises her by giving us visually arresting glimpses of her experience.

T. J. Clark, in a seminal study of Parisian Impressionism, identified the reasons for the Impressionists' sustained fascination with Parisian milieus, especially those frequented by the semi-respectable working and lower middle classes (to which Gervaise belongs before her life unravels). The petite bourgeoisie, he argued, was particularly valuable to urban artists because they

> appeared in many ways to have no class to speak of, to be excluded from the bourgeoisie and the proletariat and yet to thrive on their lack of belonging. They were the shifters of class society, connoisseurs of its edges and waste lands, and thus they became for a time the alter egos of the avant-garde – ironically treated, of course, laughed at and condescended to, but depended on for a point of insertion into modern life.[59]

This idea of the perceived inhabitability of the lower-middle-class city-dweller's point of view is crucial to the readings of 1930s literature I offer in the chapters that follow. What British fiction of the period attempted, I would argue, is a similar process of 'insertion' into modern life – except that the shadowy milieus it portrays often host extreme experiences of exclusion and humiliation not entirely unlike Zola's account of Gervaise's slide from relative respectability into complete social marginalisation.

This is not to argue that the writing examined in this book should be reclassified as Naturalist or Impressionist. After all, the period's novels neither completely conformed to the rules of Naturalism[60] (with the possible exception of Jean Rhys's novels), nor were they 'Impressionist' in the sense that the novels of Joseph Conrad and Ford Madox Ford may be called Impressionist.[61] The fiction of the 1930s does, however, have a strong affinity with the aesthetic cluster to which these modes – all of them nineteenth-century in origin – belong, and with the art form that absorbed and carried into the twentieth century the ideals and preoccupations of those earlier literary and artistic developments. The urban photography to which the 1930s novel was so often compared concerned itself, in a sustained way, with the same issues of exploring urban milieus and their inhabitants, and practising 'insertions' into their points of view. In particular, it was the genre that is now habitually referred to as 'street photography' that pursued the potentialities of the blended point of view, and of combining 'real' settings with imaginary, implied or even staged psychological effects. Clive Scott has explicitly linked street photographs to Impressionism, suggesting that the two share a sensibility, or a 'psycho-perceptuality'.[62] An even more pertinent definition of the street-photographic mode appears in Sara Blair's recent study of urban photography and the literature of post-1945 Harlem. Blair elucidates the differences between the documentary and the street-photographic aesthetics – a distinction that is also important to the readings of both fiction and photographs offered in this book.

Blair discusses the 'project', shared by photographers and writers working in New York after the Second World War, 'to relocate the meaning of social experience within everyday spaces'.[63] Blair pays particular attention to images in which the camera is used 'not as a tool for "exposure" or "enlightenment" of the conditions that produce it' (the territory of documentary photographs), 'but as an instrument for heightening our experience of its psychic depths and social meanings'.[64] She juxtaposes the documentary aesthetic with the street photographic, discussing the latter's ability to penetrate 'a certain invisibility' which is part of the condition of urban modernity in post-war New York, and which we are able to read in '[Lisette] Model's lone women in cafes', for example. Writing of Ralph Ellison's experiments with photography through the prism of Model's concept of photographic analogy, Blair argues that Ellison's photographs were an attempt to find a 'photographic correlative' for his literary work: 'The aim is neither illustration . . . nor straightforward documentation . . . but rather "analogy" in Model's quite specific sense: a negotiation of the documentary, the fictive, and the experiential as mutually mediating registers.'[65]

The photographs that I read alongside London writing in this book share this street photographic sensibility – they are not straightforwardly documentary images, but they still equate the city with the lived experiences of its citizens. Urban panoramas are discussed here, but in a minor way, as counterparts to images that focus on small urban dramas. And it is in this sense that the London novel of the 1930s may be termed 'photographic' – it is deeply invested in the power of descriptive detail that may elucidate states of 'invisibility', insecurity and alienation that proliferate in the city, but reluctant to make totalising conclusions about its subjects.

## Night and Day

The London night is a recurring and, indeed, predominant setting in the novels discussed in this book, and to a great extent the everyday vision in question is night vision, accompanied and heightened by the other senses. While representations of nocturnal London in the Victorian era have received some critical attention,[66] as has the darkness of London in the Blitz,[67] the literary and visual representations of the London night in the 1930s have been all but absent from critical assessments of 1930s fiction. Yet the decade produced literature, photography and journalism devoted to the metropolitan night in abundance. Representations of London nightlife, and especially of the artificial light that was its constant feature, were central to the period's imaginings of the modern Londoner.

Several of this book's readings rely on the material history of urban lighting in the period. I would argue that the revival of interest in the Naturalist urban tale was linked to the exposing atmospheres created within London's public (and, increasingly, private) spaces by the lighting technologies that became the feature of the nocturnal metropolis after the First World War.[68] Not only do novelists of the period frequently refer to the quality of light within a particular urban setting, but they also transcribe the effects of lighting on what their characters are able to notice. Where the soft glow of Victorian gaslight had been associated with pleasure and promise,[69] the clinical white glare of modern lighting stripped away the seductiveness, making room for less forgiving, closer observations of both the city's mechanisms of sexual exchange and their emotional toll.

The extensive representations of London's spaces of leisure after dark became a decisive criterion in my selection of authors and texts examined in this book. Storm Jameson's novels of the 1930s, especially *A Day Off* (1933) and *Here Comes a Candle* (1938), combine the form of a Naturalist case study with aesthetic depictions of London in which the shaping of urban vision by lighting plays an important role. The visual drama provided by the nocturnal city was crucial to Patrick Hamilton's trilogy *Twenty Thousand Streets under the Sky* (1935) and to Jean Rhys's fiction. In fact, if it was not for the darkness of the London night, which Rhys described as 'greasy and compelling'[70] in *After Leaving Mr Mackenzie* (1930), London – which both Rhys and her characters hate – would not have figured as prominently in her work.

The nocturnal city also dominates the photographic material under discussion in the chapters that follow. Especially where representations of London's West End and the nearby Soho are concerned, photographs of the urban night are crucial to the creation of their identities – and the mythologies that grew around these areas. From Jean Moral's dizzying double-exposure visions of the brightly lit West End to Bill Brandt's 'gritty' Soho concoctions, photographic London of the 1930s is, to a large extent, a city that comes alive at night. As in the case of literary representations of London, French influences played a part in this emphasis on the night; without Brassaï's collection *Paris de nuit* (1932), there would have been no British counterparts, such as John Morrison and Harold Burdekin's *London by Night* (1936) and Brandt's *A Night in London* (1938).

Prose dominates the account of London writing in the present study. While there are references to the poetry of the 1930s, by W. H. Auden, Louis MacNeice and Stevie Smith, its focus is firmly on prose forms and on the relationships between the novelistic, the photographic, and the prosaic and the mundane in daily life. In that sense, the 1930s poetry of MacNeice, especially the London-set *Autumn Journal* (1938), has strong affinities with prose. In a 1938 letter to T. S. Eliot, MacNeice described *Autumn Journal* as a hybrid work combining autobiography, 'rapportage' and 'ethics', and promised writing that 'is direct; anyone could understand it'. He also made an emphasis on the wide range of settings presented in the work – 'Hampshire, Spain . . . & – especially – London'.[71] MacNeice could as well have been introducing a novel written in verse.

All of the texts examined here work with a limited selection of typical London settings, and with situations that are triggered by the spatial and lighting arrangements of London during this period. One way to read this book is as a catalogue of versions of a core selection of scenes that recur throughout 1930s fiction, and many of these scenes are reproduced in different texts, and across different media, with a startling regularity. These become the stock motifs of London fiction and art in the period, and as such they acquire a wider significance than the personal and the quotidian. Or, rather, particular aspects of the personal and the quotidian are chosen as representative of the socio-political realities of the capital.

London was not the only place where the aesthetics of description this book examines were developing. One could have considered, for instance, comparable developments in the interwar literature of New York or Berlin, to give two obvious destinations. Such a broad, inter-city analysis is beyond the scope of this book,[72] the aim of which is partly to uncover what it is that makes London writing in the 1930s distinctly London, as opposed to generally urban. This task has involved incorporating much London writing from the period that is neglected or even completely forgotten. The revision of the canon of what was once referred to as 'the Auden generation' began in the 1990s, when scholars such as Janet Montefiore and Maroula

Joannou first challenged the staggering imbalance in the literary scholarship of the period, from which women writers in particular – and fiction writers more generally – had been excluded almost wholesale.[73] Such an imbalance is no longer the case, with new work on 1930s literature confining many of the myths about 'the Thirties' to scholarly history.[74] My own contribution to this process of revision aids the book's specific emphasis on urban and descriptive aesthetics, and the choice of writers, whether well known or neglected, was dictated by the need for a fuller account of the period's London writing.

Chapter 1 examines 1930s representations of women out in the West End, or 'out on the town', as this form of leisure was frequently referred to in the period. Bobbed-haired and red-lipped women appear in the period's fiction with an insistent regularity, a force to be reckoned with for anyone who wanted to write about modern London, and this chapter traces a range of responses to and representations of this female type, from a predictable wariness to empathetic identification.

Partly writing about the modern woman out on the town meant engaging in a debate about mass democracy and its perceived effects on the people's mental states. What does she think about? Is her head full of dreams about film stars and make-up? These questions inevitably crop up in even the most neutral descriptions, and even a sympathetic author like Patrick Hamilton could not resist occasionally mocking her.

There was another dimension to writing about 'the modern girl', however, one in which the striking visual effects of her face provided the material for narratives of urban life. Even writers who had little interest in her internal life noticed her intense visual presence, and this intensity often tempted narrative excesses, from the mercilessly detailed accounts of her ageing (notably in Storm Jameson's *A Day Off* (1933), to expressionistic and Gothic representations in Norah Hoult's *Apartments to Let* (1931).

Chapter 2 turns to nocturnal Soho, a favourite setting for hard-boiled fictions, and a rival to the East End as London's most exotic quarter. Soho became an important antithesis to the West End in the period, its narrow streets and small cafés a gritty and dishevelled opposite of the polished West End. The Soho nightclubs and all-night cafés accommodated the 1930s hard-boiled novel by the likes of Robert Westerby and James Curtis. There were, however, literary versions of Soho and its spaces that were far more nuanced, and a discussion of them forms the main body of the chapter. Storm Jameson's ambitious Soho-set *Here Comes a Candle* (1938), John Pudney's *Jacobson's Ladder* (1938) and Norah Hoult's *Youth Can't Be Served* (1933), about a young woman's work as a dance hostess in a nightclub, are central to this discussion. The best way to describe these works is as highly ambitious, but on a small scale. Pudney's novel and Jameson's are scathing about modern capitalism and the increasingly volatile political situation of the late 1930s, but they deliver their critique via subtle portrayals of complex interactions between people who were bound to each other by the communal, even familial, atmosphere of Soho.

Chapter 3 examines writing devoted to the London teashop. Teashops, along with cinemas, were London's most ubiquitous spaces of leisure, offering ample opportunities for people-watching and social interaction, as well as affordable meals and a pleasant environment. Because of their densely arranged seating, teashops allowed patrons to observe and eavesdrop on strangers. The abundant lighting, especially the innovative spotlighting that was used in teashops designed after the 1920s, further organised the visual experience of these spaces in ways that encouraged close looking. A scene that recurs in many 1930s visual and literary texts is of a couple in a teashop nervously and attentively observing each other, and the others around them. Often a site of romantic meetings, the teashop served as a stage for the collapse of illusions about romantic love, and communication itself.

Chapter 4 covers the phenomenon of 1930s cinema-going in London, paying particular attention to novels that worked against the commonly held assumption that going to the cinema equated an escape from reality and the associations of film viewing with distraction on the one hand, and with hypnosis or complete absorption on the other. In fact, writers discussed in the chapter, notably Patrick Hamilton and Elizabeth Bowen, took the pleasures of cinema-going seriously, and the cinema-goer is presented as anything but a passive spectator. Hamilton's London trilogy is read in relation to Dorothy Richardson's writing about inattentive cinema audiences: I argue that Hamilton, like Richardson, was concerned about representing his avid cinema-going Londoners not as unthinking vegetables, but as anxious, sensitive and highly strung people for whom cinemas ought to provide a refuge from worry and an almost excessive self-awareness, but often fail to do so.

This idea of the cinema as a refuge, a home away from home, is developed further in the chapter, in two distinct, though inter-related, directions. One concerns Orwell's contempt for the cinema as yet another bourgeois pleasure which, however, oddly coexists with his belief in the essentially decency of the sort of people who go there; the other pursues further the uneasy origins of this contempt for the cinema in general, as they are defined in Betty Miller's *Farewell Leicester Square*, a novel that mediates its telling of uncomfortable truths about the interrelations between class, nation and culture via the character of a British Jewish filmmaker.

Chapter 5 relocates from London's public spaces into the private, and examines several literary versions of lodging- and boarding-house life in the metropolis. Focusing especially on a recurring scene that involves a character looking out of the window, I explore a range of typical 1930s interpretations of lodging – as a place of confinement as well as refuge from the hostility of the outside world, as a *mise en scène* for the Naturalistic tale of tawdry sexuality, and, most significantly, as a surrealistic site that triggers memory of trauma or returns a character to the source of their state of emotional paralysis.

Most of the milieus this book examines are interiors; the effects of the descriptive passages that galvanised urban fiction during the period largely depended on the compact and dense atmospheres of spaces such as the teashop and the cinema. The first chapter, however, turns to representations of West End streets. Street culture is inseparable from urban narratives that prioritise movement and crowds; during the 1930s, however, this version of the street was increasingly being challenged by representations that emphasised West End scenes that were static and carefully staged.

## Notes

1. Richard Dennis, 'Building Suburbia', in *Cities in Modernity: Representations and Productions of Metropolitan Space, 1840–1930* (Cambridge: Cambridge University Press, 2008), pp. 179–205; Faye Hammill, 'Stella Gibbons, Ex-centricity and the Suburb', in *Intermodernism: Literary Culture in Mid-Twentieth-Century Britain* (Edinburgh: Edinburgh University Press, 2009), pp. 75–92.

2. On London cosmopolitanism, see Judith Walkowitz, *Nights Out: Life in Cosmopolitan London* (New Haven: Yale University Press, 2012), pp. 182–252; Mica Nava, *Visceral Cosmopolitanism: Gender, Culture and the Normalisation of Difference* (Oxford: Berg, 2007), pp. 32–5; Matt Houlbrook, *Queer London: Perils and Pleasures in the Sexual Metropolis, 1918–1957* (Chicago: University of Chicago Press, 2005).

3. See, for instance, T. S. Eliot, 'In Memoriam: Marie Lloyd', *Criterion*, 1 (Jan. 1923), pp. 192–5.

4. T. S. Eliot, *Four Quartets*, in *Collected Poems, 1909–1962* (London: Faber & Faber, 1962), pp. 192–3.

5. For an overview of the period's criticism of mass culture, see John Carey, *The Intellectuals and the Masses: Pride and Prejudice among the Literary Intelligentsia, 1880–1939* (London and Boston: Faber & Faber, 1992).

6. See Siegfried Kracauer, 'The Cult of Distraction' (1926), in *The Mass Ornament: Weimar Essays*, trans. Y. Levin (Cambridge, MA: Harvard University Press, 1995), pp. 323–30.

7. Louis MacNeice, 'Blacklegs' (1939), quoted in Cunningham, *British Writers of the Thirties*, p. 284.

8. George Orwell, *Keep the Aspidistra Flying* (London: Penguin, 2000), p. 107.

9. George Orwell, 'Pleasure Spots', in *Funny, But Not Vulgar and Other Selected Essays and Journalism* (London: The Folio Society, 1998), pp. 172–3.

10. On the Flapper in 1920s English literature and culture, see Billie Melman, *Women and the Popular Imagination in the Twenties: Flappers and Nymphs* (Basingstoke: Macmillan, 1988); David Ayers, *English Literature of the 1920s* (Edinburgh: Edinburgh University Press, 1999), pp. 28–58.

11. T. S. Eliot, *The Waste Land: A Facsimile and Transcript of the Original Drafts*, ed. Valerie Eliot (London: Faber & Faber, 1971), p. 141.

12. Eliot, *The Waste Land*, p. 37.

13. Amy Clukey, '"No country really now"': Modernist Cosmopolitanisms and Jean Rhys's *Quartet*', *Modernism/Modernity*, 56, no. 4 (Winter 2010), p. 438.

14. See Valentine Cunningham, *British Writers of the Thirties* (Oxford: Oxford University Press, 1989); Andy Croft, *Red Letter Days: British Fiction in the 1930s* (London: Lawrence & Wishart, 1990).

15. Maroula Joannou, *'Ladies, Please Don't Smash These Windows': Women's Writing, Feminist Consciousness, and Social Change, 1918–1938* (Oxford: Berg, 1995), pp. 6–7.

16. Chris Baldick, *Literature of the 1920s: Writers among the Ruins* (Edinburgh: Edinburgh University Press, 2012), p. 9.

17. Storm Jameson, 'Documents', *Fact*, July 1937, pp. 15–16.

18. Emile Zola, 'The Experimental Novel', in *Documents of Modern Literary Realism*, ed. George J. Becker (Princeton: Princeton University Press, 1963), p. 165.

19. Storm Jameson, *The Georgian Novel and Mr Robinson* (London: William Heinemann, 1929), p. 32. Jameson's italics.

20. Jameson, 'Documents', pp. 15–16.

21. Jameson, 'Documents', pp. 13–14. Jameson's italics.

22. On 1930s writers as political correspondents, see Catherine Clay, 'The Woman Journalist, 1920–1945', in *The History of British Women's Writing, 1920–1945*, pp. 208–12; Hopkins, *English Fiction in the 1930s*, pp. 78–85.

23. V. S. Pritchett, 'New Novels', *New Statesman*, 29 May 1937, pp. 888, 890.

24. Brian Coe and Paul Gates, *The Snapshot Photograph: The Rise of Popular Photography, 1888–1939* (London: Ash and Grant, 1977), pp. 13–15.

25. Michael North, *Camera Works: Photography and the Twentieth-Century Word* (Oxford: Oxford University Press, 2005), p. 3.
26. North, *Camera Works*, p. 18.
27. Pritchett, 'New Novels', *New Statesman*, 27 May 1933, p. 688.
28. Orwell, 'Review of *Twenty Thousand Streets under the Sky*', *New English Weekly*, 1 Aug. 1935, reprinted in *The Complete Works of George Orwell*, ed. Peter Davison (London: Secker & Warburg, 1998), vol. 10, p. 390. All subsequent references in this chapter are to this edition of *The Complete Works*.
29. Ibid.
30. Quoted in Lyn Pykett, 'Representing the Real', in *Naturalism in the European Novel: New Critical Perspectives* (New York: Berg, 1992), p. 180.
31. See, for instance, Andrew Stephenson, 'Refashioning Modern Masculinity: Whistler, Aestheticism and National Identity', in *English Art, 1860–1914: Modern Artists and Identity*, ed. David Peters Corbett and Lara Perry (Manchester: Manchester University Press, 2000), p. 142.
32. On the links between Naturalism and Modernism, see Simon Joyce, *Modernism and Naturalism in British and Irish Fiction, 1880–1930* (New York: Cambridge University Press, 2015).
33. Georg Lukács, 'Narrate or Describe?', in *Writer and Critic, and Other Essays* (London: Merlin Press, 1970), p. 116.
34. Philip Henderson, *The Novel Today: Studies in Contemporary Attitudes* (London: John Lane, 1936), p. 265.
35. Raymond Mortimer, 'New Novels', *New Statesman and Nation*, 18 March 1933.
36. See, for instance, Valentine Cunningham, 'The Age of Anxiety and Influence; or, Tradition and the Thirties Talents', in *Rewriting the Thirties: Modernism and After* (London: Longmans, 1997), pp. 5–22.
37. Chiara Briganti, '"Thou Art Full of Stirs, A Tumultuous City"': Storm Jameson and London in the 1920s', in *The Swarming Streets: Twentieth-Century Literary Representations of London* (Amsterdam: Rodopi, 2004), p. 64.

38. Phyllis Lassner, '"On the Point of a Journey": Storm Jameson, Phyllis Bottome, and the Novel of Women's Political Psychology', in *And in Our Time: Vision, Revision, and British Writing of the 1930s*, ed. Anthony Shuttleworth (Lewisburg: Bucknell University Press, 2002), p. 121.

39. Leo Mellor, 'London and Modern Prose, 1900–1950', in *The Cambridge Companion to the Literature of London* (Cambridge: Cambridge University Press, 2011), p. 201.

40. David Baguley, *Naturalist Fiction: The Entropic Vision* (Cambridge: Cambridge University Press, 1990), p. 124.

41. Baguley, *Naturalist Fiction*, p. 125.

42. Storm Jameson, *A Day Off* (London: Ivor Nicholson & Watson, 1933), p. 60.

43. Louis MacNeice, 'The Play and the Audience' (1938), quoted in Carey, *Intellectuals and the Masses*, p. 52.

44. Gregory Dart, *Metropolitan Art and Literature, 1810–1840: Cockney Adventures* (Cambridge: Cambridge University Press, 2012), p. 9.

45. Geoffrey Crossick, 'The Emergence of the Lower Middle Class in Britain: A Discussion', in *The Lower Middle Class in Britain, 1870–1914* (London: Croom Helm, 1977), p. 30.

46. George Gissing, *Letters of George Gissing to Members of His Family* (London: Constable, 1927), p. 327.

47. Susan Harrow, *Zola, The Body Modern: Pressures and Prospects of Representation* (London: Legenda, 2010), p. 6.

48. Harrow, *Zola*, p. 6. See also Christopher Prendergast, *Paris and the Nineteenth Century* (Oxford: Blackwell, 1992), pp. 40–5.

49. Katherine Mansfield, 'The Tiredness of Rosabel', in *The Collected Stories of Katherine Mansfield* (London: Book Club Associates, 1973), pp. 524–30.

50. Baguley, *Naturalist Fiction*, p. 195.

51. On non-realist elements in Naturalism, see Baguley, *Naturalist Fiction*, pp. 294–5; Harrow, *Zola*, pp. 3–9.

52. Emile Zola, *Edouard Manet, étude biographique et critique*, trans. and quoted by Susan Harrow, *Zola*, p. 4.

53. Emile Zola, *L'Assommoir* (Oxford: Oxford University Press, 2009), p. 412.

54. Zola, *L'Assommoir*, pp. 417, 412.

55. Zola, *L'Assommoir*, p. 413.
56. Ibid.
57. David Trotter, 'Naturalism's Phobic Picturesque', in *The Uses of Phobia: Essays on Literature and Film* (Malden, MA: Blackwell, 2010), p. 48.
58. Yves Chevrel, 'Towards an Aesthetic of the Naturalist Novel', in *Naturalism in the European Novel*, p. 57.
59. T. J. Clark, *The Painting of Modern Life* (London: Thames & Hudson, 1985), p. 258.
60. See David Trotter, 'The Avoidance of Naturalism: Gissing, Moore, Grand, Bennett, and Others', in *Columbia History of the British Novel*, ed. John Richetti (New York: Columbia University Press, 1994), pp. 608–30.
61. On literature and Impressionism, see Adam Parkes, *A Sense of Shock: The Impact of Impressionism on Modern British and Irish Writing* (New York: Oxford University Press, 2011); Jesse Matz, *Literary Impressionism and Modernist Aesthetics* (Cambridge: Cambridge University Press, 2001); Tamar Katz, *Impressionist Subjects: Gender, Interiority, and Modernist Fiction in England* (Urbana: University of Illinois Press, 2000).
62. Clive Scott, *Street Photography: From Atget to Cartier-Bresson* (London: I. B. Tauris, 2007), p. 37.
63. Sara Blair, *Harlem Crossroads: Black Writers and the Photograph in the Twentieth Century* (Princeton: Princeton University Press, 2007), p. 124.
64. Sara Blair, 'Ellison, Photography and the Origins of Invisibility', in *The Cambridge Companion to Ralph Ellison* (Cambridge: Cambridge University Press, 2005), p. 64.
65. Blair, *Harlem Crossroads*, p. 136.
66. See, for instance, the introductory material in William Sharpe, *New York Nocturne: The City after Dark in Literature, Painting, and Photography, 1850–1950* (Princeton and Oxford: Princeton University Press, 2008), and Jeremy Tambling, *Going Astray: Dickens and London* (Harlow: Pearson Longman, 2009).
67. See Sara Wasson, *Urban Gothic of the Second World War: Dark London* (Houndmills: Palgrave Macmillan, 2010); Leo Mellor, *Reading the Ruins: Bombsites, Modernism and British Culture* (Cambridge: Cambridge University Press, 2011).

68. For a thorough account of the different stages of the development of urban electric lighting, see Wolfgang Schivelbusch, *Disenchanted Night: The Industrialisation of Light in the Nineteenth Century*, trans. Angela Davies (Berkeley: The University of California Press, 1988).

69. On Victorian writing about gas-lit London, see William Sharpe, 'London and Nineteenth-Century Poetry', in *The Cambridge Companion to the Literature of London*, ed. Lawrence Manley (Cambridge: Cambridge University Press, 2011), pp. 134–8.

70. Jean Rhys, *After Leaving Mr Mackenzie* (London: Penguin, 2000), p. 62.

71. Louis MacNeice, Letter to T. S. Eliot, 29 Nov. 1938, in *Letters of Louis MacNeice*, ed. Jonathan Allison (London: Faber & Faber, 2010), p. 312.

72. For a comparative study of modern cities at night, see Joachim Schlör, *Nights in the Big City: Paris, Berlin, London, 1840–1930*, trans. Pierre Gottfried Imhof and Dafydd Rees Roberts (London: Reaktion, 1998).

73. See Alison Light, *Forever England: Femininity, Literature and Conservatism between the Wars* (London and New York: Routledge, 1991); Janet Montefiore, *Men and Women Writers of the 1930s: The Dangerous Flood of History* (London: Routledge, 1996); Chris Hopkins, *Neglected Texts; Forgotten Contexts: Four Political Novels of the 1930s* (Sheffield: Panic Publications, 1993).

74. See David Trotter, *Literature in the First Media Age: Britain between the Wars* (Cambridge, MA: Harvard University Press, 2013); *The Long 1930s*, ed. Leo Mellor and Glyn Salton-Cox, special issue of *Critical Quarterly* (Oct. 2015); *The History of British Women's Writing, 1920–1950*, ed. Maroula Joannou (Basingstoke: Palgrave Macmillan, 2013).

# Chapter 1

## Out on the Town

All roads led to the West End in interwar London. The area of roughly one square mile in the metropolitan Borough of Westminster boasted London's brightest street lights, the largest concentration of electric advertising, the most lavish restaurants and cinemas, and the biggest crowds. This nocturnal cityscape could rival Paris or New York, and for any writer set on modern London life as her subject matter, it was the place to be. Above all, this was where one went to look at quintessentially modern Londoners – the office workers and suburban commuters, the women and men who laboured in London's offices and shops by day, and walked the streets of the West End by night.

The West End had not always been associated with egalitarian street culture; its change in reputation, from a wealthy residential district to the centre of mass leisure, began in the early 1900s. Ralph Nevill wrote that as late as the 1880s and 1890s the West End 'was a sort of separate part of London in which the inhabitants of other districts seldom strayed': the majority of passers-by one saw in Piccadilly were not workers but people of independent means out for a stroll.[1] But at the beginning of the twentieth century West End streets became 'Londoners' premier playground for every class, from artisan and clerk to rentier'.[2] They also became the best spot in London for observing 'those who are not personages, but merely persons'.[3] This shift in interest made all the difference to the West End as a literary setting: it became a location that could rival, for the first time, the fascination long exercised on writers and photographers by the East End or the nearby Soho. By the mid-1920s the West End was firmly associated with lower-middle-class leisure – with urban workers taking a stroll or, in a fashionable interwar phrase, taking a night 'out on the town'. Observed en masse, these 'mere persons' still tended to provoke a horror of crowds in sensitive observers, a response with a long literary history.[4] George Gissing had been particularly vicious about London crowds, which inevitably exert a corrupting influence on his impressionable, middle-class heroines. In *The Nether World* (1889), the slow movement of London crowds was described as 'only a thud, thud of footfalls numberless, and the low unvarying sound that suggested some huge beast purring to itself in stupid contentment'.[5] And in *In the Year of Jubilee* (1894), the educated but penniless Nancy Lord is forced to seek employment and take to the London crowds, and her face instantly assumes a 'look of vulgar abandonment' which would have 'horrified' her if she saw it.[6] The New Woman novel also exhibited a great deal of unease about London crowds, despite often presenting London as liberating. In Isabella Ford's *On the Threshold* (1895), Lucretia's housemaid leaves her, and we watch her disappear into the London crowd, into 'the stream of men and women noisily spreading itself over the pavement . . . Horrible they looked, horrible as . . . demons, with no spark of humanity left in them.'[7] This horror of being engulfed by the multitudes proved difficult to overcome; even Dorothy Richardson's Miriam Henderson, who walks the London streets enthusiastically, finds herself observing the West End crowds and seeing 'masked life-moulded forms' with 'unobservant eyes'.[8] Women writers of the *fin de siècle* did tend to be more sympathetic in their representations of the city and the new opportunities it offered,[9] but this did not necessarily translate into an interest in people walking the streets, other than the detached curiosity of the *flâneuse*.[10]

Sensitive *flâneurs* and *flâneuses* suspicious of crowds were still abundant in London fiction of the 1930s, and this chapter does examine their versions of mistrustful fascination with street culture; crucially, however, for many writers of the 1930s, particularly for those whose literary careers were just beginning, the allure of the West End consisted in observing not the frenetic movement and anonymous flow of people, but the isolated, closely framed scenes that appeared static or even frieze-like. Panoramic and distanced views of the West End often gave way to meditations on individual figures and faces caught up, or caught out, in the strong glare of the area's many lights. West End literature of the decade engages in this back-and-forth between panoramic visions of West End crowds and lights and closely observed small dramas that required one to look more closely. Seen at a distance, the West End glittered benignly, as though it itself was a gigantic shop window offering the luxurious goods; observed more closely, it offered endless opportunities for recording the small-scale ignominies to which the less secure revellers were nightly subjected.

## City of Light

From the late 1920s onwards the West End was transformed nightly by a lighting extravaganza unseen anywhere else in London. The Borough of Westminster, now a part of the modern City of Westminster borough, was the best-lit part of London throughout the nineteenth and the first half of the twentieth centuries, and in the 1930s the West End area which it contained boasted 'the most brilliantly illuminated spot in [the] country'[11] – the Shaftesbury Memorial at the centre of Piccadilly Circus. Bathed by 60,000 watts of electricity in a 'cascade of silver', Piccadilly Circus was a dazzling display of progress and prosperity in a city many areas of which were still plunged into darkness each night. As Martin Battersby points out, 'electricity as a source of illumination was by no means common in England and, in those districts where it was available, it was expensive'.[12] Nor was the quality of gaslight – still a popular form of street lighting in the interwar period – equal across different London boroughs. The West End, once again, was ahead, with the British Commercial Gas Association providing the area with the best available high-pressure gas lamps with a power as strong as 1800 candle power, giving off a steady bright light. The company renewed its contract with Westminster City Council in 1932, pledging to replace the existing lamps across 55 miles of the borough's streets with even more powerful new versions. The light that brought the West End to life was, then, incomparably brighter and clearer than the flickering, dim gaslight in London's less wealthy boroughs, or the light of Edison's incandescent lamps that were tentatively, and not very successfully, being introduced into the capital.[13]

The West End was what much of London was not – a modern and prosperous city within a city, bustling with traffic and illuminated by large-scale, electrically lit advertisements. West End lights both mediated the city and became objects of interest in their own right. Commercial representations of the West End in the period often emphasised the bright lights as one of the area's chief attractions, on a par with the restaurants and theatres that drew in the evening crowds. A 1924 Underground poster by Harold Sandys Williamson sported inviting globular gas lamps, encouraging Tube travellers to visit a 'brighter London' (Fig. 1.1).

The colour choices are significant here: Williamson bathed his illustration in a warm yellow glow, a colour scheme that signals prosperity and commercial availability. West End street lights and advertising signs have themselves become covetable objects. West End street lights and electric ads were similarly used as shorthand for London's bustling modernity in Jean Moral's 1934 photographs of the West End. Moral made extensive use of double exposure in order to convey the dynamism of the area – and perhaps to exaggerate just how dynamic and modern the West End really was. The sleek shapes of modern neon ads do most of the work here, most strikingly in an image that superimposes an enormous cinema ad for Greta Garbo in *Queen Christina* (1933) on top of a shot of West End crowds (Fig. 1.2). The art deco shapes of the ad, together with the hypnotic, floating image of Garbo's face, create the impression of a thrilling and vibrant metropolis.

Figure 1.1 Harold Sandys Williamson, *Brighter London for Theatreland*, 1924. © TfL from the London Transport Museum collection.

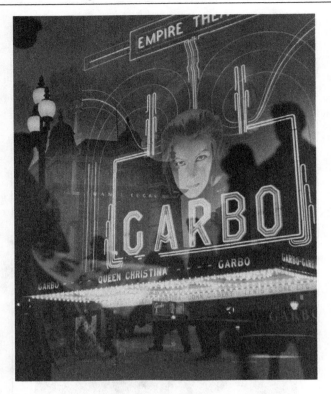

Figure 1.2 Jean Moral, *Untitled*, 1934. © Brigitte Moral Paris. Courtesy Gitterman Gallery.

Modern lighting was often used in this way – as an effective shortcut to presenting London as a vertiginous centre of modernity – in literature, as well as in cinema, advertising and photography. Gerald Kersh's *Night and the City* (1938) opens with an image of the West End that has become West Central, a city at least superficially more like John Dos Passos's New York than London:

> Up and down the street shops began to close. West Central started to flare and squirm in a blazing vein-work of neon-tubes. Bursting like inexhaustible fireworks, the million coloured bulbs

of the electric signs blazed in perpetual recurrence over the face of the West End. Underground trains from the suburbs squirting out of their tunnels like red toothpaste out of tubes, disgorged theatre-crowds.[14]

The parallels between this scene and *Manhattan Transfer* (1925) are striking, although Kersh's is a somewhat calmer version of Dos Passos's kinetic evocation of the Manhattan night:

Dusk gently smooths crispangled streets. Dark presses tight the steaming asphalt city, crushes the fretwork of windows and lettered signs . . . Under the rolling heavier heavier pressure windows blurt light. Night crushes bright milk out of arclights, squeezes the sullen blocks until they drip red, yellow, green into streets with resounding feet. All asphalt oozes light.[15]

Nothing, it seems, could be a more effective means of introducing the modern city than a reference to the transformation of its landscape at dusk. Kersh clearly borrowed a language of 'squirting', 'squeezing' and 'oozing' from Dos Passos, and, by proxy, a preoccupation with the rhythms of urban modernity. In fact, introducing London in this way was something of a given throughout the interwar period. Hitchcock included a scene in which London is made synonymous with the nightly switching on of the lights in Piccadilly in several of his early films. In *Downhill* (1927), Ivor Novello's hero Roddy's return to London after his expulsion from school is illustrated with a panoramic footage of Piccadilly at night. And in *The Ring* (1927), the fairground boxer Jack Sander celebrates his (temporary) success in a flat overlooking the blinking metropolitan lights.

In Kersh's novel, the illuminated West End functions similarly as a backdrop to a conventional narrative; the frantic flickering of the lights with which the novel so boldly opens inaugurates an unsuccessful attempt to escape an altogether more familiar West End tale, and a very English one at that. *Night and the City* is a tale of redemption – or, to be more precise, of the avoidance of disgrace – in which a character called Adam Dunne, a failed artist, finds himself mixed up with the wrong crowd in the first half of the book and proudly repudiates it at the novel's end. The novel's modern characters – transatlantic gangsters and dance hostesses – are only superficial furnishings for the main plotline, in which Adam finds his way back to a meaningful life and is born again, as it were, into sculpture.

The West End became the arena within which young British writers were able to pitch their French influences against the British novelistic tradition to which they belonged, albeit often half-heartedly. And interpretations of the relationship between urban milieu and a character's behaviour were central to this negotiation of influences. Norah Hoult's *Time Gentlemen! Time!* (1930) was the most thoroughly Zolaesque in its perfect fusion of a seductive West End and an easily corruptible character about to go under. The neon sign advertising wine goads on the alcoholic Carmichael to drink some more, 'a hand pouring red wine out of a bottle into a glass set a continuous inspiring example'.[16] *Time Gentlemen! Time!* is essentially an Anglicised version of Zola's *L'Assommoir* (1877), with a similar plot following the disintegration of a family, fuelled by the husband's alcoholism. The violent and bitter Carmichael, a near-bankrupt solicitor in a small London firm, could rival Zola's Lantier in callousness – he ruthlessly spends the family money on drink, and cannot stop thinking of other women. The red colour of neon stands in not only for hellish alcoholic vapour, but also for sexual depravity – foreign in origin, of course. In a pub overlooking Piccadilly Circus, Carmichael confides in a school friend his secret desire to abandon monogamy, and is promptly rebuked by the more sober confidant: 'This free love business. Passion considerably diluted with soda water sold under a red sign labelled "principle" and guaranteed uplifting. A nasty business.'[17] Neon-red is the colour of modern mass-culture, but also of nineteenth-century French depravity – the conversation between the two friends quickly arrives at a discussion of Parisian prostitutes. The West End here functions unambiguously as the centre of vice, to which Carmichael is irresistibly drawn, as men were drawn to the *assommoir* in Zola's novel. Before

Carmichael can sample free love, however, he is divorced by his wife and arrested for public disturbance.

Orwell's *Keep the Aspidistra Flying* could have been a very similar novel to Hoult's, and its literary sources were almost certainly the same. *Aspidistra* was Orwell's last, and unfinished, attempt, at a Naturalist novel. He wrote self-mockingly in 'Why I Write' that early in his career he wanted 'to write enormous naturalistic novels with unhappy endings', 'full of purple passages in which words were used partly for the sake of their sound'.[18] In 1946 he was professing an anti-formalist feeling, and laying a pledge to fiction where content prevails over style. Ten years earlier, however, the desire for writing a formally polished piece of fiction appears to have been strong. *Aspidistra* most probably had been initially conceived as a tale of a young writer's decline and death in the uncaring metropolis, somewhat like Zola's *L'Œuvre* (1886) or Gissing's *New Grub Street* (1891). Gordon's night out in the West End – during which he swigs alcohol out of a bottle in the middle of Piccadilly Circus, attempts to sexually assault his girlfriend, and finally passes out in a brothel only to wake up in a police cell – is an apotheosis of middle-class self-loathing that confirms Gordon's long-held desire 'to sink' into 'the ghost-kingdom . . . where shame, effort, decency do not exist'.[19]

The Zolaesque trajectory is announced by Gordon himself; his night of debauchery is punctured by maudlin self-pity and glum predictions of the future:

> He knew what folly and evil he had committed and was about to commit. And yet after all it hardly seemed to matter. He saw as something far, far away, like something seen through the wrong end of the telescope, his thirty years, his wasted life, the blank future . . . He said with a sort of philosophic interest:
> 'Look at the neon lights! Look at those awful blue ones over the rubber shop. When I see those lights I know that I'm a damned soul.'[20]

The reason Orwell did not become 'the English Zola'[21] is that he did not have quite the level of respect for his character required to follow through with the tale of decline. For Gordon, all this dissipation and despair is little more than an exercise – a chance to participate in the proletarian drama of the neon-lit West End. The total abandonment of middle-class responsibility and genteel need is a recurring theme in Orwell's fiction, and *Aspidistra* is no exception: it is a novel about the wish for total oblivion and the shedding of middle-class identity. There is nothing that Gordon wishes to escape more than the prospect of 'licit sexual intercourse in the shade of an aspidistra', and walking through a lower-middle-class neighbourhood he wishes that it would get bombed in the coming war. Gordon wishes for a chic bohemian life, with plenty of sexual adventure, fine company and the urban delights of Mayfair and Kensington. When that fantasy fails (Gordon has neither the money nor the talent to make it in the world of literary London), he wishes for the simplicity of slum life. In that sense, the glittering West End, with its infernal neon lights and its unreal atmosphere of never-ending pleasure and the slums of South London are two sides of the same coin. Despite being a Londoner, Gordon is a tourist.

Orwell saw London as an ultimately dull city, its heart located in its net-curtained quiet suburbs. The London of Naturalistic dramas under neon signs is simply a vaporous dream – there is no such London in reality. The antics one may witness in Piccadilly after midnight are nothing more than a performance. And this is where the novel's two parallel strands – Gordon's story and its metafictional meaning – come together. Gordon must finally accept that the only real London – the London where he must remain, and which he now cannot wish to see bombed in the coming war – is the ordinary London of lower-middle-class family homes. Orwell's own acceptance of this 'real' London marked the point of a conscious change of direction – the end of his literary tourism into Naturalism which had culminated in *Down and Out in Paris and London* (1932), in parts of *A Clergyman's Daughter* (1935) and in his enthusiastic reading of Henry Miller. Of Miller, Orwell would later write that 'he is writing about the man in the street, and it is incidentally rather a pity that it should be a street full of brothels':

That is the penalty of leaving your native land. It means trans-ferring your roots into shallower soil . . . you are reading about people living the expatriate life, people drinking, talking, meditating and fornicating, not about people working, mar-rying and bringing up children; a pity, because he would have described the one set of activities as well as the other.[22]

The concept of the expatriate life was central to the way that Orwell thought of the West End in the mid-1930s. To seek bohemian pleasures in the infernal lights of Piccadilly meant remaining a tourist in one's own city. In *Aspidistra*, Orwell's aim was to show that this London was simply not to be taken seriously – that the bright lights did not drive Londoners to alcoholism, and that to get disgracefully drunk underneath a neon sign was not only disingenuous but also thoroughly un-English. Several critics have noted the novel's implausible ending:[23] after getting his girlfriend Rosemary pregnant, Gor-don goes back to work and to respectability, suddenly, if hyster-ically, delighted by the prospect of clean shirts, a new kitchen and an aspidistra in the drawing-room window. Awkward as this sudden transformation seems, however, the ending was almost certainly deliberate and signalled a conscious decision on Orwell's part to write no more novels of young men pictur-esquely falling apart in the soulless metropolis. *Keep the Aspi-distra Flying* enacts Orwell's shifting views on the nature of the urban novel and, in fact, signals his overall loss of interest in urban life. It begins with an indulgence in the excesses of urban Naturalism, and ends in a satire of the mode.

Storm Jameson's *Company Parade* (1934), the first novel in the *Mirror in Darkness* trilogy, is another work that promises an investment in the life of the brightly lit streets, but eventu-ally anchors itself in the highly individualised point of view of an aspiring artist – here, a semi-autobiographical figure of a writer. Hervey Russell, who returns to London right after the Great War to work in an advertising agency – as Jameson her-self had – is by turns fascinated and horrified by the new West End, at one point compelled to walk away from the Piccadilly festivities: "'They're not enjoying themselves," she cried: "it's terrifying, it's hideous.'"[24] Much is made in the novel of the fact that London street culture died with the war, to be resurrected as disingenuous performance. 'Feeling had gone cold since the Armistice',[25] announces the narrator in *Company Parade*, and the trilogy as a whole is partly about the coldness of post-war London. There are occasional attempts at presenting the bustle of the West End in a more positive way, via Woolfian significant moments such as this one:

> She reached London after dusk and spent the evening walking with herself, in an indescribable excitement squeezed from the crowded irregular streets, the lights and darkened doorways, the gaiety, the furtive faces, the misery, the colours running pell-mell over the restaurants and theatres, the smells, all that whirl of stone and cataract of bodies caught in the forms they assumed for one moment, one evening in February 1923, once and once only, then and only then.[26]

The passage is a variation on the moment of being that Virginia Woolf had theorised in 'Modern Fiction' (1919), the moment that came 'not here but there'.[27] The arrested moment is a way of making sense of the city; it becomes a useful building block in organising the experience that otherwise would seem chaotic and shapeless. The particulars of urban life are too numerous and are tidied into generalities, assembled into one image held together by a single consciousness; the purpose of rendering the hectic street life of the West End as a whirl or cataract is the very opposite of creating the effect of disorientation. For Jameson's observer, the objects – faces, lights, buildings – that are seen as a blur never mattered individually in the first place. London is assembled into a collage and animated by Hervey's creating gaze.

Jameson's models for the London trilogy were French, Proust and Balzac, especially Balzac's vast collection of novels and stories *La Comédie humaine* (1829-55), which arguably was the first francophone sequence novel or *roman-fleuve*.[28] The term '*roman-fleuve*' was coined by Romain Roland in 1908 to describe the seventh volume of his own novel sequence *Jean-Christophe* (1904–12). The *roman-fleuve* flourished in

France between the wars, with notable examples including Georges Duhamel's *Vie et aventures de Salavin* (1920–32), Roger Martin du Gard's Nobel Prize-winning *Les Thibault* (1922–40) and Jules Romain's *Les Hommes de bonne volonté* (1932–47), which opened with a preface strikingly similar in content to Jameson's later call for fiction that might reconcile the individual and the collective in 'Documents'. Romains announced the aim of his own multi-volume exploration of French society as finding 'a means of expressing the collective life, such as we see it before our eyes, and the way in which it is associated with individual life'.[29] Jameson, however, disliked Romains intensely for his handling of the PEN presidency[30] and there is no indication that she had read his work. It was Jameson's reading of Balzac that catalysed her own *roman-fleuve*. She wrote of this impulse with ironic affection more than thirty years later:

> I am coolly certain that, *fleuve* for *fleuve*, it ran faster and deeper than any flowering now, in the sixties.
> But what a devil of an idea to set myself up as a Balzac. I must have been mad.[31]

*The Mirror in Darkness* does teem with an impressive number of subplots and characters, including a war veteran, a publishing magnate and even a budding fascist. Yet, as Jennifer Birkett puts it, Hervey's imagination is 'the focus and mediator' of the 'spectacle' of London.[32] Despite its conception as polyphonic and panoramic, the *Mirror in Darkness* is heavily invested in romantic encounters between Hervey and a number of representative urban figures – for instance, there is the obligatory Wordsworthian encounter with an elderly street vendor. By the beginning of *Love in Winter* (1935), Hervey confesses to Renn her failure to write the all-encompassing novel she had planned: 'I know what you meant when you said I must put everything into my novels – this room, that fat greedy woman, you . . . unfortunately I can't do it.'[33] Jameson does put everything and everyone into her trilogy, but not all of her London characters are convincing.

The 'fat greedy woman' is a case in point: she appears in *Company Parade* and is an outlet for a specific kind of nostalgic feeling – for the lost pre-1918 London, which from the vantage point of the mid-1930s appears noisier and smellier, but somehow less offensive than the mercantile coldness with which Jameson invests the London of the 1920s. The choice of surname – 'Hunt' – is telling, since Delia is always on the prowl for fresh experiences of London. The first chapter of *Company Parade* features Delia walking around the West End, savouring the sensory overload of London which so repulses Hervey: 'she always said that if she were blinded she could make her way from the Strand to Shaftesbury Avenue by the sounds and smells'. A middle-aged woman who had been young in the West End of the 1910s, Delia, much like Jameson, laments the passing of the old street culture, and the rise of what she perceives to be the cult of passive spectatorship – 'there were . . . more women, and they had more the air of spectators than revellers'.[34] Jameson's deep mistrust of post-1918 mass pleasures chimes with T. S. Eliot's rejection of 'cheap and rapid-breeding' cinema that threatened to erase all class distinctions – and the cultural forms to which such distinctions corresponded.[35] Honest working-class pleasures are acknowledged as having an aesthetic and a sophistication of their own, but, just as Eliot was decidedly uncomfortable about modern 'passive' pleasures such as the cinema, so Jameson makes a decisive distinction between the old, expansive street culture and the new mode of passive spectatorship. The Gargantuan Delia is of the old order – vulgar in a way that can be comprehended and embraced. By contrast, the sleek and composed modern girls out in the West End are alien; the suspicion of inauthenticity does not take long to coagulate. In Piccadilly Circus, Delia observes a young woman entertaining a Canadian officer (in the trilogy's chronology this is 1919):

She had a round laughing face, black hair cut in a fringe across her eyes, and painted lips. Delia experienced a definite conviction that the new growth had not the stamina of the old. She saw that the girl was practising a part, not, as Delia herself at that age, revelling with a nearly brutal zest in the turns of her life.[36]

The modern girl is reduced to a tableau of an insincere performance of pleasure, disapproved of by a character who appears to stand for nothing less than the pre-war West End itself – a centre of 'zesty' vernacular culture which has been irreparably damaged. In her misgivings about the girl, Jameson's suspicion of the modern city itself is rendered apparent: the young woman stands for everything that has gone wrong in London, a city Hervey traverses with a Wordsworthian horror of its perceived inauthenticity. Delia ascertains that the girl is 'practising a part' solely on the basis of the sharp fringe and the red lips. The context for this observation is the nocturnal illumination of the West End streets. An episode in the final part of the trilogy, *None Turn Back* (1936), is a case in point. Driven through London during the General Strike of 1926 Hervey observes the passing streets from inside, faintly and only very briefly amused by the celebratory atmosphere – 'the young ones counted on an adventure a day. The girls wore high heels on their shoes to be ready for it.'[37] Hervey herself no longer feels young, and the London streets and the people who walk them are increasingly mystifying and irritating. References to the sweatiness and smelliness of the city multiply in this instalment of the trilogy, and Hervey is far more fascinated by the aristocratic, sculpted face of her languorous sister-in-law Georgina Roxby than the painted faces of the young girls in the West End.

Practising parts, to which the pale, red-lipped faces were crucial, did not always automatically signal a loss of authenticity. Mask-like female faces fascinated as much as they repulsed. Norah Hoult, whose literary career began in London in the late 1920s, based an entire novel on the contradictory effects of women's faces seen in the glare of West End lights.

### Painted Faces

Norah Hoult came to London from Ireland in the 1920s, and, like many others, went into journalism, and one of the focal points of her first full-length novel was, predictably, a journalist whose walking around the West End is part pleasure, part business – the quest for suitable material for her column.

Hoult, similarly to Jameson, chose to mediate London through the point of view of a slightly older woman who remembers the city before the war, but in *Apartments to Let* there is no insistence on a stark difference between the exuberance of London pre-1918 and the coldness of modernity. On the contrary, Lena's affectionate gaze singles out continuities rather than disparities between Londoners past and present: '[In Piccadilly] . . . the sleek gliding past of motor-cars and taxis, the shouting electric signs in front of the theatres exhilarated her once more. This was the London she loved, the London which always dangled in front of her the glistening promise of romance.'[38] The journalist's knack for close observation sets the tone of sympathetic expansiveness; unlike Jameson's Hervey who dreams of becoming a great writer, the author of a novel that would 'include everything', Lena avoids harsh judgements and grand pronouncements about modern life. Instead, small observations of West End life elicit a sense of sympathy and even solidarity, such as the description of West End film extras queuing for auditions:

> The girls with their red lips, their cheap smart clothes which wanted renewing were . . . tawdry? Yes – but there was something about them . . . Crossley wondered. A sort of independence, a laugh that held real gaiety, an unconscious way they had of standing, of talking to men . . . A dog's life, of course: up the agent's stairs, 'Anything for me to-day?' 'Sorry, dear. I've got your name. Look in again.' Up the stairs again – the old, old story. All the same, say what you like, there was something – glamour, life.[39]

Lena's acknowledgement of glamour alongside the shabbiness is in direct contract with Jameson's observers' mistrust of 'the new life'; these women practise parts only once they are inside the theatre or film studio; outside, their sociability has an 'unconscious' quality. This description also differs from Jameson's in its inclusion of whole figures – and of bodies that move and are flexible. It is not just the red lips and sharply cut fringes that attract Lena's attention. Isolating the face is reserved for the novel's other female observer, Lena's fellow lodger called Josephine, whose paranoid visions of London twist the novel's tame realism into the mode of urban Gothic.

Josephine is going quietly mad in her bedsit, increasingly afraid during her ventures into the West End; where Lena sees ordinary passers-by, Josephine sees demons and ghosts, faces 'twisted' with the desire to 'hurt people'.[40] In one scene, coming up the escalator at Piccadilly Station, Josephine encounters the face of a woman, 'fashionably dressed', 'with painted eyebrows, white skin and very red lips', 'presenting herself . . . in the guise of a staring inhuman mask'.[41] The mask-like, made-up female face became a symbol of metropolitan indifference, expressed in a peculiar brand of feminine cynicism or hardness, as it was habitually referred to. That to survive London a woman must grow hard is something of a given in fiction of this period. 'Life's hard on women that are too soft',[42] thinks Hervey Russell's landlady in *Love in Winter*. Jameson reworked the same (autobiographical) motif in several novels: a young simple-faced woman from the country struggles to fit in, which is to say to cultivate a front of self-possession and even ruthlessness. Hervey makes an attempt to look like the self-assured London women she sees around, cutting her hair into the fashionable bob, but the effect is merely unflattering, 'harsh, ugly'.[43] If make-up and short hair are women's armour against the many cruelties the city inflicts on them, Hervey's attempt at cultivating such protective armour is hopelessly ineffective, though this ineffectiveness also testifies to an authenticity. Jameson was consistently ungenerous towards urban women who were good at creating a mask-like front, usually juxtaposing them with simple-faced, spirited women who come to London from up North. They are not unlike J. B. Priestley's wholesome Northern girls; Jameson disliked Priestley, but they shared at least the preference for honest countrywomen who try to conquer London by sheer perseverance and guilelessness. In Priestley's *They Walk in the City* (1936), the young Rose comes to London from the North, and moves in with a typical London girl – neurotic, stick-thin and shingled – who envies Rose her idiosyncratic beauty – long blonde hair and dark, expressive eyes. Beatrice's beauty is contrived, only a set of standard features that make her passable, while Rose's beauty is natural.

By the end of the decade, thinking about the face beneath the mask had become a well-worn cliché – though Hamilton still resorted to it in *Hangover Square* (1941), in a description of London starlets: 'they came up to the office in shoals, with their nails dipped in blood and their faces smothered with pale cocoa. And some were charming and simple beneath their masks, and some were complex and arrogant.'[44] It is, however, the complex and arrogant type that tends to be the most desirable throughout the decade's fiction (including *Hangover Square* itself). In *Entanglement* (1938), an ambitious project in which the Irish writer Henry Perrott, who wrote under the pseudonym George Buchanan, attempts a broad cross-section of 1930s Britain. Music shop assistant and socialist Kevin leaves his fiancée May who works at the shop next door partly because she is emotionally unstable, but partly because she doesn't quite look like the woman of Kevin's dreams. His doubts about her suitability are punctured with thoughts about what he perceives as the provincial simplicity of her physical beauty: when they first meet, he sees 'a nice, podgy girl with fair hair and a slightly beaming face'.[45] May's simple charm is contrasted with the seductive hauteur perfected by the enchanting debutante Vela whom Kevin spots standing outside his shop window 'with an expressionless face'.[46]

Hoult gave her novel *Apartments to Let* a sensational ending – Josephine is institutionalised after a suicide attempt involving a knife and a standoff with her fellow boarding-house residents. Josephine's madness explains her paranoid vision, but such paranoia is not unique in the London novel of the 1930s. Josephine is only an exaggerated version of disenfranchised female characters that populate many of the period's novels, most notably Jean Rhys's. Anna Morgan in *Voyage in the Dark* (1934) imagines that the faces passing her by in the London streets are the mocking Dominican carnival masks she remembers from her childhood, while Julia Martin in *After Leaving Mr Mackenzie* (1930) stares at a reproduction of a Modigliani painting of a woman with 'a face like a mask'[47] – a beautiful face that seems to be laughing at her, a synecdoche for all the mocking faces she has encountered in Paris and in London.

Josephine's madness is triggered by the relentless exposure to images and signs that promote strength, and even invincibility. While walking dazedly around the West End, she is transfixed by an advertisement for an iron supplement: 'THEY GIVE VIGOUR TO THE WEAK AND CRIMSON TO THE PALLID CHEEK. Yes, of course, she had decided to get some because she was weak.'[48] Josephine's 'weakness' can easily be read in her face – Lena gets a quick glimpse of it from her boarding-house window, 'an expression . . . so lost, so bewildered, that her heart contracted in pity'.[49] Josephine's is the face of a woman who has not learnt to look hard, the fact of which the West End signs and made-up faces constantly remind her. And Hervey, in *Love in Winter* (1935), gets a glimpse of just such a woman leaving a restaurant:

> She was young, not thirty, but her shoulders drooped, lines ran from the corners of her mouth, pulling it down, and her eyes stared round her without, it seemed, noticing anything. They met Hervey's; she received from them such a sensation of darkness and emptiness that she felt dizzy, as if, leaning from the edge of a cliff, she saw nothing beneath.[50]

The period's photographs of the West End made equally enthusiastic use of narratives in which women visibly crumble under the pressures of urban living, rather than successfully cultivating an invincible front against it. In one of *Picture Post*'s photographic essays, about the daily routine of West End models, or 'mannequins', the camera has caught one of them off guard, a frightened and pinched facial expression setting in (Fig. 1.3).

Such photographs are exemplary of the 1930s fascination with the transformation of young, confident women into older women with pinched and frightened faces. Partly the popularity of this narrative of negative transformation was due to the fact that such faces created instant drama; their faces become microcosms of the indifferent city – a myth as prevalent in the

Picture Post, December 3, 1938

FACES IN THE MANNEQUIN RESTAURANT : *A Furrier's Model*
*Her business is to wear lovely furs in a way that will make rich people*
*want to buy them. She's doing it in her spare time as well.*

Figure 1.3 *Faces in the Mannequin Restaurant, Picture Post,* 3
December 1938.

1930s as it was in any other decade. Such women also replaced,
or became conflated with, earlier stock tales involving West
End prostitutes. Although Hamilton could still get away with
writing the West End as the hotspot of luridly displayed soliciting, with Bob heading to Shaftesbury Avenue with the express

purpose to observe the women of the town – 'the poisonous horror of their bearing yet bore the glamour and beauty of the macabre'[51] – such anachronistic versions of the West End were increasingly rare. The appearance of prostitutes could conceivably have appeared 'poisonous' to a mid-Victorian observer – the made-up, gaudily dressed women would have looked unlike the women one would see elsewhere in London, during the night or day.[52] But by the interwar period West End prostitutes were known for their ability to blend in with a crowd of ordinary working women. In 1937 a Mass-Observer described his astonishment at talking to a well-dressed, 'quiet-voiced' woman for several minutes before realising that he was being 'accosted'.[53] To an extent, then, images and descriptions of women down on their luck in the West End filled in the gap left by the decline of tales of prostitution and sexual harassment. Melancholy or miserable faces were the new objects of West End tourism.

Hamilton's Bob in *The Midnight Bell* was one such tourist, wandering the West End streets in a 'vainglorious' haze of self-satisfaction, observing other people as if they were 'inexplicable objects' for which Bob feels 'a kind of beautiful pity' 'for not existing'.[54] It is in order to get away, once and for all, from this egotistical *flâneur* and his stiflingly familiar responses to the city that Hamilton turned his attention to a female Londoner in *The Plains of Cement*.

## Street Scenes

Ella is perhaps the most psychologically complex of the London girls in 1930s fiction, although her origins are in the young Hamilton's humorous sketches of a modern cliché. The first version of this character appears in 1925, in an unpublished short story about a modern woman who is described as

> a pretty girl not to be much distinguished from a hundred or so other pretty girls you see daily, who come along the pavement making a quick, hollow rapping noise with their heels, looking ahead of them, chin up, preoccupied . . . You scarcely

ever think about their minds at all – the intensive interests and plans in hats, shoes, stockings . . . the Bobbing question . . . Real Love, invincible selfishness of men, Valentino, Novarro, honeymoons in Italy, and all that.[55]

The character evolved along with Hamilton's development as a writer. In *Twenty Thousand Street under the Sky*, we are introduced to Ella as 'a dark, plain girl', her hair shingled 'to keep up with the Fashion'.[56] All the requisites of one from 'a hundred' are in this description, and the look was so ubiquitous by the time Hamilton took on this character that this description would have encouraged a set of expectations about the story about to be told. A savvy writer who made a spectacular amount of money from the vogue for Victoriana with his play *Gaslight* (1927), Hamilton would have been tempted by the character that now dominated popular narratives in literature and film. Ella's ought to be a glibly humorous story of a working girl who is unfairly neglected, though ultimately rewarded for her sheer energy and optimism. *It* (1927)[57] would have provided an obvious prototype – the story of a bobbed and dark-haired girl who, much like Ella, is not a blonde goddess, but gets the man in the end entirely by means of her irrepressible charm. A horrible version of this is enacted between Ella and an abominable ex-army bore called Mr Eccles who becomes, for a time, an unlikely marriage prospect. Eccles thinks he has bagged himself a modest working-class girl with plenty of It: Ella is by turns tempted and disgusted, and, finally, unable to marry him. During one of their strolls around the West End, Eccles suddenly acts, to Ella's great embarrassment, as a passionate lover, pinning her against the railings. She is appalled, and, at the same time, somewhat amused, by this impromptu performance of a ubiquitous nocturnal scene:

How many couples had she seen in this posture, in dim lamp-lit patches, murmuring their fervent mysteries against railings, and how little she had dreamed that she would ever be enrolled in that strange corps! But here she was, as though she had been doing it all her life.[58]

Without the imaginary passer-by, the encounter is merely sordid, but the possibility of an audience nearly transforms it into an act of reinvention. Crucially, this is a static scene: Ella is thrilled not by walking the city streets, but by being incorporated into a tableau of urban life. It is easier to become such a static figure after dark, and the pleasures of appearing as generic tableaux of London life to others is manifestly a nocturnal one. At night, faces seen briefly under streetlights all look the same: what one remembers is the posture, the dramatic unit, as it were, created by these bodies. For Ella, this diversion of attention from Eccles's face is a welcome respite from the knowledge that he is too old and too dull for her. Once the glue that had held the performance together – that is, the artificial lighting that briefly makes Eccles look younger – is gone, the fantasy collapses. Meeting Eccles on a rainy morning, Ella is nearly overwhelmed by disappointment:

> She looked at him again, and all at once she understood every-thing. He was an old man. His plodding walk, his grey hair and moustache, the harsh drawn lines of his face – all, in the grey light of the chilly sky above, revealed it. So different from the flattering artificial light of 'The Midnight Bell' . . . How emi-nently respectable and dull was her afternoon to be after all.[59]

The transitions between night and day are always more than sim-ple narrative markers in Hamilton. One way to read his London trilogy is as a meditation on the interrelationship between people's behaviour and the night/day dichotomy. *Twenty Thousand Streets* takes the basic questions of Naturalist fiction – which aspects of a person's milieus trigger their behaviours – and answers them with elaborate descriptions of urban dramas shaped by artificial lighting effects. What if people act on impulses that are aesthetic, rather than social and economic, in origin?

Hamilton poses this question in a way that shares with urban night photography an interest in scenes where people are at their least authentic, where their behaviour seems the product of the setting. Hamilton's pretend lovers have much in common with Bill Brandt's enigmatic couple in *Street Scene* (1936; Fig. 1.4).

Figure 1.4  Bill Brandt, *Street Scene*, 1936. © Bill Brandt Archive.

The photograph has a curious history. The woman is Brandt's sister Esther, the keen man – her husband. This was not a candid snapshot of London street life; Brandt's photographs of the city typically were not. Norah Wilson remarked that 'he is not so much concerned about individuals as about types'.[60] But which types the two in *Street Scene* represent is not clear. Are they arguing lovers, or a prostitute and a client? Is the woman angry with him and feigning indifference, or is she simply bored? She certainly does not appear to be pleased – and yet, I would argue that the image is about a self-conscious pleasure. The two are engaged in an elaborate role-play, and the frozen quality of Brandt's image is not the inevitable result of staging (he could easily have asked them to appear more 'natural'). On the contrary, the self-consciousness is what Brandt is recording here: the frisson between the couple is generated by their self-awareness – and by the nocturnal setting itself.

Nights in Hamilton – and Brandt – liberate Londoners from the constraints of authenticity. Far from insisting on any simple notion of a temporary escape from the real, however, these nightscapes, I would argue, reveal states of *aliveness* that only the urban night provided. The French novelist Pierre Mac Orlan wrote of the night that it presents us with an imaginative landscape – a form of the 'social fantastic', in Mac Orlan's terminology – that 'is rather naive and always easy to understand'.[61] For Hamilton, this naiveté, or crudity, of the night allowed him to tap into his Londoners' inner lives in a way that was impossible in the harshly realistic, grey light of day. Ella is the most successful example of this process; her desires are indeed figured as uncomplicated, and easy to summarise in the most basic of statements. Such a statement concludes Ella's unrequited love for Bob, whom she sees one last time in a West End street, before he hops on a bus:

> As she looked at him now, in these last few moments, it seemed that he was transfigured with almost unholy attractiveness – physical attractiveness – that was the point – sheer physical attractiveness.[62]

There is nothing more to Ella's desire for Bob than the obvious – the Rudolph Valentino-lookalike has been the content of her daydreams, and the final surge of feeling is neither more nor less truthful or sophisticated than those daydreams. But there is a sense here that even this simple confession is a difficult one for the barmaid of The Midnight Bell to make; she can only think such things within the dramatic setting of the twilit streets.

Hamilton was in the minority in his relish of the West End's pulp-fiction quality. The area irritated and repulsed writers more often than it charmed. The following chapter considers writing that turned to the nearby Soho for authenticity, where the lights were dimmer, streets narrower, and life seemingly protected from the fake glossiness of the life 'up West'.

## Notes

1. Ralph Nevill, *Night Life: London and Paris – Past and Present* (London: Cassel, 1926), p. 68.
2. Jerry White, *London in the Twentieth Century: A City and Its People* (London: Viking, 2001), p. 311.
3. Lewis Melville, *The London Scene* (London: Faber & Gayer, 1926), p. 87.
4. On the history of crowds and their nineteenth-century representations in a wider socio-political context, see John Plotz, *The Crowd: British Literature and Public Politics* (Berkeley and London: University of California Press, 2000).
5. George Gissing, *In the Year of Jubilee* (London: Hogarth, 1987), p. 68.
6. Gissing, *In the Year of Jubilee*, p. 68.
7. Isabella Ford, *On the Threshold* (London: E. Arnold, 1895), p. 50.
8. Dorothy Richardson, *Pilgrimage, vol. 3: Honeycomb* (London: Virago, 1973), p. 240.
9. Erica Rappaport, for instance, discusses the way in which women's shopping was beginning to transform the West End even before 1914, in *Shopping for Pleasure: Women in the Making of London's West End* (Princeton and Chichester: Princeton University Press, 2000). See also Liz Conor, *The Spectacular Modern Woman: Feminine Visibility in the 1920s* (Bloomington: Indiana University Press, 2004).
10. For a thorough discussion of the complexities of early twentieth-century women writers' attitudes to the city streets, see Deborah Parsons, *Streetwalking the Metropolis: Women, the City and Modernity* (Oxford: Oxford University Press, 2000).
11. *The Municipal Journal and Public Works Engineer*, 9 Sept. 1932.
12. Martin Battersby, *The Decorative Thirties* (New York: Walker, 1971), p. 96.
13. As Chris Otter explains, 'only in retrospect, with much historical simplification . . . does electric light seem inevitably poised . . . to become the dominant twentieth-century illuminate'. *The Victorian Eye: A Political History of Light and Vision in Britain, 1800–1910* (Chicago: The University of Chicago Press, 2008), p. 174.

14. Gerald Kersh, *Night and the City* (London: Michael Joseph, 1938), p. 12.
15. John Dos Passos, *Manhattan Transfer* (London: John Lehmann, 1925), p. 101.
16. Norah Hoult, *Time Gentlemen! Time!* (London: William Heinemann, 1930), p. 213.
17. Hoult, *Time Gentlemen! Time!* p. 215.
18. George Orwell, 'Why I Write', in *The Complete Works of George Orwell*, ed. Peter Davison (London: Secker & Warburg, 1998), vol. 18, p. 317. All subsequent references in this chapter are to this edition of *The Complete Works*.
19. George Orwell, *Keep the Aspidistra Flying* (London: Penguin, 2000), p. 233.
20. Orwell, *Aspidistra*, p. 192.
21. David Trotter, *The Uses of Phobia: Essays on Literature and Film* (Malden, MA: Blackwell, 2010), p. 51.
22. George Orwell, 'Inside the Whale', in *The Complete Works*, vol. 12, p. 88.
23. Rita Felski calls Gordon's 'conversion' 'largely unmotivated and singularly unconvincing', in 'Nothing to Declare: Identity, Shame, and the Lower Middle Class', *PMLA*, 115 (January 2000), p. 36. Even Loraine Saunders finds the ending 'doubtful' in an otherwise appreciative reading of the novel, in *The Unsung Artistry of George Orwell: The Novels from Burmese Days to Nineteen Eighty-four* (Aldershot: Ashgate, 2008), p. 4.
24. Storm Jameson, *Company Parade* (London: Virago, 1982), p. 109.
25. Ibid.
26. Jameson, *Company Parade*, pp. 305–6.
27. Virginia Woolf, 'Modern Fiction', in *The Common Reader, First Series* (London: The Hogarth Press, 1975), p. 189.
28. On *La Comédie humaine* as 'the first real sequence novel', see Elizabeth Kerr, *Bibliography of the Sequence Novel* (Minneapolis: University of Minnesota Press, 1950), p. 36 and Lynette Feebler, *Gender and Genre in Novels without End: The British Roman-Fleuve* (Gainesville: University Press of Florida, 1995), pp. 9–10.
29. Quoted in Chiara Briganti, 'Mirroring the Darkness: Storm Jameson and the Collective Novel', in *Margaret Storm*

*Jameson: Writing in Dialogue*, ed. Jennifer Birkett and Chiara Briganti (Newcastle: Cambridge Scholars Publishing, 2007), p. 78.

30. See Jennifer Birkett, *Margaret Storm Jameson: A Life* (Oxford: Oxford University Press, 2009), pp. 163–5.
31. Jameson, *Journey from the North* (London: Collins & Hartville, 1969), vol. 1, p. 329.
32. Jennifer Birkett, '"The Spectacle of Europe": Politics, PEN and Prose Fiction. The Work of Storm Jameson in the Interwar Years', in *Women in Europe between the Wars: Politics, Culture and Society* (Aldershot: Ashgate, 2007), p. 31.
33. Storm Jameson, *Love in Winter* (London: Virago, 1984), p. 40.
34. Jameson, *Company Parade*, p. 27.
35. T. S. Eliot, 'Marie Lloyd', in *Selected Essays* (London: Faber & Faber, 1932), p. 407.
36. Jameson, *Company Parade*, p. 25.
37. Storm Jameson, *None Turn Back* (London: Virago, 1984), p. 18.
38. Norah Hoult, *Apartments to Let* (London: William Heinemann, 1931), p. 40.
39. Hoult, *Apartments*, p. 293.
40. Hoult, *Apartments*, p. 29. For the possible Freudian context of the novel, see Chapter 3.
41. Hoult, *Apartments*, p. 170.
42. Jameson, *Love in Winter*, p. 248.
43. Jameson, *Company Parade*, p. 35.
44. Patrick Hamilton, *Hangover Square*, in *Twenty Thousand Streets under the Sky* (London: Vintage, 2001), p. 104.
45. George Buchanan, *Entanglement* (London: Constable, 1938), pp. 12–13.
46. Buchanan, *Entanglement*, p. 9.
47. Jean Rhys, *After Leaving Mr Mackenzie* (London: Penguin, 2000), p. 40.
48. Hoult, *Apartments*, p. 179.
49. Hoult, *Apartments*, p. 195.
50. Jameson, *Love in Winter*, p. 170.
51. Patrick Hamilton, *The Midnight Bell*, in *Twenty Thousand Streets under the Sky* (London: Vintage, 2001), p. 42.

52. Jerry White dates the shift towards restraint and good taste in prostitutes' appearance as early as the late 1860s. In *London in the Nineteenth Century: 'A Human Awful Wonder of God'* (London: Jonathan Cape, 2007), p. 307.

53. *May the Twelfth: Mass-Observation Day-Surveys 1937 by over Two Hundred Observers*, ed. Humphrey Jennings and Charles Madge (London: Faber & Faber, 1987), p. 101.

54. Hamilton, *The Midnight Bell*, p. 42.

55. Patrick Hamilton, 'The Quiet Room' (1925), *The Patrick Hamilton Collection*, Harry Ransom Centre, box 1, folder 1.

56. Hamilton, *The Midnight Bell*, pp. 6, 17.

57. *It*, dir. Clarence G. Badger, Paramount Pictures, 1927.

58. Patrick Hamilton, *The Plains of Cement*, in *Twenty Thousand Streets under the Sky* (London: Vintage, 2001), p. 394.

59. Hamilton, *Plains*, p. 373.

60. Norah Wilson, 'The People', in *Camera in London* (London: Focal Press, 1948), p. 43.

61. Pierre Mac Orlan, 'Elements of a Social Fantastic', in *Photography in the Modern Era: European Documents and Critical Writings, 1913–1940*, ed. Christopher Phillips (New York: Metropolitan Museum of Art and Aperture, 1989), p. 47.

62. Hamilton, *Plains*, p. 523.

# Chapter 2

# Soho Nights

For the author who had grown tired of the frenetic life of the West End, the teashops and the red-lipped girls, Soho seemed to be the natural refuge. As the West End's shabbier cousin, tucked away in the narrow streets behind Piccadilly, Regent Street and Shaftesbury Avenue, Soho was often seen as an anomaly, an island of heterogeneity and irregularity in the very heart of the commercialised central London where everything and everyone appeared to be increasingly standardised. By the 1930s Soho had long enjoyed a reputation as London's most mixed quarter, home to a heady variety of nationalities and professions. For John Galsworthy, writing in 1920, that 'amalgam' was all too much:

> Untidy, full of Greeks, Ismaelites, cats, Italians, tomatoes, restaurants, gangs, coloured stuffs, queer names, people looking out of upper windows, [Soho] dwells remote from the British Body Politic.[1]

Indeed, Soho had always seemed more French, and then more Italian, Greek and Eastern European, than it had ever been English, and the foreignness was a source of intermittent anxiety for those who, like Galsworthy, counted themselves as representatives of the 'British Body Politic'. For others, the foreignness was what made Soho appealing. According to Thomas Burke, 'when the respectable Londoner wants to feel devilish he goes to Soho, where every street is a song. He walks through Old Compton Street, and, instinctively, he swaggers; he is abroad; he is a dog.'[2] It was easy to feel tough for a time while getting drunk in a Soho boozer; Patrick Hamilton boasted to his brother Bruce about his 'wild' Soho outings, one of which, he claimed, landed him in 'a doss-house'.[3] Like George Gissing gathering 'useful ideas' at a 'die-sinker's place' in Clerkenwell before writing *The Nether World* (1889),[4] Hamilton thought of his nocturnal explorations of Soho as opportunities for making 'sociological observations'.[5] These sociological expeditions were different in kind from their nineteenth-century equivalents, which had been centred mainly on the East End and its picturesque landscapes of poverty and vice. Soho gained prominence as an alternative destination for literary slumming at least in part because it did not require writers to forego their daily comforts. No one traded their good clothes for rags in order to blend into this underworld, located only a stone's throw from the commercially glamorous West End.

One could effortlessly combine a pleasant outing in Piccadilly with a saunter through the dark streets of what was becoming everyone's favourite slum. In Dorothy Richardson's 'Clear Horizon' (1938), for instance, an Italian café bar that she frequents is presented as a place where genteel leisure can be effortlessly combined with sharp social observation. Dining at her favourite café bar called Donizetti's, Miriam Henderson makes an astute summary of her Italian host – 'a peasant, because men of that stratum when saluting or conversing with a "lady and gentleman", always, if you notice, apparently ignore the lady'.[6] Yet, despite the this uncomfortable disparity in 'manners' (that is, in culture and class), Miriam remarks to Hypo Wilson – a writer based on H. G. Wells – that she likes coming to Donizetti's because 'I never have to deal with cheap waiters with lost-soul faces'.[7] She is keen to differentiate her reasons of going Soho from Hypo's/Wells', whom she silently mocks for his 'ignorance of her perfect awareness of the conflict in him, between his bourgeois scruples and his secret, newcomer's delight in what he had called his "slum"'.[8] Richardson identifies a feature of Soho representations that is characteristic of the period: many of the self-styled sociologists (especially male ones) heading to nocturnal Soho had not grown out of the aesthetic conventions (and the inevitably accompanying pangs of guilt) of slumming; Miriam is at least aware of the fact that her evening out in a Soho Italian café bar has mixed motives: she, too, is slumming in a sense, but has fewer scruples about enjoying the pleasures, social and gastronomic, Soho offers. Richardson's differentiation between these two types of observer – the disingenuous anthropologist and the insightful hedonist – is crucial to this chapter. While several (mostly male) writers of the period still wrangled with feelings of fascination, disgust and guilt during their nocturnal expeditions, others allowed themselves to relax into Soho's nocturnal lifestyle while still remembering to take mental notes of its intriguing contradictions.

Joseph McLaughlin has suggested that 'the appeal of Soho as a new locale of the urban jungle' in the early twentieth century was triggered by a complicated phenomenon that can best be articulated as a 'crisis in mapping', whose roots he locates in London's early twentieth-century expansion.[9] I would argue, however, that this anxiety about London's stretching boundaries did not really result in a fundamental shift of representations of nocturnal London from the East End to Soho: plenty of novels set in the East End appeared throughout the interwar period, as did journalistic and essayistic accounts of the East End at night.[10] The popularity of Soho in the 1930s as a setting for London novels may have been due more to its double reputation – simultaneously as a slum of sorts, *and* as a coveted destination for dining and dancing. Despite the persistent separation of Soho from the West End in the period's fiction, and the insistence of the authenticity of the former as opposed to the glitz of the latter, many writers of the period happily combined trips to both; one could despair at the commercialisation of modern culture while surrounded by the neon glare of West End's Piccadilly, and then turn off the main streets into Soho for an instant dose of urban grit. Besides, this variation may have become necessary by the end of the First World War; as H. V. Morton shrewdly pointed out in 1936, the locations traditionally associated with slumming – the East End, the Docks and the Embankment – were beginning to bore readers:

Before us lies the mystery of dark London, of London under the glow of lamps . . . Before us, also, lies danger – the awful danger of repeating a story that has been well told already . . . I promise not to drag you through that inevitable night on the Thames Embankment or the equally ancient night in a doss-house.[11]

Relocating to Soho did not automatically guarantee novelty – in many cases, it merely offered a slightly different set of clichés. Many investigations of Soho resulted in versions that simply mirrored those of the East End, and photographic representations of Soho were as prone to this as literary narrative. *Soho* by Francis Sandwith and *Footsteps Coming Nearer*[12] by Bill Brandt are exemplary in this respect: their photographs of Soho revel in the easily identifiable markers of dissipation and disorder; each image includes a woman on her own in the empty nocturnal street, and the mess left by revellers only a few hours before – a knocked-over rubbish bin in Sandwith's photograph, and what looks like a spilt drink in Brandt's (Figs 2.1 and 2.2).

Brandt's decision to emulate scenes of prostitution resulted from the influence of Brassaï, whose collection of photographs *Paris de nuit* (1933) featured several realistic portraits of Parisian prostitutes. In fact, Brandt's collection *A Night in London* (1938) in which *Footsteps* first appeared featured French titles alongside the English ones, with *Footsteps Coming Nearer* becoming *A l'affût du client*. Brandt, however, like Sandwith, has reduced the urban night to an assembly of glimpses of its constitutive parts: we see only the woman's gleaming white shoes and the man's partially visible, anonymous figure. The rest is left to the viewer's imagination, and, I would argue, both Brandt and Sandwith opted for such broad strokes because their photographs reproduced a version of Soho that was widely circulated in the period's journalistic pieces, essays and novels.

Documenting Soho's routines of nocturnal dissipation became thoroughly fashionable during the 1930s. The writer and journalist Maurice Richardson turned an eventful night

Figure 2.1 Francis Sandwith, *Soho*, 1930s. Reproduced courtesy of the Estate of Francis Sandwith, administered by James Sandwith.

Figure 2.2 Bill Brandt, *Footsteps Coming Nearer*, 1938. © Bill Brandt Archive.

out in Soho's 'bottle-party belt' into an article for the short-lived magazine *Night and Day*, which promised its readers 'the lowdown' on 'London's Pleasure Zone' between July and December 1937. Richardson announced his report on Soho's pleasures as nothing less than a collection of 'rather gloomy little notes on the way downhill – fragments from the noct-ambulant travel-diary of an amateur sociologist'. His account of the Soho night is complete with images of 'alley cats raking over the muck in the gutters' and 'that very silly fat woman who had been mixing gin with brandy' who 'has slipped off her chair onto the floor'.[13] There is nothing new or unique in these descriptions of grime and debauchery, which echo Jack London's East End, though Richardson's unkind eye also pins down aspects of the 'contemporary Night-Town' that do seem to be specific to modern Soho, namely its easy mixing of classes and corresponding cultures of leisure:

> in even the dreamiest, most swelegant places – where the 'smart' ones move slow like chameleons in air or schizophrenes emerging from a catatonic stupor – there are sure to be some lobster-pink men and half-tight old women in funny dresses to provide a livelier, more agitated form of grotesque spectacle.[14]

Despite the snobbery of Richardson's description, it does identify the aspects of Soho nightlife that appealed to other 'amateur sociologists'. This chapter is about these numerous investigations and reports from the 'Night-Town', and about the spaces that facilitated such quests. Café bars, restaurants and nightclubs gave Soho its identity and accommodated its complex social and cultural mixes.

That leisure spaces were fundamentally important to the kind of urban experience Soho provided was first underscored in Joseph Conrad's *The Secret Agent* (1907), in a scene that involves the Assistant Commissioner dining in one of Soho's small restaurants that offer a mixed European cuisine (an early example of fusion cooking in London), a place that that exudes 'an atmosphere of fraudulent cookery'. The Assistant Commissioner is served this fake food by what appear to be fake

Europeans, no longer in possession of any distinct identity, 'as denationalised as the dishes set before them'. He, too, feels a pleasant loss of identity, 'an evil freedom', and is 'struck by his foreign appearance' upon catching a sight of himself in the restaurant mirror.[15] The prominence of Conrad's novel in recent literary criticism has placed questions of cosmopolitanism and national identity at the heart of critical discussions of Soho and its representations;[16] Conrad's novel demonstrates that these concepts had distinct spatial parameters. As Judith Walkowitz points out in a recent study of twentieth-century Soho's nightlife, Soho's cosmopolitan venues had the capacity 'to stimulate the imagination and to extend the promise of infinite possibility to men and women across the social landscape'.[17] Walkowitz's meticulous research of these spaces – their histories, meanings and significance to generations of Londoners – has proved to be an important resource for the discussions of Soho in this chapter. The focus here, however, is on the particular set of opportunities – and pitfalls – Soho spaces provided to those with literary ambitions.

## Smash and Grab: Café Bar Fictions

For many writers working in the late 1920s and the 1930s, Soho provided an answer to complaints about the lifelessness of the contemporary English novel. For example, in 1935 Cyril Connolly claimed that 'the English mandarin [writer] simply can't get at pugilists, gangsters, speakeasies, negroes, and even if he should he would find them absolutely without the force and colour of the American equivalent'.[18] Yet a writer of Soho, it seems, could. *New Statesman* reviewers were particularly fond of the new Soho melodramas, praising their vitality and colourful portrayals of local slang.[19] English versions of the American hard-boiled novel set in Soho were attempted by a number of authors during this period, including Grierson Dickson in *Soho Racket* (1935), Walter Greenwood in *Only Mugs Work: A Soho Melodrama* (1938), Gerald Kersh in *Night and the City* (1938) and James Curtis in *The Gilt Kid* (1936). Essentially, they are all melodramas, which Greenwood acknowledged in the title. They tend to feature gangsters on paths to redemption and maturity, with the sentimentality offset by curt speech and plenty of slang. Curtis's hard men, for instance, talk Cockney, and all men address each other as 'mugs', while the women are referred to as 'tarts', 'dames' or 'cows'. Such novels also seem to have made for exciting cinema: Curtis's *They Drive by Night* was made into a proto-noir film in 1938, Kersh's *Night and the City* into the classic 1950 film directed by Jules Dassin, while Robert Westerby became a successful scriptwriter in the 1950s.[20]

It is hardly coincidental that many of these Soho fictions included scenes in Italian café bars: if Soho was 'abroad', then the café bar was the furthest one could travel within its exotic atmosphere; one Soho novel of the period, George Scott-Moncrieff's *Café Bar* (1932), owed its title to this space, and set almost the entire novel within it. The novel received praise on its publication as a mercilessly realistic exposure of the Soho underworld; *The Left Review* commended it as a work that 'acidly reveals the true misery and degradation of Soho'.[21]

Degradation and, indeed, degeneration are the main themes of this melodrama which traces the decline of two respectable men as they idle their time away in the Nine, the café bar of the novel's title. The significantly named gentleman-cum-café-bar fixture Porlock partakes of the excesses of Soho life, falling for a prostitute and losing track of time, attracted to what seems to be 'a life more vital than he had found before', and unaware of 'the sucking lassitude'[22] that is concealed, at first, by the novelty.

Recalling a friend of Dr Watson's in Conan Doyle's 'The Man with the Twisted Lip' (1891) who wastes his life in the opium dens of East London, Porlock is a 'wreck and ruin of a noble man'.[23] He 'had belonged to smart society', but a hatred of 'snobbery, highbrow talk, and smugness' leads him to Soho[24] – he has much in common both with the angry young men of the 1950s, and with the Victorian addict, although his addiction is to the intoxicating atmosphere of idleness rather than to any particular drug. The feelings of revulsion and regret that inevitably follow are dramatised in a nightmarish scene which, again like Victorian opium-den writing, relies on narratives of xenophobia and degeneration, here constructed around notions of Italian, rather than Oriental, foreignness. Porlock recoils from the sight of a young Italian crook, 'utterly horrible', with 'demoniac good looks' and a 'mocking cry'.[25] Another drifter central to the novel, Harry Larkins, 'the son of a chemist in a country town' 'who had run away and changed his name, got odd jobs, got poorer – got rheumatism', also discovers the Nine, and in it his undoing. He, too, gets mixed up with prostitutes (no other type of woman is granted an existence in the novel), but repents towards the end when he bumps into a syphilitic man outside the café bar, whose appearance warns him that 'I may be like that. O the town, the murder of this London!'[26]

In his discussion of the concept of degeneration in late-Victorian England, Daniel Pick has explained that it emerged from an anxiety about 'mass democracy and the fate of the body in the city'.[27] Literary uses of the 1930s café bar such as Scott-Moncrieff's can be traced to this anxiety about the city's democratic spaces, which resulted in physiological and biological interpretations of its social problems – 'the language of "demoralisation" gave way to "urban degeneration"'.[28] Like Joseph Conrad's deformed visages in *The Secret Agent* – the cabbie's 'bloated and sodden face of many colours', or Chief Inspector Heat's 'face marred by too much flesh'[29] – the mis-shapen crooks of Scott-Moncrieff's novel construct a Soho in which the café bar hardly civilises the underworld with coffee; on the contrary, it infects the area with a brand of physical degeneration imported, as it were, from the discourse of East End writing.

Patrick Hamilton's *The Midnight Bell* also represents the Soho café bar as a den of iniquity, and relies upon images of grotesque physicality for its effect. The hard-working, self-educated barman Bob has the misfortune to have fallen in love with a prostitute called Jenny, and with Jenny he is dragged through the hell of the London underworld – dingy boarding houses, sleazy nightclubs and the worst place of them all – the Soho café bar patronised by petty criminals. 'Billy's', concealed behind 'a little curtained window', reveals 'rather a Rough

Crowd', as Jenny apologetically puts it. The interior of 'the little den' horrifies Bob, who wonders 'whether any crowd, outside a jail, could be rougher'. A dizzying list of the different types that frequent the place follows:

> [A] painted young woman of about fifty-two, with a figure about three times the size of that of the ordinary woman, and such as only the impecunious taxi driver could love . . . paper sellers, unemployed mechanics, pickpockets, Jews, a gentleman resembling a bruiser . . . a sly youth of about thirty who looked as though he lived upon the immoral earnings of women, and did.[30]

This researcher's beady eye is particularly adapted to spotting – or rather creating – caricatures. Like Scott-Moncrieff, Hamilton is relishing the atmosphere of sleaze and petty criminality, confirming with a knowing wink that the 'sly youth of thirty' not only 'looked' like a gigolo, but definitely was. The gusto with which this list tumbles on to the page reads oddly alongside the insistence on Bob's outright horror at the 'roughness' of this Soho crowd. Hamilton's bartender Bob is explicitly identified as an ex-sailor at the beginning, 'and his behaviour had been neither eccentric nor snobbish in foreign ports'.[31] It is highly unlikely, then, that a Soho café bar is the roughest place he has ever seen; Hamilton's own debauched 'research' undertaken in Soho pubs and bars has thoroughly interfered with the needs of the novel. Like Scott-Moncrieff, Hamilton ends up at the café bar not in search of the exciting 'abroad' Soho could provide, but on a quest for 'the sharp distinctions of the older kind of town', as Orwell put it.[32] Ultimately, his voracious reading of the American Naturalists such as Theodore Dreiser and Sinclair Lewis appears to have had less of a lasting effect than the inevitable influences of Dickens and Gissing.

The confined space of the café bar assaults Bob's senses with the sights and the smells of the world to which Jenny belongs; he notices the 'far from spotless' collars of the men, the 'glaring' make-up of the women,[33] and is almost overcome by nausea. Here Hamilton is every bit the egotist of the kind

Storm Jameson mocked in 'Documents' – focused only on his visceral responses to standards of living to which he is unaccustomed – 'What things I am seeing for the first time! What smells I am enduring!'[34] In order to transform the café bar into a Victorian den, however, Hamilton must not only recreate its patrons as underworld types; he also has to transform the space itself, reimagining it as a 'den'. The 'one gas mantle at the back' that illumines the café bar helps set the tone of disgust – in this bleary light, it is no wonder that all women except Jenny appear ugly, and all men rough.[35] It is true that café bars catered to a small, local clientele. These venues, which had arrived in London in the early 1920s with a wave of Italian and Greek immigration into Soho, displaced the larger, more luxurious cafés in the Parisian style that had dominated the area before the war. Nevertheless, they were set up by ambitious entrepreneurs who invested in modern, horseshoe-shaped bars, marble-topped tables and crisp lighting.[36] These were modest spaces, but not without some pretence to glamour.

Edward Burra's painting *Snack Bar* (1930) captures this mixture of seediness and glamour in a sly parody of the period's representations of café bars and of Soho in general, its foreignness, its association with prostitution, and even its famed obsession with food and coffee. Painted in Burra's signature 'enamelled' watercolour technique, the painting renders everything in the café veneered and hyper-real. Everything looks as though it has the same smooth texture, and as though everything has been assembled from perfect spare parts: one large Italian nose and pair of large hands; one ham, very pink; one prostitute, made up to look as pink as the ham, and so on; the painting pays a playful tribute to a range of Soho clichés, but it also expresses a genuine relish of the sleazy glamour of the café bar. One of Burra's influences was German New Objectivity,[37] but this painting has neither the satirical sting of a scene by George Grosz nor the despair palpable in the work of Max Beckmann. Burra was a rare kind of British intellectual during the 1930s, having embraced fully new forms of mass democracy and mass culture: he enjoyed cinema and jazz, and the vibrant urban milieus of Harlem, Marseille and Paris. In fact,

Soho seems to have been singled out as a subject for a painting precisely because it had an affinity with those other cities,
and *Snack Bar* is one of the few British scenes Burra painted
during the interwar period. This café bar – or 'snack bar', as
he chooses to call it – is not a Victorian den, but a modern,
brightly lit site of a relaxed, unforced sociability.

An Italian café bar provides one of the main settings in
Storm Jameson's novel *Here Comes a Candle* (1938), which
Jameson wrote very quickly while in financial difficulty, and
which she did not consider to be her best work. The novel
has a sensational plot involving arson and includes steamy sex
scenes and a wide range of characters including Jewish gangsters, a prostitute and a property speculator: it is every bit the
hack job Jameson thought it was, and had Jameson's plan to
turn *Candle* into a script for a film come to fruition, the book
would have made a fine proto-noir thriller.[38] Yet it is also a per-
ceptive and ambitious study of a tiny Soho community located
in the fictional New Moon Yard, and as such Jameson's most
successful attempt at what she identified in 'Documents' as an
experiment in creating 'documents' or 'records' of contrast-
ing city experiences – randomly selected areas of 'the social
body' which it is the novelist's task to 'open up'.[39] It is the type
of novel Blanche G. Gelfant would have termed 'ecological' –
focused intensely on a very small part of a large city.[40] Once a
slum, 'since the War the place had recovered a kind of spurious
prosperity, despite the decay, the want of air, the smells. Not
all the tenants were disreputable.'[41] Jameson gave New Moon
Yard a precise location, 'a stone's throw off Berwick Market',
Soho's commercial heart. This Soho is not just a destination
for middle-class slumming; it is introduced with a list not of
exotic characters, but of the numerous businesses that service
the area:

> there were dress shops, with garments made especially for
> undersized tightbottomed young women, shops selling oil,
> pâtes alimentaires, mysterious sausages, a Belgian pastrycook's,
> a herbalist. The district throbbed like an ant-heap with human,
> and insect life.[42]

Criminality and respectable work coexist matter-of-factly here, and Jameson suggests throughout the novel that the crooks and the hard-working Soho residents are often the same people.[43] The gangsters in *Here Comes a Candle* entertain dreams as banal as those cherished by the people they con or intimidate – 'they wanted the same things as other people wanted – a nice, paying little garage, a flat in Park Lane'.[44] The two Jewish con-men for hire who will carry out the arson that will wipe out New Moon Yard at the end of the novel, Ben and Franklyn, are particularly fond of Soho's bourgeois offerings: despite the fact that they are about to carry out what a policeman will call their 'dirty piece of work',[45] they take their time over coffee and macaroni at Pizetti's, the Italian café bar around which much of the novel's social interaction revolves.

Pizetti's is not a 'den', to recall Hamilton and Moncrieff, but its atmosphere of quiet prosperity is constantly undermined by 'as tough customers as he [Pizetti] had had in the place'. During one of their visits Ben and Franklyn try to gauge whether the residents might collude with the arson plan, ordered by the local nightclub proprietor in order to get an insurance pay-out. Giuseppe Pizetti notices Franklyn move his hand 'very slightly on the table', and instantly feels 'that he had been menaced'.[46] Jameson had an eye for such cinematic close-ups, and one senses that this was at least part of the reason why she gravitated towards packed London spaces such as café bars and teashops: they offered plenty of opportunities for collecting such details.[47] It seems that it was in this novel, much more than in Jameson's more ambitious London trilogy *The Mirror in Darkness*, that she was able to realise the aesthetic goals she had set in 'Documents' – to render people's emotions by means of 'fact',[48] or closely observed visual detail. There are elements of this approach in *The Mirror in Darkness*, notably in *Love in Winter*, where the dramatic scene of William Gary's rejection of Georgina Roxby is punctured with similar close-ups of hand gestures. Throughout the meal, during which William will turn down Georgina's desperate offer of marriage, he keeps looking at her nervously moving, cigarette-stained hands, wondering whether 'she was now only playing a part' and noting that '[s]he had a vivid sense of the right and dramatic gesture'.[49]

Dramatic gestures become the focal points of the most effective scenes in *Here Comes a Candle*, such as the silent, intensely uncomfortable exchange between the local prostitute Enid Jones and the visiting Franklyn. Enid is at the café bar daydreaming about a version of herself as a mysterious and sophisticated lady: 'She put on a haughty expression, and drummed on the counter with her right hand, as if she were playing a piano. She wanted to impress on anyone watching her that she played.' She hopes that this particular gesture will make her seem alluring and 'French' to the other customers at the bar. Franklyn interrupts this performance with a single cruel gesture, 'turning his thumb down, with deliberate brutality'.[50]

Franklyn and Ben will carry out their job perfectly, not simply damaging New Moon Yard, but annihilating it. At least one of the residents, a decent but unsuccessful carpenter called George Barley, knows of the plan to burn down the courtyard buildings, but does nothing to stop it. Most of Jameson's Sohoites live in a state of languor, and for them there is no escaping this mind-set simply by leaving Soho and sobering up – here, even the sober characters inhabit a kind of stupor, missing the dangerous changes that are taking place all around them. For Pizetti and his wife Maddalena, running the café bar is simply a way to make money in order to retire respectably back in Italy. It is an extension of their calm domestic life on which the external world makes little impression. One of the residents, and bar regulars, Charlotte Mannheim, catches a glimpse of Maddalena 'through the half-open kitchen door', 'scraping vegetables with her hands in a bowl of earthy water'. To Charlotte, Maddalena appears 'content': 'I have been overwhelmingly happy, she thought . . . and I know what agony of mind is – but I have never understood contentment.'[51]

Charlotte is a Soho veteran and a recognisable type – a beleaguered anarchist whose husband was killed in Hungary. In a surreal scene where Charlotte is invited to share dinner with the Pizettis, the full extent to which Charlotte's memories of extreme happiness and extreme agony clash with the imperturbable contentment that rules at Pizetti's becomes apparent:

> Charlotte Mannheim said fiercely: 'Stalin killed my husband.'
> She saw them look at her stupefied. 'What did I say?
> What nonsense! I'm mad.' She pressed her hand on her head.
> 'It is forty years since my husband was killed – and he was
> killed in Hungary, by the police. 'Don't take any notice. I was
> dreaming,'
> 'It's the heat,' Pizetti said . . .
> 'No one in this country drinks enough olive oil,' Maddalena
> Pizetti said tranquilly. 'It cures anything – sleeplessness, colds,
> stone, everything.'[52]

Jennifer Birkett has interpreted the novel as an allegory of 'a capitalism in a long-drawn-out crisis', 'of an England on the edge of conflagration'.[53] Reviewing the novel for *The Nation* in 1939, Norah Hoult proposed to read the novel's characters as 'ante-bellum, trying to grab something and run before a smash comes'.[54] Charlotte Mannheim's incoherent memory is of almost half a century ago, but 1930s Soho is London's meeting place for the Black Shirts, a fact of which New Moon Yard's residents are either unaware or unwilling to contemplate. Pizetti and Maddalena are as dreamily ignorant of what goes on around them in London as they are of the changing social landscape of Italy – the 'sacred soil'[55] of Pizetti's childhood exists only as a memory. This is a London which, in Orwell's words, is 'sleeping the deep, deep sleep of England', from which it 'shall never wake till we are jerked out of it by the roar of bombs'.[56] In fact, there is a visually compelling reference to the coming war at the novel's end when a policeman examining the fire that has engulfed New Moon Yard thinks that 'the place looked like an air raid'.[57] Jameson provocatively links the 'smash and grab' attitude of the Londoners who think nothing of destroying their city for personal gain – or are too indifferent to oppose such acquisitive madness – and the coming war.

Life in New Moon Yard triangulates between the tenement buildings, the café bar and a nightclub called The Screech Owl – for which Jameson reserves her harshest criticism. This establishment has none of the homely graces of the café bar; it is definitely seedy, a fact that is poorly disguised by genteel interior design effects, such as the 'unashamedly rosy and sentimental'[58] lights, which fail to conceal the fact that the place is full of 'hard' women who are 'so ruthless in spreading an artificial colour over their own that the lighting makes very little difference to them'.[59] These 'ruthless' women are not above stealing tips from the cloakroom, and one customer sinks as low as accusing a waiter called François of stealing her watch. François is symbolic of the routine of exploitation and indifference that underpins the festivities at The Screech Owl. He is forced to be obsequious in front of the customer – who, it turns out, has simply mislaid her watch – but is secretly indignant at the humiliation: 'she had her hand over the watch lying on the table, and the waiter concentrated all his loathing on that hand, shapeless, fat, useless'. Throughout the evening François is haunted by the image of this hand (which had almost cost him his job), and it metamorphoses into a surreal symbol of his fears of unemployment, loneliness and his wife's possible infidelity: 'he felt an anguish and loathing, like his loathing of the woman's hand on the table'.[60] Once again, Jameson puts the cinematic close-up to poignant use in this novel: here the closely observed detail acts as an objective correlative, as it were, for the ways in which the brutal economics and ugly politics that underpin the running of the nightclub intrude into its workers' most private thoughts – and into the most intimate of activities that take place here.

Sexual attraction is especially prone to such corruption. Thus the club's most glamorous regular, the young and wealthy Josephine Rapp, is instantly attracted to its thuggish proprietor, Ashton, who is a Hitler sympathiser, and it is clear that this excites her as much as the fact that he is a good dancer – '[t]he cold brutality of his voice delighted the young woman; her eyes gleamed with admiration and interest'.[61] Young and rich women are almost always suspect in

Jameson's novels of the 1930s, and tend to fall for fascists, like the gorgeous but sentimental and confused Georgina Crosby in *Company Parade*. Josephine, however, is a muddled enough thinker to be vaguely fascist herself – 'Well but, Daddy, [in Germany] the children are so *clean*. Not like here.'[62] The ease with which she has sex with Ashton in his room after the dancing testifies not to a welcome expression of female sexuality, but to a recklessness and a lack of intelligence; Ashton, for one, feels nothing but boredom afterwards, thinking only of Josephine's father's money. Josephine is desirable, and desiring, but there is something perverse about both: the sight of her body makes even her father (accompanying her at the nightclub) 'vaguely uneasy': 'Her full, vivid lips were moist, and her body seemed to him to be standing up nakedly in its dress. He was shocked by these images, and felt cold.'[63]

Intensely private, rather than politically inflected hells open up on the dance floor in Jean Rhys's *After Leaving Mr Mackenzie*, where Julia Martin has the misfortune of ending the evening of her mother's death in a nightclub, dancing with an insistent old man who approaches her in a cartoonish manner, 'on the tips of his toes'.[64] To Mr Horsfield, accompanying Julia on the joyless night, the dance seems unnatural and repellent:

> She got up. Her manner was constrained, full of an unnecessary bravado . . . How idiotic all this dancing was, idiotic and rather sinister! . . . She seemed to him to be moving stiffly and rather jerkily. It was like watching a clockwork toy that has nearly run down.[65]

Afterwards, Horsfield wonders why she danced at all, and she answers with a fatalistic maxim that applies to all of Rhys's heroines: 'sometimes one has to do things'.[66] Zolaism inflected many descriptions of nightclubs between the late 1920s and the mid-1940s, with dance hostesses making particularly frequent appearances in narratives that oversaw the progress of young women from naive girls to run-down desperados like Julia. Women who have no private incomes and spend their nights at bars or nightclubs rarely meet happy endings in the period's

fiction, and when the period's 'less soothing writers'[67] turn to
Soho nightclubs and dance hostesses for subject matter, they
gravitate towards tales of stagnation and misery, and the atten-
dant sensory overload of grime, dirt and bad breath. Gerald
Kersh indulges in a page-long description of the interior of the
nightclub, lit by a 'single flyblown electric light', couples swirl-
ing in 'an airless atmosphere, heavily impregnated with alcohol, mildew, nicotine, and the ammoniacal smell of unwashed
women'.[68] The dance hostess at this establishment, called Vi, is
suitably debauched – 'under her rouge, one could distinguish
the papery greyish pallor of the night-bird – the dead opacity
born of dank dance-halls'.[69] Vi's physical infirmity effortlessly
extends to her mental instability; she is impulsive, lazy and an
insatiable shopper. The dissolute mentality of the nightclub,
where the men's squandering of their money represents success, is mirrored in her own improvident spending. Vi's even-
tual undoing is signalled by her turn to prostitution to support
the spendthrift habit.

Alfred Hitchcock's film *Downhill* (1927) offered an interesting twist to the dance hostess tale, putting a male taxi dancer
at its centre. Roddy Berwick's last job before he is left penniless in the streets of Paris is as a nightclub taxi dancer who
is effectively pimped to rich old women by the club's (female)
proprietor. Despite the Paris setting, there are clear parallels
between these nightclub scenes and London-set tales of Soho
dance hostesses. Ivor Novello wrote the script and acted the
lead role, which explains the focus on a male dancer, and, perhaps, the misogyny. It seems that the plot was as satisfyingly
generic as stories about typists marrying their bosses, or society
women eloping with plucky working-class men. Novels detailing dance hostesses' unhappy progress certainly endured into
the 1940s. Ethel Manning's *Julie: The Story of a Dance-Hostess*
(1940) followed the 'slow degradation' of a girl from the prov-
inces who gets a job at a nightclub (in suburban Newchester,
however, rather than Soho), and has 'to get used to talking
half a crown from a man and feeling "cheap"'.[70] Julie has been
seduced by a man twice her age long before she came to London, and has had a child by him, but it is in the nightclub that

she goes 'to the devil', 'without realising it, from sheer indifference to what happened to her'.[71]

Photographic journalism, too, appeared enamoured of tales of dance hostesses bored and exhausted by their jobs, and, if not on their way downhill, certainly stuck in a rut. In 1942 the magazine *Lilliput* published a photo story by Bill Brandt titled 'Soho in Wartime'. Only one of the photographs in the sequence draws attention to the destruction of the war, with bombed buildings clearly visible in the background. The others could well belong to the 1930s Soho culture of Italian café bars and dancing clubs.[72] In fact, one of the photographs had been taken in the 1930s at Charlie Brown's pub in Limehouse (Fig. 2.3), and was then re-captioned for the 1942 story:

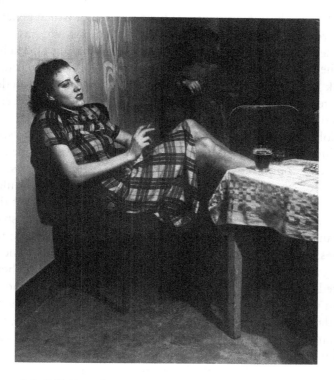

Figure 2.3 Bill Brandt, *An East-End Girl* (Brandt's caption in *London in the Thirties*). © Bill Brandt Archive.

In a night club off Newport Street, a hostess is waiting for her day to begin: her day begins after midnight. Soon she will be dancing, laughing at the jokes she has heard a hundred times, smiling at the compliments that have grown flat as the beer in front of her.[73]

The master manipulator of London settings, Brandt often showed a complete disregard for the authenticity of his locations and characters. In this photograph, however, the borrowing from one London setting in order to illustrate another is not as seamless as in other similar metamorphoses. It is as though Brandt had never been inside a Soho nightclub (which is possible), relying instead on fictional accounts of these places. The East End and Soho are unconvincingly conflated. Firstly, the woman's dress would have been far too casual for a nightclub, which generally required full evening dress; secondly, her pose would have been deemed too relaxed or 'fast' in an establishment that prided itself on the professionalism and ladylike manners of its staff. And the drink itself, the beer gone flat to match her presumed boredom, is suited more to a pub than a nightclub where champagne, cocktails or spirits would have been consumed.

Soho nightclubs did have a reputation for dubious social mixing. Robert Murphy recalled that at The Silver Slipper, one of the indomitable Mrs Kate Meyrick's establishments, one could see 'the cream of Britain's aristocracy rubbing shoulders with the roughest and toughest of the underworld'.[74] Yet these were not straightforwardly tough places; the dance hostesses certainly were not paid to have sex with their customers; their duties were limited to dancing with male patrons and encouraging them to spend as much money as possible on the (heftily priced) drinks and chocolates. If anything, working as a hostess often resulted in marriage, and Mrs Meyrick herself married off her daughters to members of the aristocracy by installing them as dance hostesses in her nightclubs.[75] Clubs generally cared about their reputations, intent on attracting as wealthy a clientele as possible. Martin Pugh points out that much of the interwar media hysteria about nightclubs had little to do with what really went on inside them, and more with the inveterate racism and class prejudice that defined the press: 'they reported . . . a white woman sitting on a black man's knees. It was this that really caused the outrage rather than the drink offences.'[76] The marriages between people of different classes provided another source of outrage for the press that made snide remarks about 'strange matrimonial alliances' that resulted from nightclub revelry.[77]

Naturalistic portrayals of these spaces had more to do with literary vogue, then, than with what really went on within them. There were other ways to represent them, however – German rather than French in origin – and a couple of 1930s writers, especially those with connections to the theatre, tried. W. H. Auden and Christopher Isherwood transformed an English hotel scene into an Expressionist tableau in their collaborative play *The Dog beneath the Skin* (1935), where the stage directions read:

> [*Enter the* Nineveh Girls. *All that is mechanical, shallow, silly, hideous and unbearably tragic in the antics of a modern cabaret chorus should be expressed here in its most exaggerated form. Crude lighting, Rowdy music.*][78]

Both Isherwood and Auden were influenced by German Expressionist theatre, especially by Bertolt Brecht and Brecht's collaborations with Kurt Weill.[79] Both intensely disliked modern entertainment, although Isherwood returned to the cabaret again in *Goodbye to Berlin* (1939), portraying it as another nightmarish, Expressionistic set. It is attended by rich men, 'lethargic, pale, probably Dutch', and their women who 'were elderly, had thick legs, cropped hair, and costly evening-gowns'. The women sit around silently, 'looking neglected, puzzled, uncomfortable, and very bored', while their rich and boring husbands talk about business, uninterested in the hired dancers' 'absurd, solicitous' performance of pleasure, which is entirely for the benefit of the wealthy customers.[80]

Expressionist influences made it in into the descriptions of a Leicester Square nightclub called The Royal in Norah Hoult's *Youth Can't Be Served* (1933). Like Hoult's other work from the 1930s, the novel is intriguingly inconsistent in its generic and stylistic affiliations. It follows the progress of a naive suburban teenager called Eileen Boyce, who moves to London in order to attend drama school and meets trouble when she finds a job as a nightclub hostess; all the elements of a Naturalist drama are in place. Eileen finishes at the Pansy drama school and promptly finds herself among the army of London's unemployed actors. Like Katherine Mansfield's unfortunate singer Ada Moss in 'Pictures', she tries the back stairs of one theatre agency after another, to no avail. During her sole interview with a theatre company, she lamely replies with 'I shall think about it' to an offer of a role as an extra, only to find out several minutes later that her interviewer was going to give the unimportant job to the first girl who would accept.

A series of mishaps finally leads Eileen to The Royal, where she auditions in a dingy ballroom, which is also a bar, is looked over by the male staff 'with what she felt was a hostile curiosity', and at one point wishes she were a prostitute: '[t]hey would be better able to cope with this than she would'.[81] Things go from bad to worse on her first night – she has to dance with a paranoid man who thinks there is a woman watching them from the corner of the room; later he deliberately offends her with a tip: 'I'll give you two pounds. Which is exactly what I'd pay a prostitute off Piccadilly.'[82] Eileen is fired after just two nights' work: she gets blind drunk and leaves with a man before she has finished her shift.

Yet, despite all the Naturalistic detailing, the many encounters described in the ten-page-long scene accumulate to produce a de-naturalising effect. The activity within the club, as the night progresses, increasingly resembles a stylised play, with dancing partners exchanging fragmented lines – or asides, as they almost read – about the Great War and its fast-approaching sequel. Hoult's version of the nightclub is not overtly political the same way Isherwood's cabaret scenes are, presenting the nightclub not as a symbol of a rife, dehumanising capitalism, but as a site where personal traumas are replayed. One of Eileen's partners is completely immersed in his feelings of regret and foreboding:

No one seems to remember the war. Well . . . you'll know about the one that's coming. I shan't be in that. One little war was quite enough for me.' He fell silent, and his eyes looked away from her. She sensed in him loneliness and hunger, and felt vaguely sorry. Was everyone around her really here because they were miserable?[83]

The Soho nightclub is gradually transformed during this long scene from a place of sensual contact between men and women (and of sexual propositioning) into a muted performance of post-war isolation. The dancing itself no longer implies the coming together of bodies; on the contrary, it expresses a disorientating disconnectedness between bodies and minds. It is as though Eileen were dancing with ghosts, on an evening that has 'the quality of a rather ugly dream':[84]

The band started: couples took the floor, tall and short, fat and thin, here a pretty girl, here a gawky one. There were eyes which looked outward, observant of the impression they were making; other eyes which were blank, showing nothing, telling nothing . . . Everything masked. It was when people – writers, saw things like that that they wrote expressionist plays, calling the background an Ultimate Reality, or something which made everything still more baffling – playing in which it seemed sense to say that what the world needed was more glue . . .[85]

Presumably, Eileen learnt her Expressionist terminology at the Pansy drama school where she is a student. Hoult gained her knowledge of it from her own, albeit indirect, involvement in experimental theatre: she lived in Dublin throughout the 1930s and worked as a theatre reviewer, and would have been familiar with the Dublin's Gate Theatre, which staged experimental, especially Expressionist drama throughout the interwar period.[86] Although the attempt to transfer her observations to Eileen's point of view does not quite work, Hoult's novel, more than any other novel of Soho from the period, testifies to an irresistible urge to twist representations of the area's nocturnal leisure into un-English shapes. Look hard enough, and you can see Berlin, or New York, in its café bars and nightclubs. Like others, how-ever, Hoult was confronted by the fact that London's 'abroad' was also still English, and the nocturnal cultures she was writ-ing about were not imported into Britain without undergoing a process of cultural assimilation. The stylisation of the dance scenes in *Youth Can't Be Served* competes with the lively, real-istic dialogue between the different dance hostesses (most of them working-class Londoners), and the mixture of cattiness and camaraderie that defines these exchanges. The women she describes are thick-skinned and resourceful, their conversations devoid of the Continental despair Eileen encounters on the dance floor. One woman, after noticing Eileen's vulnerability, cheers her up in a way that would fit well into a novel by J. B. Priestley:

> Give your face a rubbing up, a massage is often soothing and passes the time if you haven't the price of a Turkish bath or a trip to the Riviera or the Blue Mediterranean, or you feel too bored to accept the invitation you haven't got from the Duch-ess of Wandsworth Common to go to her cocktail party.[87]

While Soho may be the 'Mediterranean' – or New York, or Berlin – to those who embark on cultural tourism there, for Hoult's dance hostess the nightclub could not be further from the exoticism associated with a foreign holiday. For this host-ess, this is work at its most mundane, punctured by daydreams of a face massage imagined in the language of a magazine advertisement. These women are not wind-up dolls, and their mundane experiences are treated with considerable sympathy.

Another writer who showed a similar appreciation for, and plenty of compassion towards, Soho residents in general and its dance hostesses in particular was John Pudney, whose novel *Jacobson's Ladder* (1938), like Jameson's *Candle*, examines the lives of several Sohoites who all live in the same street. It is partly a generic Soho gangster melodrama, with a plot that involves, predictably, crooks and shady deals in nightclubs, and a murder, in which the central character gets entangled. But it is also a novel that is evocative of a way of life – familial, deeply invested in sensory memory and under threat from a capitalism that is more aggressive than the small trade that has kept Soho going for generations. The small trader Jacobson himself is in danger of surrendering to greed born of his new, 'crazy'[88] dreams of expanding his business, which he realises by undercutting the other traders, formerly neighbours and friends, in Rushlit Street. This corruption of the spirit manifests itself in a shift from Jacobson's delight in the daily sensory contact with his workshop where his parents had worked before him – 'he knew how every corner smelt from boyhood[89] – to insatiable cravings for new sensations: 'The purple and the ornate, the tessellate and the unique would be his everyday trifles. Rare fruit, flowers out of season, and women with bright lips would stand always ready to his need.'[90]

Jacobson's vulgar dream of material luxuries and red-lipped women does not interfere with his ineradicable drive to help others, however; the novel will see him help the dance hostess Annie, who accidentally falls pregnant – not to have an abortion, but to have the baby and look after it. Everyone has cinema-fuelled daydreams and mercantile ambitions in this novel, including Annie, who, while under chloroform during the birth, dreams of a private nightclub studio upholstered with pink plush. In the end, however, such fantasies coexist harmlessly with the reality of Soho life. *Jacobson's Ladder* is part allegory of modern capitalism at work, and part moral fable about avarice. Yet its observations of the fragile ecology of the Soho of small traders are gentle; crucially, the novel's language serves not disgust, but affection. One of the younger characters, Jacobson's neighbour Mark Bloom, steps into Soho upon finishing his day of work in a factory:

> He crossed into Soho: and felt at home there. The warehouses were closing, but the small tradesmen were standing at the doors of their shops because the spring evening was gentle. People were buying things for supper. There was the stale smell, the smell of streets much used, of things much handled. At this hour the little workrooms would take on a domestic character: women in pink blouses would sit at windows: lean tailors and fat sweating Jewish shopmen would swallow a glass of bitter.[91]

The emphasis on the physicality of Soho here could not be more different from the horror at unclean collars in Hamilton; the excess of matter here is humanising. Instead of Hamilton's semi-criminal 'Jews', there are 'fat sweating Jewish shopmen' – men with bodies and jobs, and a way of life; and the 'smells' of Soho do not offend, but serve as a reminder of continuous human activity. There are many such moments in the novel, where an excess of physicality is a form of exuberance – in another scene, Mark watches Jacobson eat while they are out in a restaurant, 'fascinated . . . by the quick movements of this ugly eater'.[92] Fascination, not disgust, characterises Pudney's use of Soho's sensory landscape in this novel, and the single-word qualifiers of sensory perceptions are essential to this attitude. Thus, describing the way the young dance hostess Annie smells, he writes that '[s]he smelled deliciously of cheap wall-flower scent'.[93] This sentence would have had a very different effect without the qualifying adverb – never mind that the scent is cheap, is the implication. Disgust at women's cheap scent was frequent in literature of the 1930s, including literature of the Left,[94] but it is not there in this description. Pudney's is not a particularly subtle novel, but an immensely compassionate one, revelling in the commercial spirit of Soho and in its residents' contradictions, rather than lamenting them.

## After the War

While the nightclub craze gave way to espresso bars after the Second World War, and the population included, by the late 1950s, immigrants from the West Indies, as well as from Southern and Eastern Europe, Soho remained the site of choice for a particular type of a London narrative centred around impecunious bohemian young men and women, cafés and bars, and rented rooms.[95] The building blocks, as it were, of Soho nightlife, such as women's legs on display among the rubbish, shabby bars and dim lighting, were still available to writers and photographers after the Second World War, John Deakin the most notable among them. Deakin is known mainly for his portraits of Soho habitués such as Francis Bacon and Dylan

Thomas,[96] but he also produced a number of images between the 1930s and the 1970s that are part of the same repertoire as Brandt's and Sandwith's images of Soho shopkeepers, café-bar habitués and women down on their luck. His portraits of 'unknown' women might have been taken at any point between the 1920s and 1950s.

Post-war literary versions also demonstrate continuity with interwar Soho; the teenage playground of Colin MacInnes's *Absolute Beginners* (1959), and the bohemian haven of Colin Wilson's *Adrift in Soho* (1961), was in many ways still the same place as that described by Hamilton, Pudney and Jameson. The precocious narrator of *Absolute Beginners* is aware of the continuous presence of his favourite London area's long history in its streets:

> Now, about Soho, there's this, that although so much crap's written about the area, of all London quarters, I think it's still one of the most authentic . . . in Soho, all the things they say happen, do: I mean, the vice of every kink, and speakeasies and spielers and friends who carve each other up, and, on the other hand, dear old Italians and sweet old Viennese who've run their honest, unbent little businesses there since the day of George six, and five, and backward far beyond.[97]

Soho is reassuringly 'authentic', but it is also a place that never has been anything other than a fantasy: 'one doesn't go into Soho to watch films, because Soho *is* a film'.[98] It is a genre, its 'honest' lives performances. MacInnes's teenaged narrator does not realise that he is hardly the first to point out this paradoxical quality of Soho, or that the area's Italian café bars are not the only spaces in London where one might go to watch urban life as though it were a film. The next chapter considers representations of London spaces that, throughout the first half of the twentieth century, accommodated the most self-consciously performed everyday dramas. Teashops provided their patrons with opportunities for temporarily escaping the humdrum reality of their lives. They also frequently exposed the ruthlessness underlying the fantasy. During the

1930s observing the elaborate role-play that accompanied the consumption of the proverbial tea and eggs meant observing a milieu that was defined both by dreams of glamour and by simmering aggression.

## Notes

1. John Galsworthy, *In Chancery* (London: William Heinemann, 1920), p. 28.
2. Thomas Burke, *Nights in Town: A London Autobiography* (London: Allen & Unwin, 1915), p. 253.
3. Patrick Hamilton, Letter to Bruce Hamilton, Aug. 1927, Harry Ransom Center Collection, box 1, folder 2.
4. George Gissing, *Diary of George Gissing, Novelist* (Hassocks: The Harvester Press, 1978), p. 25.
5. Hamilton, Letter to Bruce Hamilton, May 1927, box 1, folder 2.
6. Dorothy Richardson, 'Clear Horizon', in *Pilgrimage*, vol. 4 (London: J. M. Dent & Sons, 1938), pp. 329–30.
7. Richardson, 'Clear Horizon', p. 329.
8. Dorothy Richardson, 'Dawn's Left Hand', in *Pilgrimage*, vol. 4, p. 218.
9. Joseph McLaughlin, *Writing the Urban Jungle: Reading Empire in London from Doyle to Eliot* (Charlottesville: University Press of Virginia, 2000), p. 139.
10. See, among others, Simon Blumenfeld, *Jew Boy* (London: Jonathan Cape, 1935); Stephen Graham, *London Nights* (London: Hurst and Blackest, 1925) and *Twice Round the London Clock and More London Nights* (Ernest Benn: London, 1933).
11. H. V. Morton, 'Night in London', in *H. V. Morton's London* (London: Methuen, 1940), p. 307.
12. No exact date is known, but the photograph was published in Brandt's collection *A Night in London* (1938).
13. Maurice Richardson, 'The Bottle-Party Belt', *Night and Day*, 1 July 1937, p. 23.
14. Richardson, 'The Bottle-Party Belt', p. 22.
15. Joseph Conrad, *The Secret Agent* (Oxford: Oxford University Press, 2004), p. 109.

16. See Rebecca L. Walkowitz, *Cosmopolitan Style: Modernism beyond the Nation* (New York: Columbia University Press, 2006), pp. 35–54 and McLaughlin, *Writing the Urban Jungle*, pp. 133–67.
17. Judith Walkowitz, *Nights Out: Life in Cosmopolitan London* (New Haven: Yale University Press, 2012), p. 15.
18. Cyril Connolly, 'London Diary', *New Statesman*, 23 Nov. 1935.
19. See, for instance, Demon Shave-Taylor's and V. S. Pritchett's glowing reviews of novels by Frank Collins, James Curtis and Gerald Kersh: *New Statesman*, 16 April 1938 (p. 660) and 4 June 1938 (p. 958).
20. For a discussion of the Soho realism in late-1930s English cinema, see Robert Murphy, 'British Film Noir', in *European Film Noir*, ed. Andrew Spicer (Manchester: Manchester University Press, 2007), pp. 87–9.
21. *The Left Review*, Oct. 1935, p. 288.
22. George Scott-Moncrieff, *Café Bar* (London: Wishart & Co), p. 14.
23. Arthur Conan Doyle, 'The Man with the Twisted Lip', in *The Original Illustrated 'Strand' Sherlock Holmes* (Hertfordshire: Wordsworth, 1998), p. 186.
24. Scott-Moncrieff, *Café Bar*, p. 13.
25. Scott-Moncrieff, *Café Bar*, p. 141.
26. Scott-Moncrieff, *Café Bar*, pp. 55, 146.
27. Daniel Pick, *Faces of Degeneration: A European Disorder, c.1848–c.1918* (Cambridge: Cambridge University Press, 1989), p. 189.
28. Pick, *Degeneration*, p. 201.
29. Conrad, *The Secret Agent*, pp. 116, 85.
30. Patrick Hamilton, *The Midnight Bell*, in *Twenty Thousand Streets under the Sky* (London: Vintage, 2001), p. 191.
31. Hamilton, *The Midnight Bell*, p. 42.
32. George Orwell, *The Lion and the Unicorn*, in *The Complete Works of George Orwell*, ed. Peter Davison (London: Secker & Warburg, 1998), vol. 12, p. 408. All subsequent references in this chapter are to this edition of *The Complete Works*.
33. Hamilton, *The Midnight Bell*, pp. 55; 91; 90.
34. Storm Jameson, 'Documents', *Fact*, July 1937, p. 11.

35. Hamilton, *The Midnight Bell*, p. 190.
36. White, *London in the Twentieth Century*, p. 335.
37. Simon Martin, 'Introduction', in *Edward Burra* (Farmhand: Lund Humphries, 2011), p. 11.
38. Storm Jameson, *Journey from the North*, vol. 1 (London: Collins & Hartville, 1969), p. 408.
39. Jameson, 'Documents', p. 10.
40. Blanche Gelfant, 'James T. Farrell: The Ecological Novel', in *The American City Novel* (Norman: University of Oklahoma Press, 1970), pp. 175–227.
41. Storm Jameson, *Here Comes a Candle* (London: Cassel, 1938), pp. 10, 14.
42. Jameson, *Candle*, pp. 11–12.
43. Kristin Bluebell points out that Jameson herself 'never stopped working', and that her 'fiction and non-fiction is full of representations of people working'. 'Introduction', in *Intermodernism*, p. 11.
44. Jameson, *Candle*, p. 146.
45. Jameson, *Candle*, p. 275.
46. Jameson, *Candle*, pp. 132, 145.
47. On Jameson and the cinema, see Birkett, *Margaret Storm Jameson*, p. 168.
48. Jameson, 'Documents', pp. 15–16. See the Introduction for a more detailed discussion of Jameson's essay.
49. Jameson, *Love in Winter*, p. 296.
50. Jameson, *Candle*, pp. 133, 123.
51. Jameson, *Candle*, pp. 78–9.
52. Jameson, *Candle*, p. 77.
53. Birkett, *Margaret Storm Jameson*, p. 169.
54. Norah Hoult, 'Awaiting the Fire', *The Nation*, 4 March 1939, quoted in Judith Walkowitz, *Nights Out*, p. 173.
55. Jameson, *Candle*, p. 13.
56. George Orwell, *Homage to Catalonia*, in *The Complete Works*, vol. 16, p. 187.
57. Jameson, *Candle*, p. 275.
58. Jameson, *Candle*, p. 172.
59. Jameson, *Candle*, pp. 178, 189.
60. Jameson, *Candle*, pp. 188, 190.
61. Jameson, *Candle*, p. 182.

62. Ibid.
63. Jameson, *Candle*, pp. 174, 178.
64. Rhys, *After Leaving*, p. 107.
65. Ibid.
66. Rhys, *After Leaving*, p. 110.
67. V. S. Pritchett, 'New Novels', *New Statesman and Nation*, 29 May 29 1937, p. 888.
68. Kersh, *Night and the City*, p. 56.
69. Kersh, *Night and the City*, p. 91.
70. Ethel Manning, *Julie: The Story of a Dance-Hostess* (London: Jarrolds, 1940), p. 28.
71. Manning, *Julie*, p. 197.
72. Brandt occasionally recycled old material for new journalistic assignments: for instance, the photograph of a policeman on the phone, used in the 1938 *A Night in London*, was then reused for *Picture Post* in 1948. It is possible that more than one of the photographs in the 'Soho in Wartime' project had been taken in the 1930s. John-Paul Kernot at the Bill Brandt Archive shared my doubts about the dating of these photographs, but pointed out that by now it is impossible to establish with any certainty since Brandt destroyed many of his negatives.
73. Brandt, 'Soho in Wartime', *Lilliput*, April 1942 (lent by the Bill Brandt Archive).
74. Robert Murphy, *Smash and Grab: Gangsters in the London Underworld, 1920–60* (London: Faber & Faber, 1993), p. 9.
75. For an account of what some of the interwar dance hostesses went on to become, see Kate Meyrick's memoirs, *Secrets of the 43 Club* (Dublin: Parkgate Publications, 1994).
76. Martin Pugh, *We Danced All Night: Britain between the Wars* (London: Bodley Head, 2008), p. 218.
77. 'Shocking Revelations of London's Night Clubs', *Washington Post*, 28 Nov. 1926, quoted in Walkowitz, *Nights Out*, p. 212.
78. W. H. Auden and Christopher Isherwood, *The Dog beneath the Skin* (London: Faber & Faber, 1935), p. 126.
79. See Claire Warden, *British Avant-Garde Theatre* (Basingstoke: Palgrave Macmillan), p. 43; Norman Page, *Auden and Isherwood: The Berlin Years* (Basingstoke: Macmillan, 1998), pp. 80–3.

80. Christopher Isherwood, 'Goodbye to Berlin', in *The Berlin Novels* (London: Vintage, 1999), pp. 258–9.
81. Norah Hoult, *Youth Can't Be Served* (London: William Heinemann, 1933), pp. 277–8.
82. Hoult, *Youth*, p. 300.
83. Hoult, *Youth*, p. 300.
84. Hoult, *Youth*, p. 298.
85. Hoult, *Youth*, p. 299.
86. Hoult later mentioned the Gate in her article 'The Irish Theatre', in *Life and Letters Today*, 25:33 (May 1940), pp. 158–62.
87. Hoult, *Youth Can't Be Served*, p. 303.
88. John Pudney, *Jacobson's Ladder* (London: Longmans, 1938), p. 1.
89. Pudney, *Jacobson's Ladder*, p. 15.
90. Pudney, *Jacobson's Ladder*, p. 18.
91. Pudney, *Jacobson's Ladder*, p. 11.
92. Pudney, *Jacobson's Ladder*, p. 13.
93. Pudney, *Jacobson's Ladder*, p. 51.
94. See Janet Montefiore's chapter 'Vamps and Victims' in *Men and Women Writers of the 1930s*, for a discussion of Left-wing misogyny in 1930s fiction and drama.
95. See Julian MacLaren-Ross, *The Nine Men of Soho* (1947); Colin Wilson, *Adrift in Soho* (1961); Terry Taylor, *Barons Court, All Change* (1961).
96. On Deakin, see Robin Muir, *Under the Influence: John Deakin, Photography and the Lure of Soho* (London: Art Books, 2014).
97. Colin MacInnes, *Absolute Beginners* (London: Macgibbon & Kee, 1959), pp. 64–5.
98. MacInnes, *Absolute Beginners*, p. 84.

# Chapter 3

# Eating Out

In Virginia Woolf's *The Years* (1937), Eleanor Pargiter observes a lower-middle-class couple in a restaurant, enjoying their time off after work:

> She looked about her. At the next table there was a couple dining together; a young man and a girl. They had finished one course; and they were waiting too. The girl had opened her bag and was carefully and deliberately powdering her face; then she took out a little stick and reddened her lips. The young man hitched up his trousers and nonchalantly, as if half-consciously, ran his hand through his hair as he caught sight of himself in the glass. He might be a salesman in a motor-car business, she thought, and she a girl in a manicure establishment, for they were both rather lustrous and shiny. And they were both on their best behaviour. 'Preening', Eleanor said to herself with a smile. That is, she added, showing off; acting a part, naturally, she thought, after their day's work in a shop.[1]

Variations of this scene appear in many novels of the 1930s; the restaurants and teashops where London's lower middle class spent their lunch breaks and evening outings became the settings in which their behaviour, their cultural preferences and even their dreams could be scrutinised. Eleanor concludes after watching the self-conscious couple that their performance is borrowed from the movies and illustrated magazines.[2] This performance consisted of glamour and 'nonchalance' – modes incompatible with their working lives, but perfectly fitting in establishments that offered ordinary people atmospheres far removed from their mundane routines. Although Woolf does not identify it as such, the scene probably takes place in a Lyons Corner House – one of the four grand central London teashops that provided their patrons not only with affordable food, but also with a visual spectacle that could rival the glitter of the West End and the glamour of cinemas. From their beginnings in the great Victorian exhibitions, London's teashops were associated with accessible luxury. While the late-Victorian Savoy and the grand cafés of the West End initially catered only to wealthy Londoners, the expanding teashop chains, the ABC and J. Lyons and Co., soon offered atmospheres of 'regal splendour'[3] to Londoners of all social strata. Clean, bright and lavishly decorated, the Lyons Corner Houses provided a complete dining experience instead of simply serving dinner. Auspiciously situated both for leisured ladies out shopping in the West End and office workers on a night out in the Strand, Tottenham Court Road and Coventry Street just off Piccadilly, these tea palaces endured into the 1970s. In *Angel Pavement* (1932), J. B. Priestley described a London clerk's weekend night out at a Corner House, 'a teashop that had gone mad and Babylonian, a white palace with ten thousand lights':

> It steamed with humanity. The marble entrance hall, piled dizzily with bonbons and cakes, was as crowded and bustling as a railway station. The gloom and grime of the streets, the raw air, all November, were at once left behind, forgotten: the atmosphere inside was golden, tropical, belonging to some high mid-summer of confectionery.[4]

Priestley's is one of many descriptions of the larger Lyons teashops, from the 1930s and before, that stress the outlandish luxury of their décor and the richness and headiness of the all-enveloping smells of sugar and baking. The references to this space earlier in the description as 'the outpost of a new age, perhaps a new civilization, perhaps a new barbarism'[5] echo many similarly alarmist responses to mass leisure during the decade. The main charge against teashops was that they were incompatible with thinking; the secondary, though no less strenuous criticism, had to do with the teashop's reputation for generating daydreams about luxurious lifestyles in people who would never be able to afford them. Priestley's references to a new barbarism no doubt had strong class connotations, his censure reserved for poorer Londoners' aping of the manners of the upper class. In general, escapism through urban leisure was criticised harshly because it was so effective: women and men who dressed up for an evening at Lyons inhabited fantasy versions of themselves so convincingly that it worried those who, in Orwell's words, cherished 'the sharp distinctions of the older kind of town'.[6] Teashops provided a social arena for people who were adept at blurring such distinctions.

Escaping daily life in a teashop had sometimes been represented as a positive activity for the tired working-class Londoner: in *A City Girl* (1887), Margaret Harkness described sympathetically the East End seamstress Nelly Ambrose's first visit to a teashop: '[s]he felt in Paradise; work and trouble were forgotten in the joys of the present'.[7] Lower-middle-class patronage of teashops, on the other hand, attracted the suspicion that there was something deeply inauthentic about them; coupled with this social group's long-standing reputation for pretension,[8] teashops appeared to have become the epitome of a lower-middle-class inauthenticity. It did not help that, from their very inception, teashops were associated with women; despite the fact that teashop patronage was by no means restricted to women, their reputation as places full of stiflingly trivial female chit-chat endured. H. V. Morton, for instance, upon entering a Lyons, noted with some trepidation that he was nearly the only male, having to make his way 'through a jungle of musquash, moleskin, and beaver'.[9] George Orwell's Gordon Comstock in *Keep the Aspidistra Flying* suffers from a nearly pathological fear of teashops, which is really a fear of women. He lingers on the doorstep of a Lyons, but refuses to go in, lest an hour spent inhaling the sweet-smelling air kill his intellect once and for all. 'In the Charing Cross Road the tea-shops called like sirens', but Gordon must resist the temptation, if he is to prove himself to be a proper man and a serious writer. The 'hot cake-scented air' almost 'overcame him', exactly like the overwhelming scent of Parma violets exuded by one of Gordon's 'fruity' female customers at the McKechnie's bookshop where he works in order to support his writing. Comstock's violet-scented customer demands a book about cats,[10] which triggers a mood of existential despair in the already gloomy self-proclaimed poet of 'the dreadfulness of the age we live in'.[11] One of the reasons why teashops are off-limits for Gordon is that not only will he be surrounded by the smells of cakes, but he might end up rubbing shoulders with just such a woman, reading something unacceptably philistine.

Orwell's views on female literary taste are well documented, most memorably in his essay 'Bookshop Memories' (1936), where he claims that 'the ordinary, good-bad, Galsworthy-and-water stuff which is the norm of the English novel seems to exist only for women'.[12] Incidentally, the women who dominate the teashop scene in Morton's sketch have exactly the middlebrow tastes Orwell deplores: 'I heard a girl describe a bridesmaid's dress; another girl was talking about a baby; a third had discovered John Galsworthy.'[13]

Snobbery about teashops was not restricted to male writers; the connections between middlebrow tastes in literature and cinema, and trips to the teashop were further reinforced in Winifred Holtby's essay 'What We Read and Why We Read It' (1935). Holtby claimed that 'the sumptuous settings of film scenarios and the marble pillars of Lyons' corner houses both flatter the same desire',[14] which is to say the desire for luxury. Like Orwell and Priestley, Holtby makes a definitive connection between watching Hollywood films, going to Lyons teashops and reading a certain kind of novel:

> The popularity of Wild West, Foreign Legion and Gangster fiction among clerks employed in sedentary and monotonous occupations is obvious, just as 'society' novels about guardsmen and peeresses, first popularized by Ouida, provide vicarious experience of luxury to housewives and shop assistants.[15]

Holtby's is a critique of what she identifies as a lower-middle-class appetite for escapism, whetted by the lowbrow fiction in tandem with cinema-going and teashop going. Reading a novel that was a little bit like a film script in surroundings that resembled a film set (or the settings of the trashy novels read 'propped against sugar basins')[16] made the lower-middle-class experience of urban leisure doubly unreal – a process she implies to be vaguely dangerous.

There indeed was an affinity between teashops and the other great fantasy spaces of the interwar era, which included artificially constructed film sets, but also real spaces, such as hotels, ballrooms and country mansions. A former Lyons employee reminisced that '[g]oing in from the street, customers had the impression of entering a vast ballroom decorated with immense chandeliers'.[17] And the Trocadero restaurant in Piccadilly, owned by Lyons, boasted 'peach-tinted glass and gilded bronze traceries', designed by one of Britain's most coveted interior designers, Oliver Percy Bernard, who had also designed stage sets and the dining rooms of luxury ocean liners.[18]

Not all teashops were equally glamorous, however. The palatial Corner Houses aside, many were simply functional. The smaller Lyons and ABCs provided the multitudes of London's lower-middle-class workers with quick, affordable lunches and meeting space. Their look was often generic, consisting of rows of simple marble-topped tables in a neutrally painted room.[19] These less exciting spaces fostered observations of shabby lives, rather than of dazzling performances by people on their best behaviour. Accounts of boredom and sordidness were common, to the chagrin of some critics. Peter Quennell, in a caustic review of Hoult's *Youth Can't Be Served*, 'praised' Hoult's precise knowledge of 'what sort of luncheon is consumed by clerks and typists in city tea-shops, and whether the eggs they order are poached, boiled, or fried'.[20] Quennell wryly acknowledged that the pleasure of reading such descriptions lay partly in the fact that 'one is never unwilling to read about characters whose lives are perhaps even duller and less fortunately circumstanced than one's own'.[21] In contrast to the versions of lower-middle-class leisure such as Woolf's, in which dining out compensates for the dissatisfactions of daily life, many 1930s writers constructed altogether different versions of the exchanges between men and women where the teashop, far from being a setting for innocuous fantasy, becomes the stage for boredom and revulsion made disturbingly public.

This chapter traces 1930s accounts of London teashops in which daydreaming alternates with humiliation and in which performances of petit-bourgeois gentility are inseparable from Darwinian struggles for social and sexual relevance. For example, in H. V. Morton's London essays, the teashop appears as a place particularly conductive to saccharine romance with an unsavoury aftertaste: 'She is mooning at him with that you-really-are-the-most-charming-man-I–have-ever-met look in her eyes, and he . . . leans towards her and gazes at her as children sometimes look at cream horns.'[22] This look is not altogether benign; in fact, it is noted and interpreted not by Morton himself, but by 'the girl at the cash desk' who gets to witness such scenes all day, and her reaction, as Morton imagines it, is a cynical disgust at the metonymic alignment of women with the pastry produce which teashops generated.

Metonymic details are central to the teashop scenes this chapter examines. In many 1930s novels, looking around oneself often becomes an exercise in deducing social status or personality from the material details of others' appearances. To teashop patrons, the realisation that other people have inner lives often comes as a surprise, knowledge arrived at inadvertently and strangely via the examination of external detail that ought to help simplify someone's identity, not complicate it.[23] Some literary versions of teashops do put metonymy to this traditional use of locking a personality within a rigid frame of a social stratum. In what one might term the comic mode of teashop writing, men who are unfortunate to find themselves in the overbearing company of women are threatened with being reduced to the role of ineffective clowns hiding behind their hats. These comic performances of gender are juxtaposed with more experimental teashop scenes, in which sociological observation is interspersed with, or altogether dissolves into, surreal visions.

## Bored Women, Beleaguered Men

Wolf Suschitzky's best-known image, *Couple in a Lyons* (1933), is of a lovers' spat. The man is leaning over the table slightly, perhaps trying to resolve the quarrel quietly, perhaps intent on explaining himself, or simply not knowing what to say. But she is looking past him, not just angry, but completely indifferent, and possibly fixing her gaze on something or someone else altogether. Suschitzky explained later that he took the picture because 'she seemed to be giving him a hard time'.[24]

There are many versions of this scene in the fiction of the period, such as Elizabeth Bowen's shorthand of this mood in *To the North* – 'a couple who smoked in silence eyeing each other glumly . . . a blonde in a red hat being insistent angrily'.[25] And in Norah Hoult's *Apartments to Let*, a teashop provides the setting for a spectacular quarrel between the newly engaged couple Elizabeth and Leonard. The reason for the quarrel is the same as in many 1930s novels – the lady is fashionably late. Leonard is an architect trainee and has only an hour for lunch, and for seeing his beloved fiancée. The subsequent meal is rendered as a comic pantomime: she tortures him with silence over their Lyons meal, 'maintaining a bored and superior expression', while Leonard struggles to re-engage her in conversation, 'anxious and frowning'. She relishes the tension, and the obvious effect the performance has on other men: 'Looking away she caught the glance of a man at the next table. Admiring? But perhaps a trifle amused?'[26] Like the woman in Suschitzky's photo she is smoking, right before the meal, much to Leonard's displeasure. The monosyllabic dialogue between them finally peters out as she defiantly lights the cigarette with the matches she has just demanded from Leonard. He is reduced to a mere prop:

> She puffed her cigarette in a bored fashion looking away from him. Once again she caught the eye of the man behind her. Her eyelids flickered. With exaggerated precision she dropped the ash into the tray provided.[27]

For Leonard there's nothing left but to take up his hat and leave with a perplexed 'Good-bye'. The less attention she pays to him, the more inarticulate he becomes, more and more reduced to his hat, and conscious of the prying eyes of the waitresses – 'They seemed to be regarding him with combined amusement and scorn.'[28] Although Elizabeth is only playing, her relish in her performance, and her unexpected lack of guilt about the suffering it causes Leonard, makes her eventually break off their engagement.

From their earliest appearances in fiction, teashops figured as a 'new feminine constellation' that posed a 'threat . . . to a masculine subjectivity'.[29] The precise nature of this threat consisted in the relegation of masculine subjectivities entirely to the realm of the visual or, more specifically, to fragmented, metonymic feminine vision. Men lose their voices, are drowned out by female conversation, and are transformed from psychologically complex characters into two-dimensional types, bit-players in women's visual fantasies. The recurring motifs in teashop scenes from George Gissing onwards involve an emasculated, nervous man, whose only role is to watch his beloved fill herself with food. In Gissing's *The Town Traveller* (1898), Polly is taken out to a teashop by the young Christopher Parish, who 'nervously scanned a bill of fare'[30] while Polly 'quite without false modesty in the matter of eating and drinking . . . made a hearty supper'.[31] Little has changed by the time Patrick Hamilton describes Jenny's equally indecorous behaviour in *The Siege of Pleasure* (1934):

> 'I love you, Jen – that's what's the matter with me,' said Tom, when the food had come, and he was watching her delicate little teeth at work upon [the food].
> 'Don't be so silly, Tom,' she said, looking modestly at her plate. She naturally felt that it was rather inconsiderate to go on calmly filling her face after such a declaration, but common sense protested that there was no earthly use in stopping.[32]

Bob may be too in love to notice that Jenny is 'filling her face', but the expression points to Hamilton's distaste, *à la* Gissing, at the sight of a woman eating. Nineteen-thirties versions of men observing women eating range from such fairly mild discomfort to Eliotic horror. Eliot's prose poem 'Hysteria' (1915) involves a man terrified of being engulfed by his female companion's hungry mouth – 'I was aware of becoming involved / in her laughter and being part of it, until her / teeth were only accidental stars.'[33] As Colleen Lamos points out, this poem forms a 'pattern' with Eliot's other early poetry 'in which phallic types (both male and female) are juxtaposed to Prufrockian characters who are the shy, resentful, and somewhat effeminate victims of the former'.[34] Such male victims routinely appear in 1930s teashop scenes. In Priestley's *Angel Pavement*, the pale clerk Turgis is morbidly attentive to a scene that takes place at the table opposite him in a Lyons, which involves 'two stout middle-aged women, voluble, perspiring, and happy over cream buns', and their inevitable male victim, a 'very small and huddled' middle-aged man who is overwhelmed by the women, about to 'shrink to nothing but spectacles, a nose, a collar, and a pair of boots'.[35]

Nineteen-thirties versions of 'Prufrockian' men are afraid not only of women's bodies per se, but of the effects these bodies' manifold demands (for food, clothing and so on) have on the men's purses. Men tremble and shrink at the idea of financial destitution much more than they do at the Freudian horror provoked by women's eating in Eliot. The scenes of women's unrestrained eating in teashops extend the motif of the insatiable feminine appetite for material goods. Women in 1930s literature often appear as vamps with countless demands for luxury, bankrupting one man after another. Thus in W. H. Auden and Christopher Isherwood's play *The Dog beneath the Skin* (1935), the archetypal vamp Lou Vipond is defined by numerous material requirements:

> 20 cases of champagne,
> A finest pedigree great Dane,
> Half a dozen Paris frocks,
> A sable fur, a silver fox,
> Bottles of scent and beauty salves,
> An MG Midget with overhead valves[36]

and so on. For instance, Jenny in Hamilton's *The Siege of Pleasure* takes for granted a bag of Turkish Delight, purchased with the money her boyfriend 'did not have'.[37] Priestley suggests in *Angel Pavement* that Turgis's chances of finding a girlfriend are miniscule, given his perilous financial situation. His meagre teashop dinners – fish and chips and the ubiquitous eggs – are juxtaposed to the gastronomical preferences of City types who dine at steakhouses, satisfying a 'passion for large authentic juicy pieces of meat and grilled soles and the like, things that cannot be faked and that cost money'.[38] To the women in his office Turgis simply does not exist, whereas the financially solvent, bowler-hatted and steak-eating Mr Golspie has more luck with the typist called Miss Matfield.

Women reduce men to metonymic details – the only distinctions that matter within the visual economy of the teashop are the sartorial details that represent masculinity, and the value of the meal from which their income can be instantly deduced. And in Orwell's *Aspidistra*, men are further reduced to their financial predicament. Gordon is terrified of entering a Lyons because he has only small change left: 'In a vivid vision he saw the girl at the cash desk . . . grin sidelong at the girl behind the cake-counter. They'd *know* it was your last threepence.'[39]

There is something Chaplinesque[40] about these male figures reduced to images of hats, boots and newspapers, except that they toil not at assembling parts in a factory, as in the movie *Modern Times*, but at appeasing their domineering female companions. While, for Orwell and Priestley, teashops represent the emasculating, homogenising mass culture driven by women, for other writers, this capacity for an efficient summing up of men in teashops was a sign of an enviable pragmatism. In *Apartments to Let*, Lena Crossley is able to assess instantly the potential of a man whom she feels 'observing her' from the table opposite: 'Glancing with apparent casualness in his direction, she found that he was fairly young, sufficiently good-looking with shiny greased dark hair – and spoke like a gentleman. Might even be public-school?'[41] It is as though the teashop had become a set for *Gold Diggers*, with Lena's powers of observation concentrated entirely on assessing a man's financial capabilities. The glossy, well-groomed head is an essential detail that differentiates the men worthy of attention from the 'nonentities' of shabby office workers. In another scene, Lena dismisses a balding man she had mistaken for a young one at the cinema, concluding that he is 'only Corner House', and therefore probably not 'worth it'.[42] Lena's quick observations are rendered in a telegraphese of external attributes. The metonymic reduction of masculinity to disposable income is total; leisure here appears to be completely devoid of spontaneous pleasure, as efficient as account-keeping.

Whether such scenes function as outlets for misogyny, as in Orwell, or as the sites of fantasies of women having their revenge by reducing men to items of clothing, these comic scenes have plenty of counterparts in the period's fiction in which the roles are reversed; comedy gives way to unsavoury scenes that involve women under scrutiny in teashops; for female characters – especially those of a certain age – much more is at stake in such situations than for their male counterparts.

## Am I Finished?

Long before the 1930s literary representations of cafés and teashops stressed their inhospitality to women over a certain age, that is over thirty. Katherine Mansfield's 'Pictures' (1917) imported the narrative of an ageing woman reduced to prostitution from France,[43] and made the urban cafés and teashops the central settings of this tale of a woman's terrible, life-changing choice. A day in the life of Miss Ada Moss begins in a dingy Bloomsbury bedsit from which she is to be evicted by the landlady if the rent is not paid that evening. It ends, after many hours of humiliation during various theatre and film auditions, with Miss Moss leaving the Café de Madrid with a 'stout gentleman'. Mansfield's first readers would have recognised at once the significance of the character's decision to cross the road and enter the Café de Madrid, quite clearly modelled on the Café Monico, which was famous for being one of Piccadilly's 'magnets for pimps and foreign prostitutes'.[44] The man who picks her up is unceremonious and vulgar, their conversation culminating in his comment, 'I like 'em firm and well covered', and Miss Moss's voice, the beautiful contralto she dreams of showing off if she could only get an audition, becoming reduced to a set of mechanical cues: 'I'll have a brandy, if it's all the same'; 'I'll come with you, if it's all the same.'[45]

The cruel indifference of city life in this story is underlined by the protagonist's apparent denial of the true extent to which she has compromised her agency, which we partly share through the use of free indirect discourse. Miss Moss is on the threshold of the total invisibility that women over a certain age (and of a certain class) inevitably face in large cities, and every situation in which she finds herself that day painfully reminds her of this. The girls in the acting studio cruelly dismiss her as unsuitable – 'he wanted someone young'; she is also pointedly ignored in an ABC teashop, where in response to her request for a cup of tea the waitress 'sang' 'we're not *open* yet'.[46]

Although they didn't have the louche reputation of cafés such as the Monico, teashops were casually referred to as marriage markets for the waitresses who worked there, a fact cruelly emphasised in 'Pictures', where a waitress pointedly shows off her engagement ring in a way that is certain to get Miss Moss to notice. Teashops were also spaces in which women's bodies were routinely compared to the bakery and confectionery. In his version of a teashop in 'The Tea Shop' (1912), Ezra Pound condescends to a waitress who 'is not so beautiful as she was', and, in effect, to an entire class of women who have to work for a living – something in which both Pound and Eliot indulged in in their early poems.[47] Pound's narrator has come not just for the 'muffins', but also for the opportunity to consume neatly contained narratives of unexceptional lives: 'the August has worn against her . . . she will also turn middle-aged'. The woman here, no longer attractive, seems to be losing out to the baked goods, to which the 'glow' of her youth is comparable: she used to 'spread' it in the same way, it seems, her customers spread the butter on their muffins.[48]

Wrinkles and protruding veins are the damning signs of approaching the invisibility of old age; in Jean Rhys's novels women assess each other's 'freshness' with a ruthless precision. Thus in *Voyage in the Dark*, Anna's older friend Laurie sells Anna to her male friends, stressing the young woman's smooth skin: 'she's not a day older than nineteen', 'where do you see the wrinkles?'[49] And in *After Leaving Mr Mackenzie*, Julia is observed by her new lover, Mr Horsfield, in just such a way, as though she were spoiled goods. In London, he thinks, 'she looked older and less pretty than she had done in Paris': 'Her mouth and the lids of her eyes drooped wearily. A small blue vein under her right eye was swollen . . . The suggestion of age and weariness in her face fascinated Mr Horsfield.'[50] The palette of blue veins and dark circles under the eyes is taken straight out of the Naturalist tradition of writing bodies in various stages of disintegration, what David Baguley refers to as Naturalism's aesthetic of 'liquefaction'.[51] Except that in Rhys's novel, a woman's face seems to be disintegrating not in the rain in the streets, but in the hot lights of a restaurant. Women in 1930s fiction disintegrate in very specific ways – their faces melt or collapse, often as a result of their make-up literally melting in the steamy and heated environments of teashops and restaurants. And keeping one's face together, as it were, is of paramount importance to older women who are able to manipulate their faces to look younger, but not their bodies. In Storm Jameson's *A Day Off*, the ageing heroine, who works in a department store, secures a date on the strength of her face alone – 'he had had to take the lower half of her on trust as it were'.[52] When she and the man first meet, she is standing behind a shop counter, which means he cannot see her bottom half; meanwhile, the long hours of standing have taken their toll on her legs: 'they were twice their size, with veins like twisted bits of string'.[53] Jameson's most memorable metaphors tend to be about entropy; she described *A Day Off* as 'perhaps the only genuinely imaginative book I have written',[54] and this imaginative impulse is Naturalist in origin, despite Jameson's hostility towards the genre in her literary criticism.[55] *A Day Off* certainly reads like Jameson's most aesthetically coherent novel, steeped in obsessive descriptions of her unnamed character's sordid milieu – her room, which is drowning in clutter and dust, and teashops and restaurants from which she is always being ousted by arrogant waiters. As a 1930s circadian novel, it is a perfectly symmetrical response to a 1920s one, particularly Woolf's *Mrs Dalloway* (1924). Jameson's heroine, about the same age as Woolf's perfect hostess, has no parties to look forward to, and has found herself facing the terrifying prospect of loneliness and poverty, since her last lover has broken off their arrangement: 'As she pulled the hall door to after her he said that the whole house smelled of dust and females. But it was not what he said, it was his face.'[56] Her day off is really an attempt to grapple with this sudden, silent abandonment; like Woolf again, Jameson relied on anachrony for constructing her character's inner life – memories of pre-war London, when this woman was married and worked in a hotel, bleed seamlessly into the present-day shabbiness. There is nothing particularly original or imaginative here; rather, the bizarre and compelling forcefulness of this novel comes from its relentless focus on entropy and its visual manifestations. The compulsive descriptiveness cannot redeem this character, despite Jameson's attempt at sentimentality in the final lines – 'The pulse in her arm lying on the dirty sheet is one of the stages of a mystery. Look once more and you can see how beautiful she is.'[57] But the relentless focus on the material details of this woman's slow slide into oblivion effectively suspends the demands of the plot. The almost surreal sense of predictability runs parallel to the almost perverse attentiveness to her bodily existence – coming home after the long and terrible day, Jameson's heroine experiences '[t]he loosening and falling of her body' as 'an exquisite feeling of release': 'She stood with her legs apart to enjoy the new coolness. Her stained rumpled stockings were flung down with other unwashed garments in a corner between the wall and the cupboard.'[58] It is the carelessly treated objects that are the most vivid things in this novel – the 'dead' powder puff with which she tries to conceal the onset of old age every morning; the hat that 'had apparently fainted' next to her as she lies on the grass of a London park.[59] Jameson discovered, in this novel, the possibilities of Naturalist description, its unexpected points of access to the humanity of a character via the surrealism of everyday things.

Naturalist description has another function here – it is the antidote to the dreariness of dialogue. Talking in this novel, as in many other novels of the 1930s, is an exhausting and exhausted activity, and dialogue is little more than an exercise in conveying the disconnection and selfishness that defines relationships. Jameson's heroine starts her evening out with her new lover on a note of cheerful cynicism; like Lena in Hoult's *Apartments to Let*, she makes a shrewd mental summary of the man's character and social standing: 'good clothes, too, collar fastened by a gold safety pin. Or is it rolled? . . . easy with money; no patience; brags about himself – I expected that, the man hasn't been born yet who couldn't, wouldn't.'[60]

Crucially, however, this is the last time during the scene when we are offered the protagonist's first-person perspective. Jameson switches to the third person as soon as the couple begin talking, a jumbled exchange in which the woman's voice is drowned out completely. When it is her turn to talk, he does not listen, yawns and blurts out something about business and bankers. The narration then moves entirely into free indirect style, which exposes the thoughts she fails to exclude from the practical narrative of the evening that she had attempted to construct. Her vague feelings of loneliness and revulsion are only semi-acknowledged, but nonetheless they intrude into the banal conversation. 'For a moment she forgot that everything depended on the success of the evening. She looked round her and felt alone.' An almost unbearably cruel back-and-forth follows: she is so desperate that she has to carefully adjust herself to his every whim. As in other novels by Jameson, exchanges between men and women are characterised by men checking the women's laughter, piqued by their inexplicable enjoyment of surrounding reality.[61] The teashop outing momentarily brings Jameson's heroine spontaneous joy, 'people talking, laughing, reading evening papers, she felt happier than she had felt for months',[62] which is aggressively interrupted by her boorish companion:

'What are you laughing at?'
'Nothing,' she said. 'It's lovely here, isn't it?'
'If you're happy it is.'

> She saw that he didn't want her to be gay, not yet. Wants a
> little pity first, that's it. An emotion less definite than contempt
> crossed her mind; a sudden recognition, vague and familiar.[63]

For Jameson, the teashop appears to have been one of the
urban spaces in which women's minds become alert to the aesthetic patterns formed by the daily life of the city. In *Company
Parade*, Hervey enjoys sitting in the 'impersonal' space of a teashop 'where she could watch without talking. Her mind sprang
awake, like one of those table-maps on which arrows dart
from point to point.'[64] Significantly, Hervey turns to this purely
visual pleasure after the intense disappointment of a meeting
with her neglectful husband, during which she 'swallowed her
disappointment in silence'.[65] Dissatisfied and hampered in their
conversations with men, Jameson's women often enter a deeper,
more productive silence in which the visual faculty acquires
the quality of intelligence which men do not understand, and
cannot mock. The woman in *A Day Off* retreats into visual
perception, letting the conversation run parallel to her separate
experience of the evening – 'her glance wandered round the
room'.[66]

In an earlier episode, she is humiliated in another teashop,
by a waiter who, having discerned her financial insecurity, tries
to make her leave. Although she is angry, and beset by worries about rent, she becomes immersed in the geometric patterns formed by light on the glittering surfaces of the teashop:
'Points of light started wherever she looked, from the knife in
a man's hand, from his bald head, from the chandeliers, the
marble facings, from the glasses and the metal fittings on the
counter.'[67] Ultimately, these pointless observations of objects
humanise this woman, and provide the only link to the past
in which she was not old and poor. It is not the objects themselves that are important, but the tension they provide between
the realm of impersonal beauty she can temporarily enter, and
the passive-aggressive atmosphere of the teashop. The social –
and the dialogic form that expresses it most directly – is almost
always disappointing, both to the character and, one senses,
Jameson herself. Partly, then, the turn towards Naturalism

with its hyper-attentiveness to swollen veins and wrinkles provides an escape route from the Realist mode of writing the city. The unknown woman's boredom with the harsh facts of her existence, and with the inevitably harsh encounters with men she endures, is mirrored by Jameson's own boredom with her role as the observer of these facts. Naturalist description allows for whimsical departures from the strictures of Realism, temporarily suspending the predictable dramas of survival and sexual exploitation in favour of highly aestheticised detail. Abandoning dialogue was key to such escapes into intense visuality.

The total breakdowns of communication that characterise so many teashop scenes in the period facilitated literary practices that circumvent the needs of the narrative. The awkward or resentful silences that puncture leisure scenes in the period's London writing, not only Jameson's, trigger an immersion in dense description; when words fail, something else must work. Rhys's *After Leaving Mr Mackenzie* is exemplary of this use of teashop and restaurant settings. The restaurant dinner in London during which Mr Horsfield assesses Julia's attractiveness rouses contempt and boredom in Julia, who is increasingly unwilling to cooperate. The intent of this meeting is clear; the sleazy 'rosy lights' serve as a reminder of it. Julia, however, is increasingly unable, or unwilling, to concentrate on the task at hand:

> She wanted to attract and charm him. She still realized that it might be extremely important that she should attract and charm him. But she was unable to resist the dream-like feeling that had fallen upon her which made what he was saying seem unreal and rather ludicrously unimportant.[68]

Rhys's characters develop what one might term a radical inattentiveness. Unlike Jameson's unnamed protagonist, who manages to feign an interest in her companion's confidences, Julia aggressively asserts her boredom, refusing to maintain any illusion of the normality of what is taking place. Like other Rhys's characters, she is even prepared to exacerbate the 'unreality' of

the encounter through a display of something very like madness. Having reached an extreme of boredom, Julia

> took a box of matches from her bag and amused herself by
> lighting them one after another and watching them burn down
> to the end. In the midst of this proceeding she said, 'It's funny
> how you say one thing when you're thinking of quite another,
> isn't it?'[69]

Julia's behaviour puzzles Mr Horsfield and, at the same time,
fascinates him. Throughout their rendezvous, Julia behaves
inappropriately – absent-mindedly and even rudely. Her companion, however, appreciates her acknowledgement that the
situation they are acting out – the obligatory meal and drinking that are supposed to make the night that will follow seem
respectable – is ludicrous and repetitive. He is both bored by
Julia's semi-drunken antics, and pleased by the fact that she,
too, finds the whole affair boring. When at the end of the
novel Julia is asked to leave by her landlady, she simply starts
packing. Mr Horsfield cannot help saying, 'You've got some
pluck.'[70] Their fragile romance is based upon a shared sense of
the absurdity of the roles each has been assigned. Unlike the
other men in Julia's life, Horsfield is eventually attracted not to
her 'softness', but to her flashes of defiance.

Rhys's characters enjoy being anti-social in highly sociable settings, savouring encounters that are awkward or mis-
matched. Julia's modus operandi *in After Leaving* consists in
prolonging and underscoring situations in which the absurdity
of the mechanisms of urban sociability is pushed to the extreme.
The setting is familiar, and for a moment it might seem as if
Rhys had decided to introduce a typical teashop description
into the novel: 'A band filled the vast room with military music,
played at the top of its voice. Grandiose.'[71] Instead, the scene
resembles a bizarre exchange of monologues, as though no one
is really aware of the person they are talking to. Julia sits down
at a table next to a 'little man' who 'in the midst of his meal
uttered an exclamation, seized his bill, and rushed off'. Just as
suddenly he reappears, talking to Julia 'excitedly':

'A most extraordinary thing! I've just seen a man I thought
was dead. Well, that's an extraordinary thing. A thing like that
doesn't happen every day to anybody, does it? A man I thought
was killed in the Japanese earthquake.'
   'Were you pleased to see him?' asked Julia . . .
   'Pleased to see him?' echoed the little man cautiously. 'Well I
don't know. But it gave me a bit of a turn, I can tell you.'
   Julia left him talking to the waitress, who was making
clicking, assenting noises with her tongue.[72]

Beneath the triviality of the encounter, which is left unfinished
because neither party is really interested in the other, lies a
strange alternate reality. Julia's sense of the scene around her
grows progressively stranger as she focuses on details – from
the women 'with the naïve eyes of children' sitting opposite
her, to the conspicuous tongue of the waitress. The people
she observes look unfamiliar, perhaps resembling mechanised
objects rather than human beings. In the teashop scene, Rhys's
Naturalist version of the city expands into its adjacent mode of
surrealistic dream-sequence.

## A Chelsea Bun

Naturalism also spills into a surrealism in a teashop-set short
story called 'A Chelsea Bun' (1935) by Frank Baker, who subse-
quently made a career as a writer of thrillers and supernatural
tales in the style of Arthur Machen. Baker's more conventional 'A Chelsea Bun', a short story published in *New English
Weekly*, was written with the paper's preference for naturalistic settings and characters in mind, and resembles such works
as 'A Fragment of London' by J. S. Collis, published in *New
English Weekly* in 1933:

> Mark Lane got his ticket and reached the platform at Aldgate
> in time to catch the shoddy New Cross train. The carriage was
> blowing with the usual cold draught. Cigarette-ends lay on the
> floor as thick as gravel on a drive – the assault of the reeking
> refuse inviting a closed mouth.[73]

Many of the stories published in *New English Weekly* had melodramatic plots in which husbands are abandoned by wives, and women are stuck in doomed relationships. Thus Leroy Charles Fleischer's 'And She Waited' (1933) is stringed together with bleak sentences such as 'he pecked her forehead with a lifeless kiss'.[74]

Baker's story at first glance answers all of these requirements – its setting is recognisably and vividly that of a London teashop on a rainy day:

> There are people at most of the tables, many of them gloomy and taciturn because so uncomfortably wet. Two young men play chess over an Eccles cake they have perfunctorily nibbled. There is a thick smell of doughnuts, old coffee, fish and washing-up . . . The waitresses move with rapid boredom from table to table, their pencils and little chit-pads swishing from their belted waists.[75]

The opening announces both the story's Naturalist credentials, with references to the smells and dampness of the place, and suggests an affinity with Mass-Observers' recordings of city life, especially in its use of snappy, present-tense sentences. The main characters are, suitably, two ageing, stolid ladies, and one of them proceeds to tell the other the story of her son, who ran away and ended up in jail. And yet gradually the naturalistic fabric of the story disintegrates, leaving us with an absurd encounter that leads nowhere, and has no purpose. Mrs Willis is in the teashop on her own, and longing to speak to someone. She spots a woman reading at a table opposite although it is hard to examine her satisfactorily since she is almost entirely obscured by the evening paper:

> A podgy pink hand with long orange nails curved round the edge of the racing page; a ring with a fat red stone like a beetle's back. And above the paper, the crown of an elegant green hat, one of those bowlers with a little feather at the side. Not like the old feathers they used to wear. This is a more discreet reference to the bird that had been plucked. The sort of hat, thinks

Mrs Willis, you see stuck all alone on a stick in Bond Street, the sides of the shop-window fringed with tasselled beige curtains, which fall conclusively upon the hat as night comes. Three guineas at least.[76]

The true life in this story is the life of objects: the stranger's ring lives; so do her nails, and hat. Mrs Willis's shrewd calculation of the woman's wealth is headily mixed with a compulsive anthropomorphosis of her possessions that recalls Katherine Mansfield's short stories. In 'Pictures', the man with whom Miss Moss leaves is referred to as 'the little yacht' after the shape of his hat, and in 'An Indiscreet Journey' (1915) the narrator cannot stop staring at the woman who shares her train carriage, wearing 'a black velvet toque, with an incredibly surprised looking sea-gull camped on the very top of it',[77] which, the narrator imagines, interrogates her about the (illicit) nature of her trip. The scene then erupts into a real, tense interrogation of Mansfield's indiscreet traveller by the wearer of the 'sea-gull'. Moments of mischievous looking that prioritises objects over people can temporarily hold unpleasant encounters at bay, but the emphasis on decoding another life is eventually reinstated.

Baker's story works against the assumption that the urban chance encounter necessarily involves the attempt to construct a story of the stranger's life. The narrative in which objects take on, and take over, their owners' identities is antithetical to the type of encounter which defines the pleasure of urban looking as one of placing and categorising strangers, of unlocking others' lives. In 'A Chelsea Bun' any curiosity Mrs Willis may have had about the woman is replaced with her fascinated contemplation of her hat. One way to read the story is as a woman's daydream about a covetable fashion accessory. It is similar to the many 1930s teashop scenes in which women sip their tea in a state of mental anguish over another woman's better clothing; for example in Hoult's *Apartments to Let* where Lena is 'eyeing the well-tailored black coat' of another teashop patron.[78] However, there is something surreal about the way in which in Baker's story the interest in the hat excludes the possibility of any interest in its owner. And the lack of interest is mutual: Mrs Willis, having initiated a conversation with the hat's owner, embarks on a dramatic account of her past marriage and her son abandoning her and ending up in jail – 'She wipes an eye. The moment of her life story is coming. The stranger, beginning to be bored, looks about and half listens.'[79]

In both Mansfield's and Baker's stories, sartorial objects mock a whole literary genre of urban encounter. In particular, the vivid descriptions of hats playfully invert the tradition of writing the spaces of urban modernity as the theatres of female rivalry and the implicitly deplorable female obsession with clothes and the social status those clothes are presumably designed to display. Instead, these unexpected literary uses of the hat recall the Surrealist tradition of transforming objects of haute couture into *objets d'art*. As Richard Martin puts it, 'fashion and its instruments were at the heart of the Surrealist metaphor, touching on . . . the correlation between the world of real objects and the life of objects in the mind'.[80]

Discussions of hats in Surrealism have been dominated by Freudian theory,[81] and several Surrealists in the 1920s and 1930s did write in terms of a (barely) repressed sexual dimension of modern life. Tristan Tzara's 'Concerning a Certain Automatism of Taste' (1933), with its meditation on the resemblance of hats to genitalia, is frequently cited. However, this emphasis excludes different strands of Surrealist art that were more interested in the idea of the hat's ultimate uselessness. Once an accurate barometer of class, by the 1930s the woman's hat (though not yet the man's) was becoming a luxury without any meaning other than the wearer's love of fashion. An expensive hat was worn by the woman who was unaware it was wearing her. For a Surrealist artist like Eileen Agar this idea of the hat taking over its owner seemed to connote not so much the shallowness of modern materialism, as a possibility for radically reconfiguring one's public self. Agar appropriated the world of haute couture with a light touch and a shrewdness that has only recently begun receiving the critical attention it is due.[82] She modelled for Schiaparelli, looking chic in their stylised hats, and at the same time appeared in the

Surrealist magazine *Minotaure*. Always impeccably dressed and made-up, she balanced a buttoned-up, conventionally feminine appearance with a Surrealist's ridicule of its very foundations. In 'Am I a Surrealist?' (1936), Agar stressed that 'the juxtaposition . . . of a Schiaparelli dress with outrageous behaviour or conversation was simply carrying the belief of Surrealism into public existence'.[83] The hat was the sort of object that could look at once elegant and outlandish, both fashionable and completely unwearable, like the Schiaparelli shoe-shaped creation from 1937, designed by Salvador Dalí, or the extravagant pyramidal hat Greta Garbo wears in *Ninotchka* (1939). Of all fashion objects, the hat seems to be the most likely to lead a life of its own, as it were, not complimenting its wearer, but diverting the attention from her.

In 'A Chelsea Bun' the hat too leads a life of its own, an object the narrator imagines displayed in a shop window, glamorous in a way quite independent of any wearer. This extravagant object introduces a surreal element to the clichéd narrative of a teashop encounter – it makes a mockery of the idea that the urban milieu is suitable for confidences and psychological assessments of strangers. The banality of teashop chatter is rendered unfamiliar, even absurd. In 'A Chelsea Bun', close observation thwarts the potential for psychological involvement; moreover, it releases the participants of the teashop encounter from the burden of faking an understanding.

The sociological impulse behind setting a story or novel in a teashop often led writers and image-makers in non-realist, Surrealist and abstract directions. Teashops and cafés, it turns out, often encourage modes of observation that have little to do with an interest in people and relationships between them. In Hoult's *Apartments to Let*, for instance, even the practical journalist Lena finds herself fascinated by the sight of a man's 'shiny greased dark hair', a detail in that instance quite irrelevant to what she makes of his social status and potential suitability as a lover. The same detail – a man's greased dark hair – appears in *Youth Can't Be Served*, where its meaning appears to be quite different from a simple denotation of social status. The young drama student Eileen Boyce frequents the Isolde tearooms with an older and more experienced friend, Flora. The Isolde is a step-up from Lyons, mainly because it is visited by 'quite a number of real men, not the pale-faced nonentities of clerks who said, "Coffee and poached egg, please, miss", and then hid themselves behind newspapers'.[84] At the Isolde tearoom Eileen is 'intrigued' by a couple sitting on

> the couch which ran at right angles to their tables . . . though she could only see two heads: a glossy dark male head; and a smart little feminine white straw hat on one side of golden hair . . . The heads were always coming very close together . . .[85]

Flora explains that what she and Eileen are witnessing are assignations, 'the Isolde was one of those places where men took women who weren't their wives'.[86] But it is less the obvious relationship between the observed couple that intrigues Eileen than the aesthetic quality of the image they form. They are kissing and whispering caressing words to each other, yet Eileen's gaze is fixed on the neat geometric arrangement that they form within the interior of the café, and on the reflective surfaces of their shiny hair. Her attention to detail goes beyond its uses for social classification. Paradoxically, this releasing of female looking from the mercantile is achieved by rendering it even more highly stylised and dehumanising than before. Teashop gazing is no longer about spotting potential lovers, but about looking at unfamiliar objects. Rather than rehabilitating women's looking by making it idiosyncratic, Hoult presents it as focused on symmetries and repetitions of the typical visual elements of teashops. The appeal of these places is no longer that of a stage of the social dramas of the city, but of an austere combination of geometric lines and corresponding textures.

There is a striking contiguity between Hoult's experiments with teashop observations and a photographic exploration of a Parisian café by Brassaï. *Couple d'amoureux dans un petit café parisien – Place d'Italie* (*Lovers in a Small Paris Café, near the Place d'Italie*) (1932; Fig. 3.1) is a fascinating document of Parisian culture during 'the crazy years', but it also is about urban looking more generally, a meditation on the reasons one might want to take a camera to a café in the first place. Like Hoult's stylised observations, it prioritises the aesthetic appeal of cafés over the sociological content of the interactions that happen within them. What one notices immediately about this image is its shininess, and almost perfect symmetry. The framing locates the couple right in the centre of the image, and they are emanating glamour. The woman's made-up face is lifted triumphantly, as though she were at the very end of a brilliant performance. Doubled in the café mirror, it has the quality of a theatrical mask, a summary of so many performances of urban gaiety. The man is less important to the atmosphere

Figure 3.1 Brassaï, *Couple d'amoureux dans un petit café parisien – Place d'Italie*, 1932. © Estate Brassaï – RMN–Grand Palais.

the photograph creates, except as a necessary component, the other half of the couple. His glossy, reflective hair gives the image the aura of an occasion, of eventfulness. Everything here is perfectly balanced, everything has its counterpart: the two mirrors on each side of the lovers, the sharp corner of the table, the reflecting teapot that is the same in tone as the man's reflecting hair – everything looks as though it were meant to be framed in precisely this way.

Brassaï captured an essential component of the pleasure of café life: the dazzling performances not so much by people as by objects. The drama of this image is partly created by the amorous couple, their self-conscious postures and gestures, but it is also intrinsic to the overall iridescent quality of the scene. The photograph is at once a record of Parisian life between the wars, and an abstract observation of purely visual correspondences. In other words, the emphasis on the luminous surfaces and metonymic details in this image lift it from the mode of mere 'documenting'. As Michael Sheringham puts it, 'in Brassaï, an ostensibly unmanipulated, indexical image can convey a "double vision" which both documents and transforms the real'.[87]

Brassaï is known as the master of the 'small dramas' of urban life, and at least one practitioner of the London street photograph, Bill Brandt, learned this observational style from Brassaï, to whom he had been apprenticed in Paris before coming to London.

However, the significance of Brassaï's image is not just in its direct influence on British photography. Lovers in a Small Café, near the Place d'Italie illustrates the compulsions behind 1930s 'documentary' or 'sociological' descriptiveness of urban spaces; it points to an impulse that is anti-realist in nature, to defamiliarise and even dehumanise the people one observes in cafés or teashops. Partly the fascination of these spaces is provided by the gendered exchanges they host; but partly observing people in such settings allows one to become detached from the sociosexual components of those exchanges, focusing instead on the overwhelming appeal of the textures and visual contrasts that frame them.

Teashop writing tested the boundaries of describing social interactions, pushing the social further and further into the background of scenes set in public spaces. What always seems to be taking place in 1930s teashop scenes are performances that come undone or become overwhelmed by too much observation. This happens in the Corner House scenes in Patrick Hamilton's *The Plains of Cement*. Here Ella attempts to make the most of her outing with the boring Mr Eccles by temporarily inhabiting the role of a Hollywood seductress:

> She knew there was no mistaking her soft and coaxing tone. She was more than 'encouraging' him now. She was what they called 'vamping' the man! Never had she dreamed that she could play such a role – or that she could enjoy it as she was enjoying it.[88]

Ella's cinematic fantasy stands little chance against the hyperreality encouraged by the teashop setting. What kills pleasure in Hamilton is, in the end, the presence of other people: objects and interiors create auspicious and forgiving environments; people always puncture through them with clumsy or cruel remarks. Ella would have had a perfect time had she been able to concentrate on the mental image of herself in the role of a cinematic vamp. Ella's temporary conviction that Eccles may be a suitable candidate for marriage is dependent on what becomes a refrain of sorts in Hamilton's trilogy – 'he looked young, just now in this light'.[89] That is until he opens his mouth to speak. Their outings become progressively less enjoyable as Eccles talks more and more, boring Ella with prissy talk about his fondness for religion and his disapproval of swearing and exposing throughout the monologue a crooked tooth on which she, struggling to ignore the talking, fixates to the point of becoming nearly delirious with irritation: 'What a fool, and what a Tooth!'[90]

If the primary reason for setting fictional scenes in teashops was social commentary, this practice almost always opened up the surreal potential of these spaces. Women's pragmatic summaries of the economic potential of male teashop visitors, and male appraisals of women's sexual attractiveness mutate into observation that is compulsive and dehumanising. These intensely sociable spaces paradoxically inspired writing about profoundly anti-social states of mind and modes of navigating the city that depended upon reducing interaction with other people to a fixation on isolated details. In the context of writing the petit-bourgeois Londoner, this has an intriguing effect: the lower middle classes were typically mocked for their mercantile attitudes and clichéd aspirations based on film scenarios and popular newspapers. Teashop writing, on the other hand, locates the typical attitude of this group of Londoners in an everyday surrealism.

The next chapter considers the ways in which these new assumptions about Londoners' reactions to leisure milieus shaped 1930s representations of cinemas. Far from facilitating a total immersion in the art of film, as was often assumed by the period's intellectual elite, cinemas accommodated a complex and often conflicting set of engagements – with what was happening on the screen, but also with the interior of the cinema and with the other patrons. These were, like the teashops, intensely sociable spaces, but, as the following chapter will demonstrate, this sociability was frequently represented as undesirable, aggressive – the chiaroscuro environment of the cinema tended to exaggerate social tensions, rather than neutralise them.

## Notes

1. Virginia Woolf, 'Galley Proofs of Episodes Excluded during Final Revision of *The Years*', in Grace Radin, *Virginia Woolf's The Years: The Evolution of a Novel* (Knoxville: The University of Tennessee Press, 1981), pp. 227–8.
2. Woolf, 'The Years', pp. 217–18.
3. Aldous Huxley, 'Notes on Liberty and the Boundaries of the Promised Land', in *Music at Night and Other Essays* (London: Chatto & Windus, 1931), p. 123.
4. J. B. Priestley, *Angel Pavement* (London: Granada, 1980), pp. 154–5.
5. Priestley, *Angel Pavement*, p. 154.

6. George Orwell, 'The Lion and the Unicorn', in *The Collected Essays, Journalism and Letters of George Orwell*, vol. 2: *My Country Right or Left*, ed. Sonia Orwell and Ian Angus (London: Penguin, 1970), p. 77.

7. Margaret Harkness, *A City Girl: A Realistic Story* (London: Vizetelly & Co., 1887) p. 47.

8. See Geoffrey Crossick, 'The Emergence of the Lower Middle Class in Britain: A Discussion', in *The Lower Middle Class in Britain, 1870–1914*, pp. 1–60.

9. H. V. *Morton's London* (London: Methuen, 1940), p. 37.

10. George Orwell, *Keep the Aspidistra Flying* (London: Penguin, 2000), p. 17.

11. Orwell, *Aspidistra*, p. 178.

12. George Orwell, 'Bookshop Memories', in *The Complete Works*, ed. Peter Davison (London: Secker & Warburg, 1998), vol. 10, p. 512.

13. H. V. *Morton's London*, p. 38.

14. Winifred Holtby, 'What We Read and Why We Read It', *The Left Review*, 1, no. 4 (Jan. 1935), p. 114.

15. Holtby, 'What We Read', p. 113.

16. Ibid.

17. Peter Bird, *The First Food Empire: A History of J. Lyons & Co* (Chichester, West Sussex: Phillimore & Co., 2000), p. 99.

18. Martin Battersby, *The Decorative Thirties* (London: Studio Vista, 1971), p. 45.

19. See Bird, *The First Food Empire*, pp. 108–21.

20. Peter Quennell, 'New Novels', *New Statesman*, 4 Nov. 1933, p. 555.

21. Ibid.

22. H. V. *Morton's London*, p. 276.

23. Susan Harrow defines 'the metonymic instant' as 'envision[ing] the individual as inescapably defined by social class, profession, gender, and ascribed or acquired values', *Zola, The Body Modern: Pressures and Prospects of Representation* (London: Legenda, 2010), p. 165.

24. Quoted in David Clark, *Photography in 100 Words: Exploring the Art of Photography with Fifty of its Greatest Masters* (London: Argentum, 2009), p. 92.

25. Elizabeth Bowen, *To the North* (London: Vintage, 1999), p. 113.
26. Norah Hoult, *Apartments to Let* (London: William Heinemann, 1931), pp. 70, 72.
27. Hoult, *Apartments*, p. 73.
28. Hoult, *Apartments*, p. 77.
29. Scott McCracken, *Masculinities, Modernist Fiction and the Urban Public Sphere* (Manchester: Manchester University Press, 2007), p. 121.
30. George Gissing, *The Town Traveller* (London: The Harvester Press, 1981), p. 32.
31. Gissing, *The Town Traveller*, p. 33.
32. Patrick Hamilton, *The Siege of Pleasure*, in *Twenty Thousand Streets under the Sky* (London: Vintage, 2001), p. 248.
33. T. S. Eliot, 'Hysteria', in *Collected Poems, 1909–1962* (London: Faber & Faber, 1962), p. 24.
34. Colleen Lamos, *Deviant Modernism: Sexual and Textual Errancy in T. S. Eliot, James Joyce, and Marcel Proust* (Cambridge: Cambridge University Press, 1998), p. 84.
35. Priestley, *Angel Pavement*, p. 156.
36. W. H. Auden and Christopher Isherwood, *The Dog beneath the Skin* (London: Faber, 1935), pp. 138–9.
37. Hamilton, *Siege of Pleasure*, p. 249.
38. J. B. Priestley, *They Walk in The City* (May Fair books, 1961), p. 107.
39. Orwell, *Aspidistra*, p. 77.
40. For a provocative discussion of *Modern Times*, and of the inherent conservatism of the comic mode, see Michael North, *Machine-Age Comedy* (New York: Oxford University Press, 2009).
41. Hoult, *Apartments*, pp. 39–40.
42. Hoult, *Apartments*, p. 44.
43. On the links between 'Pictures' and Colette's *L'Envers du music-hall* (1913), see Gerri Kimber, *Katherine Mansfield: The View from France* (Oxford: Peter Lang, 2008), pp. 118–19.
44. Walkowitz, *Nights Out: Life in Cosmopolitan* London (New Haven: Yale University Press, 2012), p. 197.
45. Katherine Mansfield, 'Pictures', in *Collected Stories of Katherine Mansfield* (London: Constable, 1972), p. 128.

46. Mansfield, 'Pictures', p. 123.
47. See Ezra Pound, 'In the Garden', in *Personae: Collected Shorter Poems of Ezra Pound* (London: Faber & Faber, 1952), p. 93; T. S. Eliot, 'In the Department Store', in *Inventions of a March Hare*, ed. Christopher Ricks (London: Faber & Faber, 1996), p. 56.
48. Ezra Pound, 'The Tea Shop', in *Personae*, p. 127.
49. Jean Rhys, *Voyage in the Dark* (London: Penguin, 2000), p. 106.
50. Jean Rhys, *After Leaving Mr Mackenzie* (London: Penguin, 2000), p. 66.
51. Baguley, *Naturalist Fiction: The Entropic Vision* (Cambridge: Cambridge University Press, 1990), p. 201.
52. Storm Jameson, *A Day Off* (London: Ivor Nicholson & Watson, 1933), p. 229.
53. Jameson, *A Day Off*, p. 230.
54. Jameson, *Journey from the North*, vol. 1, p. 285.
55. See, for instance, her essay 'Has the novel gone into decline?', in *Parthian Words* (London and Glasgow: Collins, 170), pp. 17–41.
56. Jameson, *A Day Off*, p. 40.
57. Jameson, *A Day Off*, p. 219.
58. Jameson, *A Day Off*, p. 214.
59. Jameson, *A Day Off*, pp. 147–8.
60. Jameson, *A Day Off*, p. 231.
61. I discuss this motif more fully in Chapter 5.
62. Jameson, *A Day Off*, p. 230.
63. Jameson, *A Day Off*, pp. 230–1.
64. Jameson, *Company Parade*, p. 29.
65. Ibid.
66. Jameson, *A Day Off*, p. 232.
67. Jameson, *A Day Off*, p. 217.
68. Rhys, *After Leaving*, p. 63.
69. Rhys, *After Leaving*, p. 67.
70. Rhys, *After Leaving*, p. 124.
71. Rhys, *After Leaving*, p. 49.
72. Rhys, *After Leaving*, p. 50.
73. J. S. Collis, 'A Fragment of London', *New English Weekly*, 14 Dec. 1933, p. 205.

74. Leroy Charles Fleischer, 'And She Waited', *New English Weekly*, 14 Dec. 1933, p. 205.

75. Frank Baker, 'Chelsea Bun,' *New English Weekly*, 2 May 1935, p. 51.

76. Baker, 'Chelsea Bun', p. 51.

77. Katherine Mansfield, 'An Indiscreet Journey', in *Collected Stories of Katherine Mansfield* (London: Constable, 1972), p. 633.

78. Hoult, *Apartments*, p. 38.

79. Baker, 'Chelsea Bun', p. 52.

80. Richard Martin, *Fashion and Surrealism* (New York: Rizzoli, 1987), p. 11.

81. See Rosalind Krauss, *The Optical Unconscious* (Cambridge, MA: MIT Press, 1993), pp. 162–3; Robert Belton, *The Beribboned Bomb: The Image of Woman in Male Surrealist Art* (Calgary: University of Calgary Press, 1995), pp. 101–3.

82. See Brigitte Libmann, 'British Women Surrealists – Deviants from Deviance', in *This Working Day World: Women's Lives and Culture(s) in Britain, 1914–1945*, ed. Sybil Oldfield (London: Taylor & Francis, 1994), pp. 155–67; Ann Simpson and David Gascoyne, *Eileen Agar, 1899–1991* (Edinburgh: National Galleries of Scotland, 1999).

83. Eileen Agar, 'From "Am I a Surrealist?"', in *Gender in Modernism: New Geographies, Complex Intersections*, ed. Bonnie Kime Scott (Urbana: University of Illinois Press, 2007), p. 795.

84. Norah Hoult, *Youth Can't Be Served* (London: William Heinemann, 1933), p. 106.

85. Hoult, *Youth*, p. 106.

86. Hoult, *Youth*, p. 106.

87. Michael Sheringham, *Everyday Life: Theories and Practices from Surrealism to the Present* (Oxford: Oxford University Press, 2006), p. 102.

88. Hamilton, *Plains*, pp. 388–9.

89. Hamilton, *Plains*, p. 388.

90. Hamilton, *Plains*, p. 477.

# Chapter 4

# Going to the Cinema

Going to the cinema was the single most important pastime in 1930s Britain. Cinemas boasted 'some eighteen to nineteen million attendances every week', with 'nine hundred and three million cinema tickets . . . sold in 1934'.[1] 'From flea-pits to fairy-palaces',[2] cinemas were everywhere. The picture-palaces were styled as Grecian temples, Spanish villas, baroque mansions and art deco ocean liners. One patron described the Astoria in Finsbury Park as a Moorish paradise: 'the air was faintly perfumed . . . overhead one could see what appeared to be a night sky with stars twinkling'.[3] Going to the cinema, then, was not just about seeing films. In recent decades a number of studies have explored the multi-sensory nature of the movie-going experience, especially its tactile, olfactory and aural dimensions. Jeffrey Richards pioneered the empirical, case-based approach to writing the cultural history of inter-war cinema-going in his monumental *The Age of the Dream Palace* (1984), which not only discussed the significance of the films themselves to the 1930s generation, but also drew on his own personal sensory memories of cinemas – 'most of all one remembers the feel of the faded plush, the distinctive smell of disinfectant and orange peel, the cheer that greeted the lowering of the lights'.[4]

The notion of the cinema as a physical environment defines many literary descriptions of going to the movies during the 1930s and also figures prominently in critical writing about film. Elizabeth Bowen's 1937 essay 'Why I Go to the Movies' is exemplary of this tendency to emphasise the ambient qualities

of cinemas. It is not only, or even not so much, the films themselves that exercise such a powerful appeal on audiences. In
Bowen's account, the two-dimensional world on screen is not
necessarily the main event: 'I go because the screen is an oblong
opening into the world of fantasy for me; I go because I like
story, with its suspense; I go because I like sitting in a packed
crowd in the dark, among hundreds riveted on the same thing.'[5]
Bowen's account emphasises not only the pleasure offered by
the alternate reality of the film, but also the sensory experience
of a 'packed' cinema which is not subordinated to the fantasy
world on the screen, but interacts with it.

The number of scenes set in cinemas increased, it seems,
proportionately to the increase of the new medium's popularity and to the rise in interest in what the masses did with their
spare time. As Valentine Cunningham has pointed out, after
1930, 'suddenly, fiction was cluttered with cinemas' and going
to the cinema was 'abruptly taken for granted'[6] as an everyday
activity for fictional characters. It was also taken for granted
that characters went to the cinema to dream. Cinema audience were often referred to with disdain by writers both on
the Left and Right, all of them claiming more or less the same
thing – that once an ordinary woman or man entered the cinema, she or he stopped thinking. In some instances this anxiety
was tempered by sympathy; in *Autumn Journal*, Louis Mac-
Neice made a rare acknowledgement of the cinema as 'escape
by proxy / From the eight-hour day or the wheel / Of work
and bearing children'.[7] More often, however, the cinema craze
was denounced in hostile terms, as an addiction that resulted in
the loss of political and intellectual agency. In C. Day Lewis's
'Newsreel' (1938), 'this loving darkness' of the cinema is 'a fur
you can afford'[8] – the epicentre of the commodity culture that
insulates his generation from thinking about the horrors of the
coming war. And in Graham Greene's *The Confidential Agent*
(1934), sitting inside a cinema is likened by the central character not just to a dream, but to a hypnotic, subhuman state:

> He felt her hand rest on his knee. She wasn't romantic, she had
> said: this was an automatic reaction, he supposed, to the deep

seats and the dim lights and the torch songs, as when Pavlov's dogs saliva'd.[9]

While the movies were assumed to promote sentimental and 'unreal'[10] ideas about life, the movie theatre itself was also thought to work on the minds of viewers on some psychosomatic level. For Greene, cinemas were culpable of triggering purely sensory or physiological responses in their audiences, appealing to their basest instincts. Paradoxically, these instincts or reflexes were figured as both animalistic and mechanical. The immediate, subhuman response to the warmth and comfort is unhesitatingly opposed to sophisticated thought processes. In W. H. Auden and Christopher Isherwood's *The Dog beneath the Skin* (1935), cinema audiences 'gape at the tropical vegetation', themselves in a vegetable state,[11] while Aldous Huxley rages against a culture in which cinema audiences 'soak passively in the tepid bath of nonsense'.[12] George Orwell's explanation, in *The Road to Wigan Pier*, for cinema's popularity with the unemployed is that at the pictures they can keep warm.[13]

Yet cinemas were not exclusively represented as opulent spaces threatening ordinary people's ability to tell fantasy from reality. Not thoughtlessness, but an excess of thoughts and worries, dominated accounts of going to the cinema that are discussed in this chapter. 1930s representations of cinemas were as varied as people's experiences of these dark spaces, and while some focused on youthful couples touching in the back seats, others made cinemas the settings for tense psychological dramas and discreet unhappiness. A cinema is presented as a site of betrayal and disillusionment in Elizabeth Bowen's *The Death of the Heart* (1938), for instance. During an afternoon at the pictures, the novel's central character, the teenage Portia, is forced to observe, during a perversely aestheticised, painfully prolonged moment, her lover's callous betrayal:

> The jumping light from Dickie's lighter showed the canyon below their row of knees. It caught the chromium clasp of Daphne's handbag, and Wallace's wrist-watch at the end of the row . . . Those who wanted to smoke were smoking: no one

wanted a light. But Dickie, still with the flame jumping, still held the lighter out in a watching pause – a pause so marked that Portia, as though Dickie had sharply pushed her head round, looked to see where he looked. The light, with malicious accuracy, ran round a rim of cuff, a steel bangle, and made a thumb-nail flash. Not deep enough in the cleft between their fauteuils Eddie and Daphne were, with emphasis, holding hands.[14]

This scene functions as a cruel metonym for what happens to Portia elsewhere in the novel: she is being manipulated and scrutinised for reaction by people who do not care whether she has 'a heart'. Portia's heartbreak is illuminated for others' entertainment. The tense atmosphere of this scene is hardly the passivity-inducing tepid bath denounced by Huxley or Orwell. It is a dangerous and vertiginous environment, not because it cuts all ties with reality, but because it reinforces and magnifies reality to an overwhelming effect. No one in this scene is interested in what is happening on the screen: their attention is directed firmly to the real-life drama that unfolds inside the cinema.

This chapter has a dual purpose – on the one hand, it examines 1930s writing about cinema-going that, like Bowen's description, emphasises the role of cinema as a site of bitter realism, where dreams are destroyed rather than generated. On the other hand, it considers scenes that are indirectly dependent on characters' cinema-going for the particular acts of visual framing that they perform.

The reputation of the cinema as a dream palace rests, crucially, on the idea of its complete insularity and separateness from the city outside. This chapter turns to literary versions of cinema-going in the 1930s that on the contrary conceive of the activity as *continuous* with the London life outside. Cinematic experience in the works examined here is presented not as uniquely different from all other urban experience, but as contiguous with it. Importantly, the emphasis in the discussion that follows is on writing that does not *liken* the urban experience to cinematic vision or film aesthetic, but, rather, suggests that the two are concurrent, that they overlap.[15]

Roland Barthes presented the relationship between cinema-going and urban life as one of exchange and continuity in his essay 'Leaving the Movie Theatre' (1975) where he writes that

> it's not in front of the film and because of the film that he *dreams off* – it's without knowing it, even before he becomes a spectator . . . the darkness of the theatre is prefigured by the 'twilight reverie' . . . which precedes it and leads him from street to street, from poster to poster, finally burying himself in a dim, anonymous, indifferent cube where that festival of affects known as a film will be presented.[16]

Although Barthes still conceives of film as dream, and a hypnotic Freudian dream at that, his emphasis on the unity of urban experience and that of the movie theatre resonates with the ways in which authors such as Patrick Hamilton and Jean Rhys wrote about cinema-going. Their characters do not come out of the cinema thinking that they are in a movie, nor is leaving the cinema portrayed as a shock of reality after the dream. In a novel such as Hamilton's *The Midnight Bell*, the movie theatre never creates the expected distance between the world of cinema and real life. Even Bob's ardent visual consumption of a beautiful movie star reminds him of a real woman he has already met, and not, as we might expect, the other way around – the actress is like 'the little beauty to whom he had given a pound two nights ago'.[17]

There is a brief and somewhat cryptic remark in Bowen's 'Why I Go to the Movies' that characterizes the relationship between people's daily lives and the movies as one of subtle influence the effects of which are not immediately felt, and which are activated later, by reality itself:

> To reject, as any kind of experience, a film that is acting powerfully on people around seems to me to argue poverty in the nature. What falls short as aesthetic experience may do as human experience: the film rings no bell in oneself, but one hears a bell ring elsewhere.[18]

Bowen offers an original interpretation of cinema's 'influence' on the daily lives of ordinary people, a much-debated topic between the wars. She suggests that cinema has the ability to sharpen people's perceptions of daily life, not only through the viewing of the film itself, but also through exposure to the environment of the cinema. The most intriguing effects of this exposure will be felt outside the picture palace. Several writers on cinema in the 1920s and 1930s appear to have shared this interest in film not as an autonomous art, but as a continuation of daily life, or a medium that showcased daily life at an unprecedentedly close range. Thus Alistair Cooke, whose essay 'The Critic in Film History' appeared alongside Bowen's in the 1938 collection *Footnotes to the Film*, praised film as an art form in which 'we may be moved at one moment by a line of dialogue, at the next by the look of the veins on somebody's hands, by the sound of a train's siren fading as the countryside fades'.[19] Film presents us with magnified versions of 'the beautiful confusion of life itself'[20] – surprising the eye with rapid successions of images and now suddenly erupting with sound, cinema was hailed by sympathetic critics as the new medium for the poetry of daily life.

Writing about film throughout the 1920s and 1930s explored the effects that cinema-going, and watching even aesthetically inferior films, have on audiences. *Footnotes to the Film* as a collection offered a much more nuanced view of what such effects were, presenting cinema-going not as a totally engrossing experience of an imagined world of which critics such as T. S. Eliot were wary, but as an activity that, although it is mundane and unremarkable in itself, effects a subtle enhancement in people's perceptions of their daily lives. Walter Benjamin wrote about a similar quality of indirect influence of cinema on daily living in the essay 'The Work of Art in the Age of Mechanical Reproduction' (1936). He describes film as a catalyst for the unsuspected sharpening of the city-dweller's senses that transforms her or his dull reality 'by focusing on hidden details of familiar objects', and 'by exploring commonplace milieus under the ingenious guidance of the camera':

Our taverns and our metropolitan streets, our offices and furnished rooms, our railroad stations and our factories appeared to have us locked up hopelessly. Then came the film and burst this prison-world asunder by the dynamite of the tenth of a second, so that now, in the midst of its far-flung ruins and debris, we calmly and adventurously go travelling.[21]

The cine-camera reveals the qualities of the urban landscape that have been invisible to the naked eye. Benjamin presents the consequences of cinema's fracturing of the visible world into minute details as no less than revolutionary, but stresses further in the essay that the full potential of this new way of seeing can only be achieved via irreverent, casual film viewing – 'the public is an examiner, but an absent-minded one'.[22]

The idea that distracted or absent-minded watching held the potential for social and political change was also explored by Dorothy Richardson in her writing for the cinema quarterly *Close Up*; Richardson insisted that film audiences approached the viewing of films with far more sophistication than the near-hypnotic absorption of which they were frequently accused. She defined cinemagoers' talking at the movies as a politically significant act. As Laura Marcus points out, Richardson's references to the 'audible running commentary'[23] of the female viewers have an affinity with Benjamin's positive assessment of 'a non-bourgeois mode of visual and sensorial experience'.[24] Richardson, too, presents the distractedness of the cinemagoer as a form of sophistication and mental dexterity, as well as a sign of a quickly developing aesthetic fastidiousness: 'They come level-headed and serenely talking through drama that a year ago would have held them dizzy and breathless.'[25] For Richardson, this vital reinvention or restructuring of ordinary sensibility is associated primarily with female consciousness and female forms of socialisation; in her portrayal of the cinema audience, it is the women who talk, destroying in the process the illusion of art as a separate activity from life, while the male portion of the audience tut-tut irritably:

If her casual glance discovers stock characters engrossed in a typical incident of an average mind, well known to her for she has served her enthralled apprenticeship and is a little blasé, her conversation proceeds uninterrupted. And to this we do not entirely object. The conversation may be more interesting than the film.[26]

Women who pay more attention to the people around them rather than to the film are 'amateur realists'; the 'dreadful' talker 'unconsciously testifies that life goes on, art or no art and that the onlooker is a part of the spectacle'.[27]

Richardson's observations about the gender divisions implicit in cinema-going practices chime, somewhat unexpectedly, with Patrick Hamilton's portrayal of going to the cinema in *The Midnight Bell*. The cinema in that novel is, like Richardson's, a site in which a woman's incessant talking testifies to her keen awareness of both the film's artifice and the poignancy of the real-life situation, which the nervous conversation is meant to suppress.

## Inattentive Viewers

In one of the opening chapters of *The Midnight Bell*, Bob and Ella spend an afternoon at the cinema, or, rather, a fraction of the afternoon – they must soon get back to work. They sit through a silent Western starring Richard Dix, and see the beginning of Fritz Lang's spy melodrama *Spione* (1928), 'but knowing that they could not watch the thing artistically, and as a whole, they were unable to take it seriously and were . . . flippant and talkative'. Hamilton's characters are devoted cinemagoers, as Hamilton was himself. Ella's adulation of Richard Dix is likened to worship 'at the shrine of pure beauty and romance', and the comparison is only partly tongue-in-cheek. Not just romance, but also 'pure beauty' constitutes the pleasure of cinema, and Ella's dreams are not only of impossible love, but are also 'aesthetic'.[28] At one point Hamilton describes cinema-viewing as an impersonal and disembodied experience in which the picture-goers' faces 'had abandoned every trace of the sensibility and character they had borne outside', becoming 'blank,' 'calm' and 'inhuman'. And yet such solemn consummation of cinema is not to be: Ella starts talking almost as soon as the programme has begun, fidgeting and whispering to Bob.[29] The trifling conversation between them is ostensibly about Gerda Maurus, who plays the leading role in *Spione*, but it really is about their mutual knowledge of Ella's yearning for Bob: 'This is your type, ain't it Bob?' said Ella at the appearance of the leading lady. It was true. It was his type – a large-eyed, slim and shingled blonde.'[30] Ella is not 'his type', and Bob, looking at Ella as they leave the cinema, thinks 'You either had it or not. She had not.'[31] The mundane conversation and the ensuing awkwardness are indeed more interesting than the film, a situation that is reversed when Hamilton describes Ella and Bob's nightly routine as workers at The Midnight Bell pub. Work is aestheticised; leisure, on the other hand, is marred by awkwardness, as elsewhere in Hamilton. When his characters are supposed to relax, they find themselves bored, talking nervously and inelegantly. The nightly routines at the pub, on the other hand, have a dizzyingly complex and dazzling choreography to them; they are presented as a clever montage of expressive body language and sound, and Hamilton explicitly announces the sequence as cinematic:

> an acoustic background of deep mumbling and excited talk without which its whole atmosphere would have been lost – without which, indeed, the nightly drama of the Saloon Bar would have been rather like a cinematograph drama without music.[32]

*The Midnight Bell* was written before the arrival of the talkie, and it is the aesthetic of silent film that supplied Hamilton with the ideas and techniques for effectively conveying the atmosphere of this space. However, the attention to aural detail in the pub scenes anticipates the GPO Film Unit director John Grierson's call for a 'dramatic' use of sound in film and literature that may reveal the 'poetry' of everyday life. Grierson had primarily urban life in mind when he wrote hopefully about the 'development there might be if the often beautiful formulae of sound and word which occur in life were to be given dramatic value'. A talented filmmaker's task, according to Grierson, is to notice what he refers to as 'the poetry which, in the case of the streets, say, will arrange some essential story in the mumble of windows, pub counters and passers-by'.[33] Grierson's idea is of daily life arranging *itself* into a meaningful pattern; in other words, urban life is already cinematic, and the film director, or writer, must know it well and be especially attuned to it if he is to discern its poetic quality. Hamilton positions himself as just such a discerning observer of patterns of everyday sounds and gestures. More intriguingly, he ascribes a similar capacity for the aesthetic appreciation of daily life to the novel's central characters. The pub descriptions use free indirect discourse to blur the line between the narrator's/Hamilton's perceptions and those belonging to Ella and Bob. For instance, the sound of the 'continual crash of the till' that punctures the 'blurred noise and fuss' of the pub's busiest hours is simply announced;[34] it is not clear who singles out this aural detail. Ella is introduced in the previous paragraph, and it seems that Hamilton's attentiveness to the acoustics of the pub is shared with hers. Free indirect discourse here allows for a rare moment of a seamless transcendence of class distinctions: Hamilton is identifying with his pub workers in a way that prioritises aesthetic experience; for a moment, the pedantic mockery of their cliché-laden speech has been set aside.

Hamilton's characters are keen and sensitive observers, alert to subtle shifts of mood within the spaces they occupy. Objects provide the material for particularly poignant examples of Ella and Bob's emotional intuitiveness. Bar bottles, mirrors, clocks, even the materials and textures of the rooms become objective correlatives, as it were, for their exceptional astuteness; they also become actors in the 'cinematograph drama' of pub life, taking centre stage at the end of the evening, when the pub is quiet. Eloquent objects have been identified as one of silent film's most effective tropes from early film criticism onwards. Elie Faure wrote in 1923 of 'the commotion that I experienced when I observed, in a flash, the magnificence there was in the relationship of a piece of black clothing to the grey wall of an inn'.[35] Béla Balázs, in the classic study on cinema *The Theory of the Film* (1952), described the cinematic art of the close-up as the art of exposing 'the face of things': 'the close-up . . . shows the speechless face and fate of the dumb objects that live with you in your room and whose fate is bound up with your own'.[36]

There is an unmistakable sense in which the relationships between objects and people are intimate and even fateful in *The Midnight Bell*, although Hamilton typically stops short of defining the precise nature of these relationships. The role of inanimate objects in this novel is to provide more than what Roland Barthes termed 'the reality effect' where their sole purpose is to 'finally say nothing but this: we are the real'.[37] Balázs's definition is more appropriate in its emphasis on a shared fate – and, in the case of Hamilton's novel, a shared melancholy. Ella is surrounded by what Hamilton describes as 'bottly glitter'[38] – a felicitously tactile phrase that imparts pathos where otherwise would have been only Ella's unremarkable boredom. The dramatic iridescence of the environment that frames her is another aspect of pub life that elevates it to the status of cinematic drama.

In fact, the material arrangements of spaces such as The Midnight Bell were as sophisticated as those of a film set. Many London pubs were extensively refurbished in the late 1920s to early 1930s, with the ornate Victorian interiors often replaced with more restrained alternatives in the art deco style. Lighting played a central part in making the pub look attractive, with the highest concentration of electric lights usually in the bar area, just above the bartenders' heads. The effect would have been similar to that achieved by strong lighting from above that was often used in the cinema and in film stars' publicity photographs. Behind the brightly lit bar Ella appears as though she were in the spotlight, but the effect is not to make her imagine that she is in a movie. On the contrary, the bar setting only emphasises her feelings of isolation; even her frequent looking at herself in the small overhead mirror behind the bar is referred to as a half-conscious melancholy gesture that is not even prompted by a concern for beauty – 'she was always glancing at herself in the glass. This was not the result of vanity, but rather of a general despondence.'[39] Ella is not a woman at her toilette, in the process of self-creation or makeover.[40] Nor is this a mechanical gesture like that made by Eliot's typist in *The Waste Land* – 'she smoothes her hair with automatic hand'[41] – an easy-to-read sign of the lifelessness of modern sexuality. The meaning of Ella's radiant sadness is more difficult to define.

Perhaps the closest one can approach to decoding Ella's habit is by looking at a film that was contemporary with Hamilton's writing of *The Midnight Bell*. Alfred Hitchcock's *The Lodger* (1927) repeatedly shows women anxiously smoothing their hair, in front of mirrors and in empty rooms. *The Lodger* is a thriller in the Jack-the-Ripper style, and female hair plays a crucial part in the plot – the killer is only interested in blondes. On a surface level, then, the scenes in which young women touch their hair simply illustrate the anxiety that spreads across London as the killings multiply. Yet there is something wistful about these gestures, something cinematic in a pure sense. As Balázs put it, film can show us 'a quality in a gesture of the hand we never noticed before . . . a quality which is often more expressive than any play of the features'.[42] So are the hands of Hitchcock's women involuntarily more expressive than their faces (Figs 4.1 and 4.2).

These gestures expose more than fear, however; they are pensive in a way that seems to have been provoked by the passing of time itself. Tellingly, in the scene where Daisy's mother listens for her lodger to come back at night, she is surrounded by clocks. The fact that the younger woman's gesture is then precisely reproduced by her mother – a less subtle reference to time elapsing via the juxtaposition of their age. Throughout the film Daisy's physical vitality is juxtaposed with her mother's slow and tired movements about the house. Daisy is a fashion model and a coquette – we see her this way in the film's opening scenes – often preening in front of the mirror, but in the scene where she worriedly smooths her hair she is suddenly without vanity, and her hand takes centre stage. Her hand will become like her mother's hand one day, and that idea seems to provide the real connection between the two scenes.

Figure 4.1  Alfred Hitchcock, *The Lodger*, 1927.

Figure 4.2  Alfred Hitchcock, *The Lodger*, 1927.

This is both an intimately personal moment, and a radically externalised one; it is both a premonition of Ella's future loneliness – after all, the trilogy concludes with 'the sound of the barmaid weeping' – and an evocation of a de-personalised, almost existential sadness, one of many such odd moments that are scattered throughout *Twenty Thousand Streets under the Sky*. *The Midnight Bell* has the highest concentration of such reveries; they are fewer in the last instalment of the trilogy, in which dreaming, even of a melancholy kind, must give way to a flatter, more consistently realist vision.

## Alone in an Afternoon Cinema

The long-suffering Ella is honoured in Hamilton's trilogy with an instalment all to herself. This volume traces the courtship of Ella by the horrible Eccles and the final rejection by Bob of her passion for him. Jenny's instalment, called *The Siege of Pleasure*, has all the thrills of a Naturalist tale, including a night of debauchery and a drunken car accident. By contrast, the novel about Ella adopts a realist, rather than Naturalist, course.[43] It is an account not of decline, but of a grey life that is haunted by muted feelings of regret. In the final pages of *The Plains of Cement*, Ella comes to accept that she probably will always be alone, a realisation which is rendered in the classic realist mode of negation that emphasises and dramatises the sheer insignificance of the events that have just taken place: 'And, indeed, what had taken place in those dull months? Nothing, really, whatever – nothing out of the common lot of any girl in London.'[44] Significantly, this quiet drama of disillusionment is set in a cinema.

Ella goes to the cinema in the afternoon, to escape the rain and her room, 'or she would go mad'. She chooses not any cinema, but the expensive West End 'Capitol', 'a tremendous extravagance'.[45] But even the extravagant plush surroundings fail to impress her, and the experience that is meant to dazzle instead depresses her. In place of a luxurious 'loving' darkness, there is a darkness that allows one to be discreetly miserable. Hamilton turns the description of Ella's visit to the movies into an elegiac meditation on the endless turnover of unhappiness in the city:

> It is a sad pass when a solitary young woman in London is so low in spirits and miserable in her thoughts that she decides she must buy herself some sweets and go by herself to the pictures and sit in the gloom, to hide from the roaring world, and try to divert her mind from its aching preoccupations by looking at the shadows. You will sometimes see such lonely figures, eating their sweets and gazing gravely at the screen in the flickering darkness of picture theatres, and it may well be that they are merely other Ellas, with just such problems and sorrows in their grey lives as hers.[46]

The gnomic address to the reader reasserts the novel's realist agenda. There will be no more theatrical excesses, as there had been in the scene where Ella was 'vamping' Mr Eccles in a teashop.[47] Ella's chances of becoming someone else are now firmly in the past, while the future bodes only dullness from which there is no escape. After the cinema scene Ella will only appear in the novel working; as the prospect of marriage to Mr Eccles falls through, she will probably have to continue as the barmaid of The Midnight Bell indefinitely. Already in the cinema scene she is rendered less as an individual and more as a statistic – one of the hundreds of working girls who hide in cinemas from work and worry. Ella herself has become a shadow, a silhouette that is exactly like so many others that simply illustrate a general truth about living in the city. At the beginning of *The Midnight Bell*, Ella was watching 'the two-dimensional ghost of Mr Dix',[48] and the world of shadows was portrayed as the opposite of the noisy and full-blooded reality she and Bob had inhabited as the barman and barmaid of The Midnight Bell. Siegfried Kracauer defined the spectacle of silent cinema as a procession of 'pale apparitions', 'the limbo through which the deaf are moving'.[49] And yet, at the end of Hamilton's trilogy, Ella is herself in a limbo. Life itself is rendered as a pale reflection of what life could, or ought to, be.

Ella performs the familiar ritual of the escape from life's difficulties into the dreamland of the movie theatre, but life follows her there, her unhappiness amplified, not cancelled out, by the darkness. Even the cinema sweets that had so delighted women in other episodes of the trilogy here fail to please – 'to have come to a stage of hopelessness and isolation wherein the sole remaining consolation is to be found in sweets!' In *The Siege of Pleasure*, Jenny consumed Turkish Delight at the rate of 'a pound an hour', opening the brown paper pack with 'a delicious, almost salacious rattle', which was typical of Jenny's innocent sensuality.[50] 'As far as Jenny was concerned, sensuousness advanced little beyond the realms of Turkish Delight',[51] much to her boyfriend's dismay. This Jenny still lives the disembodied life of fantasy; the visits to the cinema are associated not with touching, but with the childish pleasure of sweets. A picture of Rudolph Valentino adorns the young Jenny's room, his 'sensuously ominous gaze followed her around the room';[52] but this again is sensuality imagined by a very young woman, at a safe distance. This innocent idolatry of a film star's image is juxtaposed with the sleazy photographs of Jenny's numberless 'admirers' that make Bob queasy when he visits the bedroom she occupies years later as a prostitute. The ritual of worshipful gazing has been tainted by Jenny's profession, with the roles reversed – now it is as though the men in the photographs were looking at her in her private space. The arrangement of the photographs in the room no longer mirrors Jenny's fantasies, but the reality of her daily life.

Ella's taste for cinema sweets is similarly spoiled by the collapse of fantasy. She tries 'to concentrate upon the show and enjoy her Italian Cream', but 'she soon found her mind wandering and her heart sinking'. The disappointment is so intense that she eventually has to leave – 'with a cold feeling all over her body, she sprang impulsively from her seat'.[53] The experience of the cinema is intensely, and unpleasantly, physical. Ella's sensory perceptions sharpen rather than dull her inner life. While many 1930s writers associated the cinema with a comfortably passive state of mind, Hamilton portrays it as a place where anxieties are not carried away on 'the waves of silliness',[54] but are so keenly felt as to become almost palpable. Afternoon cinemas were similarly figured as uncomfortable and hostile spaces in Jean Rhys's London novels. In her 1930s fiction, the cinema is figured as a microcosm of the cruel world outside in which women are constantly humiliated, not least by being looked at. Having just arrived in London, Julia goes to the cinema in the afternoon (like Hamilton's Ella, she has to go somewhere or go mad in her dingy room). *Hot Stuff from Paris* is on, but Julia pays more attention to other women in the audience:

> The girls were perky and pretty, but it was strange how many of the older women looked drab and hopeless, with timid, hunted expressions. They looked ashamed of themselves, as if they were begging the world in general not to notice that they were women or to hold it against them.[55]

The scene undercuts the cliché of women losing themselves in dreamland during their afternoons off at the cinema. Here the 'dream palace' does not provide an escape from daily life; on the contrary, everyday burdens feel especially heavy within its dark interior.

The clichéd definition of the cinema as dream palace is similarly debunked in Rhys's *Voyage in the Dark*, where an odd, almost supernatural exchange between the world on screen and that occupied by the audience takes place. Anna Morgan and her flatmate Ethel are watching an episode of *The Three-Fingered Kate*, a popular British crime series that screened just before the First World War. Kate, played by the French actress Ivy Martinek, is an unrepentant leader of a criminal gang, constantly baffling a parodic version of Sherlock Holmes, Sheerluck Finch.

As Elizabeth Miller has suggested, 'Kate becomes an exaggerated version of Rhys's victimized protagonist . . . The fictional film audience's pleasure in Kate's punishment mirrors the casual sadism that Anna faces from men.'[56] The detailed description of the film Anna is watching was not an accurate description of an existing episode of *Kate*, but a scenario created by Rhys for the novel:

> A pretty girl was pointing a revolver at a group of guests. They backed away with their arms held high above their heads and expressions of terror on their faces. The pretty girl's lips moved. The fat hostess unclasped a necklace of huge pearls and fell, fainting, into the arms of a footman. The pretty girl, holding the revolver so that the audience could see that two of her fingers were missing, walked backwards towards the door. Her lips moved again, you could see what she was saying. 'Keep 'em up . . .'[57]

The *Three-Fingered Kate* series ran between 1912 and 1913, but there seems to be little difference between the pre-war London Rhys describes and the London of the 1930s. The choice of a silent film seems to have more to do with the sinister dynamic between the miming heroine and the coarsely laughing audience. It is their laughter that transforms Kate from a plucky, 'pretty' and unconventional heroine to a maimed girl cruelly mocked. In this scene, the screen heroine is retreating from the guffaws that accompany the film, and that fill Anna with contempt for the audience: 'Damned fools . . . Don't you hate them? They always clap in the wrong places and laugh in the wrong places.'[58] Even a cinematic fiction becomes vulnerable to real cruelty. Anna's commentary on the film also resonates painfully with the real plot of her disgrace. The audience laughing at Three-Fingered Kate's demise becomes a menacing allegory for the cruel fun that not just lovers, but, it seems, the city itself collectively has at her expense.

The sneer or smile becomes a recurring motif, not only in the fiction, but also in Rhys's unfinished autobiography *Smile, Please* (1979). Like Anna Morgan, the young Rhys trained as an actress, and her reminiscences of the training read like a blueprint for all the incongruous laughing and crying in her fiction. Rhys described one of her first acting lessons as a lesson in laughing and crying, in which she did not do well:

'And now, watch me,' said Miss Gertrude. She turned away for a few seconds, and when she turned back tears were coursing down her face which itself remained unmoved. 'Now try,' she said. The students stood in a row trying to cry ... I looked along the line and they were all making such hideous faces in their attempts to cry that I began to laugh.[59]

In a sense, Rhys's protagonists are all extensions of this portrait of an uncooperative drama student. Rhys described the expectations placed on her when she first arrived in England as quite similar – to smile on cue, to respond politely and so on. There is a clear correlation between the doll-like behaviour that was taught her at drama school and by her family, and the way her protagonists find themselves having to act. Men certainly expect such doll-like behaviour from them, becoming angry and cruel when the right automatic responses do not come. Rhys's women often feel as though they are competing with better designed, inanimate versions of themselves. The route to success in life is to resemble a 'dummy' as much as possible. In *Good Morning, Midnight*, Sasha remembers the mannequins in a Parisian shop where she used to work, with a sneer: 'damned dolls . . . thinking what a success they would have made of their lives if they had been women'.[60] In the earlier 1930s novels, however, the joke works in reverse order: if Rhys's women could only be more like dolls, they would perhaps have been more successful.

The trope of the glamorous woman as doll was pervasive across different cultural forms during the 1930s, and to women from different social strata. Upper-class women and film actresses were regularly described as dolls, from Auden's summary of the eponymous heroine of 'Sue' (1937) as 'a doll with everything money can buy'[61] to Rudolph Putnam Messel's reimagining of the world of film as a mechanical play of sexed-up automata, or human puppets:

Take the ordinary young woman . . . Train her until she can smile or look wistful at a moment's notice . . . emplant in her emptied head the idea that she must get, and having got, must keep her man. Endow this puppet with a name . . . set it in motion, and the film heroine is created.[62]

Messel's portentous tone of the knowing critic does not conceal the fact that his account of 'this film business' has much in common with the decade's popular journalistic narratives about the film heroine's less glamorous cousins. Under the banner of documenting the lives of modern women in bohemian professions such as acting and modelling in a detached, documentary mode, a normalisation of their status as eroticised dolls was taking place. In the late 1930s *Picture Post* exploited the motif of women of 'bohemian' occupations as part of its 'Day in the Life' series, running pieces on the artist's model and the film extra. *Picture Post* took inspiration from the even more salacious comparable features about working women in the French magazines *Vu* and *Voilà*[63] – the film extras appear semi-clothed, the smutty undertones made obvious. At the same time, the 'A Day in the Life' photo-essays insisted on the women's physical stamina and a detached attitude to their work. Thus we are told that Miss Walker, the artist's model, has 'no shyness', prefers posing for 'professionals' and 'considers herself successful, although the life is a little uncertain'.[64] A film extra, in a similar vein, lives a life of 'a minimum of glamour and a maximum of hard work', getting up early – although we are informed about just what items of clothing – 'brassiere, panties, and petticoat' she is 'fumbling' for 'in the half-dark'.[65] These women are represented as supremely adaptable, twisting their faces and bodies into whatever shape necessary for the job (the photo-essay about the artist's model features particularly odd photographs of the woman posing for an advertising artist, her body in a clearly uncomfortable position).

Nineteen-thirties doll worship reached its apogee in the story of Cynthia,[66] a life-sized fashion mannequin created by the American sculptor and artist Lester Gaba. Cynthia was lavished by gifts from fashion houses and real-life stars, and taken by Gaba everywhere – to cocktail parties and to the cinema, in what was at once an ironic commentary on the contemporary world of fashion, and a somewhat disturbing assumption about modern femininity. 'She' was photographed with Gaba for *Life*, cigarette in hand, looking exactly as a woman taking part in conversation – or, rather, of a woman physically present in a place where someone else's conversation was taking place. Urban settings were crucial to Cynthia's success – cocktail bars, city streets and theatre booths within which the mannequin was inserted made the effect especially eerie, as did the sleek, high-contrast photographs that clearly emulated Hollywood film stills. Cynthia was the ultimate doll, completely unencumbered by the indignities suffered by her less successful real-life counterparts; while the hard-up starlets of *Picture Post*'s features were 'fumbling' for clothes in dark rooms, Cynthia was photographed as she was being dressed for dinner.

The inconveniences of a real body – and a head that is not empty – for a young woman aspiring to be a film star provide the subject matter for Betty Miller's circadian experiment *The Mere Living* (1933). The novel traces a day in the lives of a lower-middle-class family, in particular the young hairdresser's assistant called Nancy, who dreams of becoming the next Greta Garbo and is having an affair with an older, middle-class man called Oliver. The rendezvous are consistently disappointing; Nancy is thrilled by the proximity of her almost-lover, but she is also embarrassed by the less glamorous aspects of physicality, such as 'stomachs making a rumble' during her and Oliver's kissing on the sofa – 'petty things which hurt and humiliated her to quite an extraordinary degree': '[h]er dramatic instinct demanded that events should have the ease, the significance and the poise of things rehearsed on the high impersonal brilliance of a stage'.[67] There is no doubt that Nancy's 'dramatic instinct' has been developed by devoted cinema-going. The innocent Nancy knows nothing about sex and is disturbed when Oliver attempts to go too far in his caresses. Unlike Rhys's bitterly experienced heroines, Nancy has imbibed the cinematic ideal of love as the epitome of elegance and poise. To be doll-like and still is to be perfect, and Nancy does not yet know that the price of such perfection is going along with being patronised. To Oliver, her youthful prettiness translates automatically into inferiority; he is openly snobbish about her cultural tastes: 'She could see that he derived a superior amusement from her taste in music: because she was flooded with easy thrills at the rich harmony of "In a Persian Market".'[68] The cinema itself, from which Nancy derives her youthful dreams, is presented in Miller's novel as also vulnerable to such snobbish dismissiveness:

> But now the doors of the cinema were open, and a charwoman was scrubbing the floors and dustmen at the back carted away refuse bins overflowing with cigarette ends and rubbish. The orchids were invisible, packed away in the round tin box: the powerful illusion of the film, the dark man in evening dress and the blonde woman and the champagne and the glittering New York lights, all lay coiled away in that round box: waiting to be unpacked by the grimy hands of the operator, waiting for the hour when the film's uncoiling could begin, when its dreamy poison would grow and unfold and thickly blossom in the hothouse darkness congenial to its strange erotic sensibility, which a bite of intellectual frost from the outside world would instantly shrivel and kill.[69]

The inscription of the world of the 1930s cinema as exotic and erotic, artificially maintained and attractively insulated from the outside world, shares with many other 1930s literary accounts of the cinema an association with dreaming and fantasy. The equation of the cinema to a dream palace became a cliché in the period's fiction, but here it is undercut by an insistence on the fragility of this dream. The 'powerful illusion' is, in fact, rather delicate. The grimy physicality of London's streets is an aggressive and unforgiving environment in contrast with the delicate fantasy world of film, which is easily reduced to the unexceptional two-dimensional physicality of a roll of film stored in a box. The hothouse or jungle metaphor so often used in writing about cinemas is used with a difference here – the implication is of vulnerability, rather than cloying seductiveness.

Miller's other London-set novel of the 1930s, *Farewell Leicester Square*, expands this juxtaposition of whimsical fantasy and 'intellectual frost', in a tale of a London-based (but Brighton-born) film director Alec Berman. With this novel, Miller went deeper than any other novelist of the 1930s into the socio-political implications of popular cinema, but she chose to mediate this examination of the most popular of all the arts via the person closest to the process of filmmaking. And although it has at its centre a male consciousness, this novel is about someone like Nancy: a person who is observant and astute, but whose gifts are never fully accepted by those whose intelligence is legitimised by class.

*Farewell Leicester Square* was finished in 1935, but not published until 1941, its treatment of Jewish assimilation into British life too bold for Miller's publisher Victor Gollancz. The novel follows the progress of Alec Berman from the son of a working-class shopkeeper to one of Britain's best film directors; he assimilates fully into what appears to be a neutral or nonspecific British identity, and marries his once-mentor's daughter Catherine Nicolls. Alec achieves all of this only to realise that it was all a mistake – that his painstaking journey to becoming as English as the Anglo-Saxons whose family he enters cannot erase the profound, if almost completely suppressed, prejudice that eventually destroys his marriage. The deep-seated beliefs which Alec is unable to reshape are class-bound as well as race-bound; in fact, the novel's disconcerting message is that a certain kind of British anti-Semitism and a certain kind of class prejudice are two sides of the same coin.

After a hard-won apprenticeship at a film studio in London, Alec rises in the world of filmmaking, mainly due to his talent for close observation of lower-middle-class English life, which is noted throughout the novel, and which earns him somewhat resentful praise from film critics, one of whom writes a review for *The Observer*, expressing a wish that Alec Berman would 'rid himself of his aesthetic fixation on the Kilburn High Road'.[70] Alec's latest picture premieres at the start of the novel, and this new film is another such study of the London life Alec knows so well:

> There was no doubt, of course, had been none, from the first moment that the production went on the floor, that *Farewell Leicester Square* was going to be a success. The sort of picture of middle-class London life that Alexander Berman could be trusted to do with his eyes shut. A trivial but well-constructed story, adapted from a recent lending-library success, redeemed,

brought alive, by his loving insistence on detail, his genius for
putting the commonplace on to the screen and somehow illu-
mining it with his own passion of observation. Hetty, the heroine, blonde waitress in a Corner House restaurant, improbable,
but lovely. A curious contrast to his other characters: his dowdy
suburban housewives, typists, shopkeepers . . .[71]

Miller cleverly folds the stock narratives of the London novel
(which she herself attempted with *The Mere Living*) into Alec's
cinematic work. There is a suggestion here of a humility and
authenticity that characterise Alec's films because they are
based on 'observation' rather than the pure fantasy of a Hollywood film. Alec always has been sharply observant, even as
a young man in Brighton, and hence the art of film comes easily to him. Miller resists the clichés that often accompanied
literary assessments of cinema-going, especially the persistent
assumption that urban-dwellers had their perceptions of reality shaped, or even distorted, by too much cinema-going. In
Miller's novel, it is always life that shapes Alec's filmmaking,
and the reason for his success is this lifelike quality. *Farewell
Leicester Square* also advances the argument that the trusted
and admired Britishness of Alec's films is partly dependent on
his status as a semi-outsider, both British and Jewish.

Alec leads a carefree lifestyle in his house near Regent's
Park, maintaining a no-strings-attached affair with his leading
lady, Hetty Follet. But it is with Alec's courtship of the painter
Catherine Nicolls that the novel's drama begins to unfold. The
tragic failure of Alec and Catherine's marriage is triggered by
the growing atmosphere of anti-Semitism in Britain; in the end,
it is too much for Catherine, who takes the painful but cowardly decision to raise their son as a gentile, divorcing Alec
shortly after the boy is taunted for being Jewish at school.
Alec finds himself in a peculiar position – as a disembodied
omniscient creator of a film he is admired, but as a Jewish man
out in Piccadilly he is not only despised, but physically unsafe.
Perhaps, he thinks, 'even his right to appreciate' London, 'the
streets and characters and shadows of this city which he loved'
might be 'denied to him'.[72]

This disconcerting double experience extends to Alec's new family relations; Basil Nicolls – Catherine's Cambridge-educated brother – admires his films to the point that he plans to write Alec's biography; yet upon meeting him, Basil dislikes Alec not only or not simply because Alec is much more Jewish than he had expected, but because Alec's cultural tastes are middlebrow – sensual and sensory, and broad: Miller insists throughout the novel on Alec's love of popular song and dance. Alec does not fulfil Basil's expectation that he would be, like himself, an intellectual, and therefore an artist whose portrayals of the lower-middle-class London milieu are part of the intellectual elite's fascination with this new character type. That Alec is really one of the people whom he portrays in his films is his gravest offence, which his Jewishness exaggerates even further. Alec's fundamentally unintellectual outlook, the un-patrician concreteness of the way he experiences the world aligns him both with the characters he presents in his films, and with female novelists whom Basil despises:

> Basil had an aversion to the inchoate; the emotional. He sought, never the direct experience, but its abstraction. Refinement: essence. For him, the actual was always the vulgar: Alec understood now Basil's frequent condemnation of modern feminine novelists with their 'tedious catalogues'.[73]

Alec occupies a position equivalent to these women novelists – and that of an alter ego for Miller, within which she was able to articulate her preference for a creative mode opposed to any narrowly defined intellectualism. She aligns herself with what was (and still often is) frequently dismissed as 'the middle-brow'[74] – without sacrificing intellectual rigour or sliding into sentimentality, as a middlebrow novel might be expected to do by its detractors. While Miller identifies with Alec's appreciation of popular cultural forms, she makes no lazy equation between it and the director's class or cultural background – an equation that was made frequently during the 1930s.

In Priestley's *Angel Pavement* the clerk Turgis's 'second destination' of the evening, after the Lyons Corner House, is 'the

Sovereign Picture Theatre, which towered at the corner like a vast spangled wedding-cake in stone. It might have been a twin of that great teashop he had just left; and indeed it was; another frontier outpost of the new age', a 'monster' Priestley imagines to have been concocted by '[t]wo Jews, born in Poland but now American citizens . . .'[75] Jewish film moguls also appear in Priestley's non-fictional *Midnight on the Desert* (1937), where he describes them as 'unique in their mixture of shrewdness and ignorance, bombast and humility'; they are referred to as 'emperors of make-believe' and 'tailors turned caliphs', 'whirled from three back rooms in Brooklyn to a pseudo-Spanish castle in Southern California'.[76] Priestley's satirical outbursts, with their hefty dose of prejudice, are directed at the middlebrow habitus which produces the men who have miraculously arrived at the heart of modern culture from 'back rooms'. The satire is not without an element of jealousy; Priestley's 1930s fictions try to produce exactly the effects he associates with the Jewish filmmaker – a combination of bombast and humility, and of melodrama and a meticulous attention to detail. He occupies a similar cultural stance to Orwell's: styling oneself as a 'serious' writer meant the need to express one's wariness of middlebrow and popular culture. While both Priestley and Orwell felt very keenly that this middlebrow, or petit-bourgeois, culture represented the future, because it could reach the widest possible audience, both writers actively distanced themselves from it.

## A Home Away from Home

For many cinemagoers of the 1930s, the picture palace became a home away from home, where one could dream that one's address was a baroque mansion, a country house or a Mediterranean villa. But nothing, it seems, made quite the same sensory impression as the red velvet seat – a material object of publicly available luxury that thrilled the movie-made generation. Elizabeth Bowen described her pleasure in climbing 'the sticky velvet seat': 'I am . . . home again.'[77] And C. A. Lejeune offered a gendered reading of the comforts offered by the velvet seat: 'the small cushioned seats' are 'women's seats'. According to Lejeune, they gave female cinemagoers 'the chance to relax unseen' and indulge in 'pleasures which no man, however tired he may be, [can] ever quite appreciate or understand'.[78]

For George Orwell, the velvet seat was, if not exclusively for women to enjoy, certainly detrimental to the intellectual faculties of a thinking man. In the typical language of Left-wing anti-cinema writing of the 1930s, he attacks cinema as a 'soggy' attraction in which a man's mind is at risk of getting bogged. It is unsurprising that the would-be great poet Gordon Comstock in *Keep the Aspidistra Flying* decides against watching Garbo in *The Painted Veil* (1936):

> He yearned to go inside, not for Greta's sake, but just for the warmth and the softness of the velvet seat. He hated the pictures, of course, seldom went there even if he could afford it. Why encourage the art that is destined to replace literature? But still, there is a kind of soggy attraction about it. To sit on the padded seat in the warm smoke-scented darkness, letting the flickering drivel on the screen gradually overwhelm you – feeling the waves of its silliness lap you round till you seem to drown, intoxicated, in a viscous sea – after all, it's the kind of drug we need.[79]

The suggestion here is that Orwell does not need this drug, but Gordon does. As a literary character, he may eventually be elevated to the status of MacNeice's tired worker who has earned his time in a plush seat with the eight-hour working day. Orwell's contempt for the cinema is well documented,[80] and in 'Inside the Whale' he included 'Hollywood films' in a list of modern horrors alongside 'machine-guns' and 'political murders'.[81] It may be, however, that in *Aspidistra* the judgement extends beyond the cinema and towards the class that consumes it. In particular, Orwell mocks what he perceives as Gordon's arrogant self-belief that he is the future of literature. It may be that the biggest distraction for Gordon is not the cinema, but his literary aspirations, which prevent him from fulfilling his civic duty of working and raising a family.

Gordon never will become a good writer, even if he sinks as low in everyday comfort as the London slums. Instead, he will go back to work, marry and probably go to the cinema once a week, now with his wife Rosemary. If the cinema is a place where one can rest after a long day's work, then Gordon's return to work at the advertising agency, as well as the hard work of bringing up baby, will legitimise going to the movies. Orwell's point seems to be that that is the life that Gordon is destined to lead. In *Down and Out in Paris and London*, he had confessed to his enjoyment of the simple life of working as a *plongeur* in Paris, defined by 'a sort of heavy contentment'[82] derived from a repetitive work routine followed by the simple pleasures of food, wine and sociability in the bar. Gordon's comparably predictable routine will involve a steady shuttling between the office, the suburban home and the local cinema. And Orwell's point towards the end of the novel may be that upon such contented men the health of the nation will finally rely.

From a disgusted denunciation of feminised mass culture Orwell works towards a definition of peculiarly English forms of domesticity at the end of *Keep the Aspidistra Flying*, for which the movies, somewhat unexpectedly, provide the material. The novel closes with the newlyweds' first quarrel, which is presented in the form of verbal fencing in a screwball comedy. Gordon and Rosemary are quarrelling about an aspidistra, playing ball with 'yes' and 'no':

'Anyway we aren't going to have that aspidistra.'
'Yes, we are.'
'We are not, Gordon!'
'Yes.'
'No!'
'Yes!'[83]

Orwell's characters jokingly bicker about shared property, like William Powell and Carol Lombard bickering about the wallpaper at the end of *My Man Godfrey* (1936). But, crucially, they argue about an aspidistra, the symbol of lower-middle-class English life that Gordon had so detested. It is a distinctly English comedy that Orwell has in mind, one that perhaps more closely echoes the all-English *Sing as We Go* (1934), a sentimental panegyric to community and family, with Gracie Fields singing a song about 'the biggest aspidistra in the world'. Gordon thinks in a similarly heightened comic-sentimental mode that 'the aspidistra is the tree of life'.[84] As Michael Levenson points out, 'Orwell conceives of his character as the ordinary self on which civilisation was founded and on which it could thrive again.'[85] The newly reformed Gordon who no longer wishes the bombs to fall on the houses of 'the common men . . . behind their lace curtain, with their children and their scraps of furniture and their aspidistras'[86] is Orwell's unlikely figure of hope on the eve of the Second World War, clinging with a heroic optimism to the comforts of family and home, which the freshly employed Gordon now finally owns. He comes to resemble the clerk Traddles in *David Copperfield* (1850), whose life of drudgery in the City is conveniently compensated for by his dreams of housekeeping and married life; he shows the visiting Copperfield the modest furniture, a marble-topped table and a 'flower-pot and stand' his fiancée has bought 'herself', 'with great pride and care'.[87]

The newlyweds Gordon and Rosemary cannot stop looking at their newly acquired domestic possessions; because 'neither of them had ever owned furniture before . . . living in furnished rooms ever since their childhood', 'they fell into absurd raptures over each separate stick of furniture'.[88] Orwell implies that Gordon and Rosemary own this flat, and are therefore able to decorate and furnish it according to their taste. This implication reads oddly alongside the flat's location, which Orwell specifies as Paddington. The young couple with a baby on the way would have found greater domestic bliss in the London suburbs, which were expanding at a staggering rate in the 1930s. Orwell is clearly ready to leave London behind – and will in his next novel, *Coming Up for Air* (1939) – but *Aspidistra* allows its characters a suburban happiness in central London.

The next chapter examines 1930s writing that, like Orwell's novel, displays mixed allegiances: to the pleasures of suburban living on the one hand, and to the promises of bohemian freedoms offered by renting rooms in central London on the other. For characters in such novels, by Norah Hoult, Rose Macaulay and Rosamond Lehmann, the crisis is one of personal identity: can one be a free-spirited bohemian while longing for the comforts of a suburban villa or country home? For the writers themselves these tales of confused allegiances often provide opportunities for metafictional investigations into the descriptive practices that are required by setting a novel in a domestic space. Central London bedsits were highly charged spaces with long literary histories, just as the rooms themselves often contained the material traces of generations of previous occupants. For any writer still wishing to describe such rooms, there were decisions to be made about the legacies of Dickens, Gissing and even Zola. These decisions required solutions more complex than the choice between imitation and rejection. Finding new ways of representing spaces that were old required a sophisticated way of imagining how these rooms were being appropriated by new generations of lodgers.

## Notes

1. Juliet Gardiner, *The 1930s: An Intimate History* (London: Harper Press, 2010), pp. 3, 659.
2. Valentine Cunningham, *British Writers of the Thirties* (Oxford: Oxford University Press, 1989), p. 280.
3. Muriel Peck, quoted in Annette Kuhn, *An Everyday Magic: Cinema and Cultural Memory* (London; New York: I.B. Tauris, 2002), p. 141.
4. Jeffrey Richards, *The Age of the Dream Palace Cinema and Society in Britain, 1930–1939* (London: Routledge, 1984), p. 19.
5. Elizabeth Bowen, 'Why I Go to the Movies', in *Footnotes to the Film* (London: Lovat Dickson, 1937), p. 205.
6. Cunningham, *British Writers of the Thirties*, p. 281.
7. Louis MacNeice, 'Ode', in *Collected Poems* (London: Faber & Faber, 1966), p. 54.

8. C. Day Lewis, 'Newsreel', in *Overtures to Death* (London: Jonathan Cape, 1938), p. 17.

9. Graham Greene, *A Confidential Agent* (London: Vintage, 2006), p. 73.

10. See, especially, Richards, *The Age of the Dream Palace*, for an overview of the contemporary criticisms of cinema that denounce it for feeding viewers with 'unreal' ideas, values and expectations, pp. 55–9.

11. W. H. Auden and Christopher Isherwood, *The Dog beneath the Skin* (London: Faber, 1935), p. 54.

12. Aldous Huxley, 'Pleasures', in *On the Margin: Notes and Essays* (London: Chatto & Windus, 1923), p. 49.

13. George Orwell, *The Road to Wigan Pier* (London: Penguin, 2001), p. 74.

14. Elizabeth Bowen, *The Death of the Heart* (Harmondsworth: Penguin, 1986), p. 195.

15. For a succinct discussion of the ways in which urban life was compared with the cinema in modernist fiction, and beyond, see Laura Marcus, *The Tenth Muse: Writing about Cinema in the Modernist Period* (Oxford: Oxford University Press, 2010), pp. 140–3. See also Thomas Burkdall's *Joycean Frames: Film and the Fiction of James Joyce* (London: Routledge, 2001), pp. 31–48 and Donald James, *Imagining the Modern City* (Minneapolis: University of Minnesota Press, 1999).

16. Roland Barthes, 'Leaving the Movie Theater', in *The Rustle of Language* (Basil Blackwell, 1986), pp. 345–6.

17. Patrick Hamilton, *The Midnight Bell*, in *Twenty Thousand Streets under the Sky* (London: Vintage, 2001), p. 81.

18. Bowen, 'Why I go to the Movies', p. 103.

19. Alistair Cooke, 'The Critic in Film History', in *Footnotes to the Film*, ed. Charles Davy (London: Lovatt Dickson, 1938), p. 238.

20. Cooke, 'The Critic in Film History', p. 238.

21. Walter Benjamin, 'The Work of Art in the Age of Mechanical Reproduction', in *Illuminations*, trans. Harry Zohn (London: Fontana Press, 1973), p. 229.

22. Benjamin, 'The Work of Art', p. 234.

23. Dorothy Richardson, 'Continuous Performance VII: The Front Rows', in *Close Up, 1927–1933: Cinema and Modernism* (London: Cassell, 1998), p. 173.

24. Marcus, *The Tenth Muse*, p. 357.
25. Richardson, 'Continuous Performance VII', in *Close Up*, p. 174.
26. Dorothy Richardson, *Close Up*, 2:3 (March 1928), pp. 51–5.
27. Ibid.
28. Hamilton, *The Midnight Bell*, pp. 81, 79.
29. Hamilton, *The Midnight Bell*, p. 81.
30. Hamilton, *The Midnight Bell*, p. 81.
31. Hamilton, *The Midnight Bell*, p. 82.
32. Hamilton, *The Midnight Bell*, p. 9.
33. John Grierson, 'The G.P.O. Gets Sound', *Cinema*, Summer 1934, p. 217.
34. Hamilton, *The Midnight Bell*, p. 21.
35. Elie Faure, 'The Art of Cineplastics', trans. Walter Pach (Boston, MA: The Four Seas Company, 1923), p. 25, quoted in Laura Marcus, *The Tenth Muse*, p. 182.
36. Béla Balázs, *The Theory of the Film*, trans. Edith Bone (London: Dennis Dobson Ltd., 1952), p. 55.
37. Roland Barthes, 'The Reality Effect', in *The Rustle of Language*, trans. Richard Howard (Oxford: Basil Blackwell, 1986), p. 148.
38. Hamilton, *The Midnight Bell*, p. 9.
39. Hamilton, *The Midnight Bell*, p. 13.
40. See David Trotter's *The Uses of Phobia: Essays on Literature and Film* (Malden, MA: Blackwell, 2010) for a wide-ranging discussion of images of women at their toilette throughout the history of art and literature.
41. T. S. Eliot, *The Waste Land*, p. 141.
42. Balázs, *Theory of the Film*, p. 55.
43. Not that the definition of Naturalism is quite so simple. See the Introduction for a discussion of David Baguley's definition of the 'comic strain' of Naturalism that is quite different from the classic Naturalist tale of dramatic decline. Of the writers' considered in this book, Jean Rhys's fiction approached the classic Naturalist mode the closest, while the other writers tended to switch between modes, often within the same work.
44. Patrick Hamilton, *The Plains of Cement*, in *Twenty Thousand Streets under the Sky* (London: Vintage, 2001), p. 526.

45. Hamilton, *Plains*, p. 518.
46. Ibid.
47. Hamilton, *Plains*, p. 389.
48. Hamilton, *The Midnight Bell*, p. 80.
49. Siegfried Kracauer, *Theory of Film* (Oxford: Oxford University Press, 1960), p. 135.
50. Patrick Hamilton, *The Siege of Pleasure*, in *Twenty Thousand Streets under the Sky* (London: Vintage, 2001), p. 249.
51. Ibid.
52. Hamilton, *The Siege of Pleasure*, p. 252.
53. Hamilton, *Plains*, pp. 519–20.
54. George Orwell, *Keep the Aspidistra Flying* (London: Penguin, 2000), p. 78.
55. Jean Rhys, *After Leaving Mr Mackenzie* (London: Penguin, 2000), p. 50.
56. Elizabeth Miller, *Framed: The New Woman Criminal in British Culture at the Fin de Siècle* (Ann Arbor: University of Michigan Press, 2008), p. 121.
57. Jean Rhys, *Voyage in the Dark* (London: Penguin, 2000), p. 93.
58. Rhys, *Voyage*, p. 93.
59. Jean Rhys, *Smile Please: An Unfinished Autobiography* (London: Penguin, 1979), p. 102.
60. Jean Rhys, *Good Morning, Midnight* (London: Penguin, 2000), p. 16.
61. W. H. Auden, *Sue: A Ballad* (Oxford: Sycamore Press, 1977), p. 57.
62. R. P. Messel, *This Film Business* (London: E. Benn, 1928), p. 53.
63. On these publications in relation to Bill Brandt's photo-stories for *Picture Post*, see Paul Delany, *Bill Brandt: A Life*, pp. 147–54; 175–86.
64. Robert Burnett, 'A Day in the Life of an Artist's Model', *Picture Post*, 28 Jan. 1939, p. 37.
65. *Picture Post*, 14 Jan. 1939, p. 20.
66. On Cynthia, see Vanessa Osborne, 'The Logic of the Mannequin: Shop Windows and the Realist Novel', in *The Places and Spaces of Fashion, 1800–2007*, ed. John Potvin (New York: Routledge, 2009), pp. 190–3.

67. Betty Miller, *The Mere Living* (London: Victor Gollancz, 1933), p. 28.
68. Miller, *The Mere Living*, p. 71.
69. Miller, *The Mere Living*, p. 70.
70. Betty Miller, *Farewell Leicester Square* (London: Persephone Books, 2000), p. 198. Miller's italics.
71. Miller, *Farewell Leicester Square*, p. 63.
72. Miller, *Farewell Leicester Square*, p. 177.
73. Miller, *Farewell Leicester Square*, p. 99.
74. On middlebrow fiction and culture, see *Middlebrow Literary Cultures: The Battle of the Brows, 1920–1960*, ed. Erica Brown and Mary Grover (New York: Palgrave Macmillan, 2012); *Middlebrow and Gender, 1890–1945*, ed. Christoph Ehland and Cornelia Wächter (Leiden: Brill Rodopi, 2016); Nicola Humble, *The Feminine Middlebrow Novel: Class, Domesticity, and Bohemianism* (Oxford: Oxford University Press, 2001).
75. Priestley, *Angel Pavement*, p. 157.
76. J. B. Priestley, *Midnight on the Desert: Being an Excursion into Autobiography during a Winter in America, 1935–1936* (New York: Harper & Brothers, 1937), pp. 142–3.
77. Miller, *Farewell Leicester Square*, p. 54.
78. *Manchester Guardian*, 15 Jan. 1926, quoted in Marcus, *The Tenth Muse*, p. 304.
79. Orwell, *Aspidistra*, p. 78.
80. Alok Rai, *Orwell and the Politics of Despair: A Critical Study of the Writings of George Orwell* (Cambridge: Cambridge University Press, 1988), p. 94; John Rodden, *George Orwell: The Politics of Literary Reputation* (New Brunswick, NJ: Transaction Publishers, 2002), p. 232.
81. George Orwell, 'Inside the Whale', in *The Complete Works*, ed. Peter Davison (London: Secker & Warburg, 1998), vol. 12, p. 91.
82. George Orwell, *Down and Out in Paris and London* (London: Penguin, 1989), p. 95.
83. Orwell, *Aspidistra*, p. 276.
84. Orwell, *Aspidistra*, p. 268.
85. Michael Levenson, 'The Fictional Realist: Novels of the 1930s', in *The Cambridge Companion to George Orwell*,

ed. John Rodden (Cambridge: Cambridge University Press, 2007), p. 71.

86. Orwell, *Aspidistra*, p. 268.

87. Charles Dickens, *David Copperfield* (Oxford: Oxford University Press, 2008), p. 394.

88. Dickens, *David Copperfield*, p. 274.

# Chapter 5

# Staying Home

Rented rooms make unhappy homes. The literature of 1930s London abounds in tales of dull routines set in cheap lodgings, their inhabitants clinging to dreams of a better job, a nicer room and a romance that would put the end to their financial misery as well as their loneliness. For the period's literary lodgers, London bedsits are always defined in terms of what they lack: space, style and any sense of cosmopolitan freedom. While complaints about the dullness and conformity of the suburbs had become standard by the early 1900s,[1] after 1918 the experience of renting in central London no longer provided a cosmopolitan antithesis; central London lodging was perceived to be as grim as suburban life.

That renting flats in London is a dreary experience was by no means an interwar discovery. George Moore, in *Confessions of a Young Man* (1886), professed his unreserved hatred of his London lodging house – 'eggs and bacon, the fat lascivious landlady with her lascivious daughter . . . I can do nothing, nothing; my novel I know is worthless'[2] – sentiments reproduced almost exactly in Orwell's *Keep the Aspidistra Flying* half a century later. And in Gissing's *New Grub Street* (1891), Edwin Reardon suffers the ignominy of trying to write in the shabby rooms he rents with his wife and child, unable to cope with the squalor and the constant reminder that he has to support the family. The stifling atmosphere of London lodgings also figures prominently in New Woman novels, most notably in Ella Hepworth Dixon's *The Story of a Modern Woman* (1894) where the protagonist, Mary, hoping to make it as a journalist, takes up rooms 'giving on a grimy back-yard'.[3] And Dorothy Richardson's Miriam Henderson, a direct descendant of the New Woman, feels her heart sink as she enters her Bloomsbury room at the beginning of 'The Tunnel' section of *Pilgrimage*: 'This is the furnished room; one room . . . The awful feeling, no tennis, no dancing, no house to move in, no society.'[4]

The trials of young writers by grim living conditions were still a prominent subject for London writers in the 1920s and 1930s, a continuity ensured partly by the fact that the rooms they occupied were often the same as the ones that had been inhabited by their predecessors. There is a scene in Jean Rhys's *Voyage in the Dark* when Anna, having just moved into one of the many London bedsits she will inhabit throughout the novel, discovers someone's badly written poem, redolent of early T. S. Eliot, in a drawer, that refers to London as 'a vile, stinking hole'.[5] The melodramatic lines could well have been written by George Moore, or a young T. S. Eliot, or George Orwell, and Rhys seems to be poking fun here at the generations of men who built literary reputations on complaining about the bleakness of London. Where the adolescent Anna is concerned, however, the bad poem is not an altogether inaccurate description of her own, deeply negative relationship with London. The bohemian identities assumed even by the older women in novels such as *After Leaving Mr Mackenzie* and *Good Morning, Midnight* are inseparable from an intense aversion to the city. Anna's recurring thought on arriving in London, 'I'm not going to like this place', becomes a self-fulfilling prophecy, and broadly defines all of Rhysian women lodgers' relationships with London where streets and houses are 'exactly alike'.[6]

Nineteen-thirties fiction often returned to central London lodging and lodgers, and to the formal conventions of the realist *Bildungsroman* that these dingy spaces had accommodated for so long. Franco Moretti has written that the English *Bildungsroman* always tends to portray youthful experiences as 'negative' – 'they will not teach what one could be, but always and only what one is not, does not want to be, and should not be'.[7] Characters in novels by Jean Rhys, Patrick Hamilton, Rosamond Lehmann and Rose Macaulay prove unable to move on to a more mature existence, an impasse partly, but not entirely, caused by financial constraints. The bedsit novels, then, are frustrated *Bildungsromane* in which the pursuit of the bohemian dream is inseparable from an inability to grow up. It makes a certain kind of sense that these writers were read as amateurish or 'photographic' realists, given the fact that the formal choices they made to tell tales of not growing up were themselves frequently identified as both immature and, simultaneously, out of date. Their novels are not about living conditions, neither do they offer a straightforward record of the material difficulties of aspiring writers or artists, in the way that Gissing's *New Grub Street* had. This is because none of the characters involved are committed to any creative pursuit in the way that the fin-de-siècle lodgers had been. The descriptions of their rooms are not there to elicit our sympathy; rather, more than anything characters in these novels do or say, they expose their mixed allegiances and their bad faith in the anti-domestic, anti-suburban lives they have chosen to lead.

By the 1930s writing about rooms was routinely dismissed as passé – the modernists of the 1920s (or at any rate some of the more vocal representatives of that decade) thoroughly discredited the practice of describing rooms as both aesthetically unsatisfactory and ideologically suspect. This vocal denouncement of writing rooms, however, coexisted with an undiminished flow of descriptive passages about rooms in their own work.

In his *Manifesto of Surrealism* (1924), André Breton condemned 'the purely informative style' of literature, of which he made a description of a shabby room in *Crime and Punishment* (1866) an example. For Breton, such descriptions 'are nothing but so many superimposed images taken from some stock catalogue, which the author utilizes more and more whenever he chooses'. What irritates Breton even more than what he calls Dostoevsky's 'laziness', however, is his reduction of the character to an avatar of the author's ideology:

> The author attacks a character and, this being settled upon, parades his hero to and fro across the world. No matter what happens, this hero, whose actions and reactions are admirably

predictable, is compelled not to thwart or upset – even though he looks as though he is – the calculations of which he is the object. The currents of life can appear to lift him up, roll him over, cast him down, he will still belong to this *readymade* human type.[8]

Breton likens the exhausted Naturalist style to postcards or 'clichés' (that is, photographic negatives), positioning Dostoevsky at the centre of a failed representational mode. Breton's critique of *Crime and Punishment* resembles Virginia Woolf's criticisms of the realism of 'Mr Wells, Mr Bennett, and Mr Galsworthy' in 'Mr Bennett and Mrs Brown', in which the harshest judgement is reserved for Bennett, who opened *Hilda Lessways* with detailed descriptions of what Hilda could see from the window of her house. According to Woolf, Bennett 'is trying to hypnotise us into the belief that, because he has made a house, there must be a person living there'.[9] Woolf concedes that 'the convention' of introducing a character via 'house property' had worked for the Edwardians – a luring device of sorts, in order to make one read on and into the more challenging, psychological content of a novel, that is to make one 'willing to co-operate in the far more difficult business of intimacy'[10] – but, she claims, it could not possibly work in 1924, since, as is famously established at the beginning of the essay, 'on or about December 1910 human character changed'.[11]

Like Breton, Woolf objected to the realists' presumption that an inner life could be deduced from or equated to a sum of external facts – what furniture one has, how much one pays in rent. Yet Woolf never denied her own characters' relationships with their environments. Clarissa Dalloway, after returning from her walk around London, welcomes the sequestered atmosphere of her home – 'the hall of the house was cool as a vault'.[12] And in *To the Lighthouse*, the Ramsays' seaside family home is described in much detail, including the kinds of objects and substances the Ramsay children bring back with them from the beach – sand, shells, insects. Woolf does not object to realism per se, but the 'sooty blankets' Hilda Lessways observes from her window (a passage which Woolf quotes in her essay) could only represent, to Woolf, a blunt social realism that has nothing to offer the modern novelist whose concerns are psychological. Breton and Woolf both treat passages of domestic description as a convenient marker of Naturalism, understood broadly as social realism at the time. For Woolf and Breton, describing a room was too safe, when what was needed was stylistic boldness. Writers whose work is central to the discussion in this chapter, rather than rejecting descriptions of domestic spaces altogether, used the descriptive passages in their work to pose questions about both the possibilities of description and its limitations. The practice of detailed literary description per se was not problematic for Rose Macaulay, Norah Hoult and Jean Rhys. For these writers, London rooms – particularly ones that are shabby and messy – can and do give the sense of a person that is there; once again, they become suitable preludes to 'intimacy' with the people who inhabit them, because the people in whom they are interested only get to experience intimacies of the most fleeting kind: they inhabit milieus in which intimacy is as remote a concept as that of home.

## Semi-bohemians

Rosamond Lehmann's *The Weather in the Streets* (1936) is one such melodrama about perpetually withheld intimacies, centring on Olivia Curtis, who has become stuck in a lodger's life following the breakdown of her marriage. Much of the woeful uncertainty of her life is the result of her indeterminate class status. Olivia grew up in an upper-class family in the country and was educated at Oxford, but life in London proves tough: the family have not enough money to support Olivia and her husband Ivor, both of whom have come of age with an illusion of privilege, but ultimately have to work for a living. The domestic spaces that Olivia occupies, all of them temporarily, triangulate in this novel in a way that leaves the central character in a complete impasse. Olivia is stuck, wedged impossibly between the genteel domesticity represented by her family, her upper-class, married rake of a cousin called Rollo Spencer, and the bohemian lifestyle represented by her friends – all of them, like Olivia, without fixed incomes, but, unlike her, free of the shame and embarrassment with which she responds to her domestic discomforts. The love affair that forms the novel's backbone is based largely on two people's extreme discontent about their domestic lives. This love affair is doomed from the beginning not only because Rollo is married, but also because Olivia falls not as much for him as for the upper-class stability he represents. She is a reluctant bohemian who has all the insight of her intellectual friends, but cannot decide whether to direct this perceptiveness against Rollo's upper-class set or against her friends' idealism. Ultimately, Olivia is a cynic in love, and only being in love holds the cynicism at bay, temporarily. When Rollo finally meets Olivia's artistic friends, he lets slip a philistine comment about Colin – a brilliant intellectual who is unable to find his true calling:

> 'Too much in the brain-pan, I expect, to settle down,' said Rollo comfortably – the silly. For the first time I realised it's no use telling him really what people are like . . . If I weren't in love with him, would this matter rather? Might I get irritated? Bored?[13]

As a matter of fact, Olivia does get irritated, more frequently than she admits, but the irritation is always directed at Rollo's way of life, and especially at his pompous country mansion with its glass-fronted bookcases stuffed with 'smart editions of the classics bound in calf' and a 'shockingly bad pastel portrait' of Rollo's wife Nicola, 'the kind they always seem to have of their wives in these houses: too meaningless to be upsetting'.[14] Olivia is expertly contemptuous of the upper-class pretentiousness of Rollo's dwelling and its 'meaningless' display of cultural capital, where books and paintings, entombed in expensive furniture, are reduced to the status of decorations. But her rage is ultimately futile; because there is no 'we' with whom she is able to identify in opposition to 'them', she mistrusts her friends' commitment to lives without possessions in equal measure. About halfway through the novel, Olivia moves into her friend Jocelyn's flat – a welcome change from

sharing an apartment with a female friend Etty, an arrangement that becomes intolerable as Olivia's affair with Rollo
gains pace. The difficulties of sharing a flat are not entirely
resolved by moving; Jocelyn's flat is uncomfortable and aesthetically wanting:

> The room seemed quite the wrong shape – too high – square –
> what? . . . I don't like bed-sitting rooms, specially at night . . .
> And Jocelyn's windows, large, bald, vacant with his long dis-
> mal unlined butcher-blue curtains, trailing down like a giant's
> boiler-suit . . . He hasn't any taste in decoration; not that he's
> indifferent, he likes his room; he just hasn't any eye. Writing
> young men often haven't . . . Not uncomfortable, or downright
> ugly; undeveloped more, student-like. Not puritanical exactly,
> but, anyway, a hint of a moral attitude.[15]

A feeling of being confronted not by a simply furnished room
but by 'a hint of moral attitude' is at the heart of Olivia's
inability to commit to inhabiting the 'we' that might provide
an alternative to the upper-class 'them' that will never accept
her as one of their own. A single-minded, committed way of
life, whether Rollo's or Jocelyn's, is unappealing to the restless
Olivia. In different ways, both lack the solidity of middle-class
family life exemplified by her mother and sister – a sister who,
unlike Olivia, is married with children and, Olivia believes, is
fundamentally calmer and saner than herself. *The Weather in
the Streets* is a novel about not wanting to grow up – and one
that seems unable to quite decide what to make of such an
unwillingness. Olivia might just be able to escape the cycle of
bedsits and disappointments if she breaks off with Rollo and
reunites with her husband Ivor – the only person who nurses
her through her abortion at the end of the novel (the marital
reunion is not to be). Lehmann positions her narrator ambigu-
ously in relation to her character: tellingly, the final section of
the novel is narrated in the third person, in contrast with the
first-person chapters that detail Olivia's affair. It is as if Lehmann eventually tires of her character's mind; or, perhaps, she
comes to the conclusion that Olivia's inconsistencies are better

served by the details of her surroundings than by her (rather clichéd) thoughts about love and class. Olivia is more present in the descriptions of the ways in which she inhabits indoor spaces than in her musings. The descriptions of rooms come as a relief from the obsessive daydreaming about Rollo and the worries that the sex might be 'sordid' after all:

> The fittings are distinctly casual; queer mattresses, and a stormy, capricious plug, and a rough little bright-green bath in a blistered bathroom so small you soon can't see for steam. Personally, I like it – cosy and secretive – hardly able to see one's own legs. Back to the womb with a vengeance. Anna says if I could sublimate my bath-lust I might become adult. She's sublimated hers all right, if she ever had one. I had that bathroom practically to myself.[16]

Olivia's bath-lust – the temporary obliteration or numbing of the self offered by the steam – similarly becomes a trope in Henry Green's *Party Going* (1939), and in Louis MacNeice's *Autumn Journal* (1938):

> We lie in the bath between tiled walls and under
> Ascending scrolls of steam
> And feel the ego merge as the pores open
>     And we lie in the bath and dream;
> And responsibility dies and the thighs are happy
>     And the body purrs like a cat . . .[17]

Baths are somewhat like cinemas, and indeed often provide the metaphor for describing pleasures offered by the latter. Both of these activities are repeatedly associated with infantilism in the period's fiction, although bathing itself comes under less criticism, perhaps because it has at least the functional use of keeping bodies clean. In MacNeice's version, both cinemas and baths offer a welcome, if only temporary, escapism. Such moments of pure bodily pleasures are welcomed in a work as anxious as *Autumn Journal*, and as merciless in its self-scrutiny; the uncomplicated happiness of bathing is a luxury for the self-conscious poet. Olivia's day-dreaming in baths, however, is tinged with guilt, since she believes her love of physical comfort to be a form of immaturity. Being grown-up would mean being, like Jocelyn, able to forget about one's discomfort, or, like Olivia's sister Kate, who is a mother of two young children, becoming too busy to care. Olivia is neither mother nor artist, and her shame about the break-up of her marriage is as much about her inability to save the relationship, as about the inability to withstand the squalor in which she and Ivor had found themselves:

> Thinking that was the worst of my marriage; not enough money to have privacy, places of one's own; Ivor's clothes and comb and toothbrush mixed up with mine, Ivor lying in bed, bored, watching me dress.[18]

This intolerance of squalor becomes more than simply the material underpinning of marital discord: it hints at a moral attitude of the kind Olivia professes to mistrust. Ultimately, it is the dinners in opulent restaurants and Rollo's impeccable shirts that convince her Rollo is the love of her life. During Rollo's first visit to her room, she thinks 'it must not be sordid', arranging the space as neatly as she can. The obsession with things not being sordid is by far the most convincing motivating desire for everything that happens in the novel; *The Weather in the Streets* is, finally, not about romance, but about various forms of squeamishness.

Squeamishness about social class – that is snobbery – also forms the subject of Rose Macaulay's *Keeping Up Appearances* (1928), a novel about a suburban woman with complicated inter-class parentage who is torn between an intense love for her mother and a sense of shame about her social standing.

Daisy, like so many heroines in London novels from the late 1920s and 1930s, is a journalist. A professional dealer in types, she semi-successfully resists the habits of mind her job imposes upon her throughout the novel. Daisy's ability to remain healthily detached from the artificial taxonomies she has to create for her articles depends upon her continued closeness to her suburban family in East Sheen, and especially to her mother who belongs to 'ordinary people' who 'went about their business, cynical, indifferent, and patiently sceptical'. Daisy's mother is particularly sceptical about Daisy's articles about modern life and modern women – about cocktails, fashion and hairdressing, and 'fast' morals – she 'read what Daisy wrote in the papers, and thought it fine, but all the finer in that it had no relation to real people or real life'.[19]

Daisy is able to write for a paper only via the accident of her birth: she is an illegitimate child of a working-class mother and an upper-class father who, although he never married her mother, ensured that Daisy received a good-quality education in a public school. From this uneasy mixture of suburban dreaming and a more specific cultural aspiration born of having had a taste of a privileged upbringing stem all of Daisy's troubles. Her identity is split in two: as Daisy, she relishes the suburban home life of 'her jolly, common, philistine family' which is described as the only place where she 'could be utterly herself'; as Daphne (the name her father had preferred and by which she is known in London), she has lofty aspirations and falls in love with an upper-class, Oxbridge-educated young man she meets through her father's side of the family. Daisy's move to a bedsit in Great Russell Street in Bloomsbury is an opportunity to reinvent herself as Daphne. The differences between the London bedsit and the suburban family home are not limited to the predictable idiosyncrasies of bohemian house decoration that mark Daphne and her friends from the net-curtained homogeneity of the rest of the building they occupy. There is a conspicuous absence in the London scenes of any voice that is not educated, and indeed all sounds of the city are muffled in order to make way for the conversations between the young bohemians. By contrast, the East Sheen house where Daisy has grown up is filled with music: the sound of the Savoy Havana band played through 'a loudspeaker' which reaches Daisy's bedroom upstairs and her mother's 'crooning' voice.[20] These sounds are part of the aural landscape of the suburban life of which Daisy is both ashamed and which she is unable to renounce. This is another novel about a woman who will not grow up. At thirty, Daisy nearly marries Raymond Foylot, who stands by her after the revelation of Daisy's class background – yet it is Daisy who breaks off the engagement, unable or unwilling to accept that the 'shame' of her lower-middle-class roots is self-imposed. Daisy's radical remedy is to leave Britain altogether; the ending sees her off to America on a liner, full of ambitions to become a writer, and with a new name – Daphne Daisy Simpson.

## Rebels and Escapees

In *Keeping Up Appearances*, central London is the exciting antithesis of the drab suburbia the central character can finally only leave behind by making a transatlantic journey. To characters raised in inner London, however, even the most cosmopolitan areas appear as suffocatingly dull as East Sheen. One of the central characters in Norah Hoult's *Four Women Grow Up* (published in the 1940s, but set in the 1930s), a recent school graduate, Elsie Henderson, listens with a mixture of pity and contempt to her mother's talk of Mr and Mrs Vevey, a booking clerk and his wife who live near Paddington station. The description of their domestic arrangements might as well be of a lower-middle-class suburb:

> Without bothering to reply Elsie thought scornfully of Mr and Mrs Vevey. He took his wife's arm when they went out; she saw them arm in arm in their drab clothes going into their little house in Acacia Avenue, a house with a big pot of palms in the window, shutting out the heat and the dust and life. Mr Vevey spoke of the government, of wars, of turbulations, in the words of the leading article he had read in his morning paper. And Mrs Vevey listened and admired.
> . . . Would she herself ever be old enough, dull enough to covet such drabness![21]

Rebellion against marriage, money and potted plants in net-curtained windows was by no means confined to Orwell's novels – the disdain for petit-bourgeois suburban family life is a recurring motif in the period's fiction. Orwell's solution to this youthful rebelliousness was a pragmatic resignation to what he believed to be the essential dullness of English life, in or out of London. For other writers, only political radicalism could revive their characters' (and often the authors') interest in London; in 1930s fiction, political commitment is often what differentiates central London from the suburbs, and it is one of the few things that still makes London a great metropolis, rather than simply a collection of net-curtained houses. Politics also encourage sexual behaviour that is the opposite of the net-curtained marital bliss that so many 1930s characters find so depressing. Orwell's complaint, in *Aspidistra*, that 'it is never the time or the place' in London for unmarried lovers reads oddly against the many narratives in which sexual unions fuelled by political radicalism blossom without encountering any intervention from nosy landladies or a lack of places to go. In George Buchanan's *Rose Forbes*, the suburban housewife Rose leaves her husband for her intense lover, whom she first encounters at a Communist Party meeting. She comes straight to his flat – where she has already been many times – only to discover that he is there with another woman. And Storm Jameson, in her autobiography, recalled the pleasure of living in the house of 'a pleasant slightly louche young woman' in north-west London.[22] Even Orwell exaggerated when he described the overbearing Mrs Whisbeach in *Aspidistra*; Orwell himself had an easy time with landladies in the mid-1930s. In an entertaining letter to one of his girlfriends, Orwell recounted the conversation between him and his prospective landlady about his needs:

> When I came she asked me what I particularly wanted, & I said, 'The thing I most want is freedom.' So she said, 'Do you mean to have women up here all night?'
> I said, 'No', of course, whereat she said, 'I only meant that I didn't mind whether you do or not.'[23]

The repressive atmosphere of London lodgings was a myth, which served Orwell's fictional version of London in which nothing exists between total squalor and genteel misery.

Hoult's characters find a space between such extremes in acts of sexual rebellion that encounter no obstacles from forbidding landladies – or from their blissfully unaware parents. In *Four Women Grow Up*, Elsie eventually loses her virginity to her boyfriend Julian in a drab hotel close to Paddington – an act prompted as much by defiance as by desire: she and he are 'isolated from the everyday world with its cowardly smug grown-ups who only saw love in terms of marriage . . . who believed that what alone was real was money in the bank'.

Like Storm Jameson's *Mirror in Darkness* trilogy and John Sommerfield's *May Day* (1936), *Four Women Grow Up* is a polyphonic novel showcasing the diversity of urban points of view, but Hoult focuses only on women, and the novel's politics are entirely filtered through their personal lives. As well as the socialist Elsie, we encounter upper-class Joan McComb who works as a journalist for a women's magazine – and who does end up married and suburbanised; Rachel Sweetman, who must somehow reconcile her longing for experiment and adventure with her conservative Jewish roots; and Evelyn Wright – an aspiring writer, the only one out of the four former schoolmates who moves not into, but out of, the suburbs and into a Soho bedsit, fleeing a violent husband.

Evelyn's story is the central one – the character's aspirations, as in so many other novels of the period, channel the writer's own struggle to work through her literary influences before finding an original voice. In this novel, Hoult was searching for a way out of imitating Zola's Naturalist melodramas of Paris on the one hand, and Dickens's London novels on the other. Evelyn, on her way to an independent life, must first learn to live without her husband, which means leaving behind the daily melodrama of arguments, tears, sex and blows, a life described brilliantly as a gradual 'surrender' to 'emotional debauch': [t]he senses knew restraint, could be satiated: the emotions indulged became greedier and greedier, feeding on quarrels, feeding on reconciliations'.[24] When Evelyn finally leaves, she heads to central London, where she meets an impoverished actress Sally who offers her a room in her home. Evelyn initially rejects the room, struck by its messiness, which instantly triggers literary associations:

> It was Charles Dickens; it was Fleet Street, it was Little Nell, it was London slum and all that goes with lack of dress. A little girl about ten with a nose that badly need wiping, wearing a red dress that came far above her skinny and dirty knees, was sitting up to a centre table covered with newspaper . . . The floor was partly disguised by two strips of threadbare carpet. The planks that could be seen looked damp, and there was a smell, that yet was not a clean smell, of soapsuds.[25]

Like Patrick Hamilton's description of Jenny's room in Doughty Street in *The Midnight Bell*, with its 'large double bed, whose sheets were grey' and towels 'several grades greyer than the sheets',[26] this version of the shabby London bedsit explicitly announces its literary origins, although the description itself owes as much to Zola as it does to Dickens; like Bob, Evelyn is looking at a London setting that is unreal despite the visceral disgust provoked by the sights and the smells. It is almost impossible to disentangle these characters' perceptions of the city from their reading of Dickens. But this is what Evelyn must do, if she is to make London home. She only decides to move in with Sally once she is able to mentally transform the Dickensian interior – a picturesque still life in which nothing is out place, despite the mess – into a place where people live, and which can be cleaned up and changed:

> *But* the smells, and the dirt! 'Haven't you two hands, and can't you do a little scrubbing and dusting?' she asked herself angrily . . .
>
> A girl came towards her, and she found herself thinking of Sally; Sally would teach her something; she was gay; she had a sort of wisdom.[27]

The suburban housewife's experiences are transferred to the bedsit rather than discarded altogether – Evelyn's project of becoming an independent woman still involves making a room a home; her ultimate challenge is to reconcile the metropolitan and the suburban in order to make something new. Continuing to write about London requires moving beyond Dickensian and Zolaesque still lives, preventing these literary sources from weighing down her novels with descriptions that have become museum exhibits.

The process of working through the nineteenth-century influences was more complex than a question of, simply, abandoning or 'growing out of' descriptions of interiors per se. The wholesale abandonment of 'atmosphere' Storm Jameson advocated (but never practised) in 'Documents' was in the same spirit as Woolf's earlier calls to discard descriptive excess. For Jameson, one way of engaging with bedsit life that would avoid revisiting Dickensian or Zolaesque versions of the urban was to concentrate on the one material detail of the domestic interior that does not fully belong to it: the window.

## Looking Out

Jameson's novel of Soho, *Here Comes a Candle* (1938), is partly about women's claustrophobia, and the disappointment, rather than exhilaration, of moving to London. In this novel, most trips outside the Soho location of New Moon Yard are brief and merely functional – characters go to work, for medical examinations, to shop, but that is all. Life shrinks to a repetitive shuttling between home and work, in a way that recalls Orwell's *Down and Out in Paris and London*. Orwell described his experience as a Parisian *plongeur* as one where the city 'has shrunk to the hotel, the Metro, a few bistros and . . . bed'.[28] Jameson's characters simply do not have the time to enjoy the metropolis at a leisured pace; even the young and unmarried, working Harriet walks between her Soho room and the advertising firm in Covent Garden where she works without pleasure, hungry and tired, her clothes sticking to her in the heat.

For the female characters in *Here Comes a Candle*, life in London resembles life in a small village that is nightly disrupted by the bizarre spectacle of a crowd of strangers arriving at The Screech Owl nightclub. Watching the revellers right below their

windows crystallises these women's frustrated sense of isolation from metropolitan life. Thus the carpenter's wife Sally Barley observes the stream of arriving couples with a mixture of
envy and contempt:

> She lifted a corner of the blind and watched an elderly man
> in evening dress help two women out of a car in front of the
> door. One of the women slipped her cloak off in the doorway,
> displaying bare shoulders and back.
>     She's as old as I am, Sally Barley thought. Older, probably;
> they look after themselves.[29]

Jameson repeatedly taps into the provincial prejudices that are
preserved in pockets of the metropolis that are neglected and
unprogressive. One of Jameson's aims in *Here Comes a Candle*
seems to have been to debunk the myth of cosmopolitanism's
availability to all, and the free exchange between the street and
the house that this type of urbanism presupposes. The domestic
sphere, in Jameson's fiction, almost automatically stands for
deeply conventional (and anti-urban) thinking and behaviour,
of which the bitter and narrow-minded Sally is an embodiment. Sally's daily life is so far removed from the opportunities offered by cosmopolitan London that she experiences the
city as a hallucination of sorts: 'The noise of cars coming and
going, changing gear, went on outside. It was another world.
Her world was this room, this bed, the man lying drowned in
sleep beside her.'[30] The city enters this room with its noises,
but not in order to establish a porosity between the domestic
space and the city; on the contrary, the demarcations between
inside and outside are emphasised. The man sleeping next to
Sally is her husband, who is a carpenter and whom she married
because 'he charmed the young woman by his tales of what he
was going to do in London at the end of the War'. They end
up in three shabby rooms in Soho – 'she would die of shame if
any of her friends visited her' – and Sally's daily life becomes
permanently steeped in barely controlled anger with a husband
who 'looked like a workman's son'.[31] Their marriage is one
of many in Jameson's fiction where women marry below their

social status or intellectual level, and end up in shabby interiors with windows looking out on to dusty backyards.

The most ruinous aspects of these fictionalised accounts of marital unhappiness, however, have less to do with material hardship than with husbands' constant intrusions into their wives' complex inner lives. Jameson's female protagonists often experience the sensation of having their imagination ridiculed and invaded by male callousness. Harriet's absorption in the nightly activity outside the nightclub is not even registered on a conscious level until her fiancé notices her habit of looking out of the window:

> 'You don't want to look at them,' Randall said.
>
> He watched Harriet with a slight smile. She dropped the curtain across the window and turned to him.
>
> 'A lighted doorway at night, and people going in – I like it.'
>
> 'Why?'
>
> 'I don't know.' She looked at him with a self-conscious smile. She was not always at ease with him ... She wanted him now to feel that her love of lighted doorways at night was interesting. She tried to think of a witty or a poetic explanation, but nothing occurred to her.[32]

This is a point at which communication between them breaks down – because what she is saying is merely descriptive, not 'witty' or 'poetic'. In fact, all of Jameson's semi-autobiographical characters possess the sophisticated ability to distil scenes of ordinary lives into moments of aesthetic absorption, but like the ideal novelist of 'Documents' they cannot, nor do they feel the need to weigh down their observations with moral or critical judgements, or to explain their significance. Such moments of disinterested perception are the best in Jameson's writing – in describing them, she appears to have been able to achieve the detachment and power of 'striking angles' she theorised. Windows frame the city in ways that privilege the fragment and the small-scale urban drama, as opposed to panoramic visions of the 'tumultuous city' in *The Mirror in Darkness*.

Windows also frame characters' reflections in Rhys's work of the 1930s, though in very different ways from Jameson's experiments. For one, there is nothing much that Rhys's characters want to see – rather, they choose to concentrate on the other senses, especially sound and smell, and the indirect ways in which those senses trigger uncomfortable feelings and suppressed memories.

In *After Leaving Mr Mackenzie*, Mr Horsfield stands by the window in Julia Martin's room, having just spent a night with her: 'He looked out. A freshness came up from the garden. It was light enough to see the leaning trees and the bare brown patches of earth trodden by the feet of children playing.'[33] In Rhys's novels, views from, and sounds coming from, windows allow their characters moments of disinterestedness – half-chances to reclaim lost innocence. Such moments of purely sensorial registering of the sounds, smells and sights of the outdoors almost always go hand in hand with the queasy business of living, where one must come into contact with other people. In another, similar scene in *After Leaving Mr Mackenzie*, Julia herself prefers thinking about what is outside the window while she sits by her dying mother's bedside. In this scene, Mr Horsfield is allowed a brief respite from his rather shabby affair with Julia, which is consummated in her bedsit, in a section of the novel subtitled 'It Could Have Been Anywhere'. The room resembles many other rooms Julia has temporarily occupied, in a house that looks exactly like the others in a street where Julia keeps getting lost. And even to Horsfield himself the unknown building appears to be oddly familiar as he goes up the communal stairs:

> They mounted silently, like people in a dream. And as in a dream he knew that the whole house was solid, with huge rooms – dark, square rooms, crammed with unwieldy furniture covered with chintz; darkish curtains would hang over the long windows. He knew even the look of the street outside when the curtains were drawn apart – a grey street, with high, dark houses opposite.[34]

This is one of the oppressive English interiors that Rhys's female characters detest, but it hardly oppresses Horsfield. On the contrary, this dark English house in a grey London street appears to him ephemeral and unreal. This section of the novel exceeds the requirements of a tawdry tale of sex in a shabby room – it is clear that Rhys saw such encounters as emblematic of a fundamental problem with the English version of urban life. However, rather than merely attacking English hypocrisy – something which she tended to represent as boringly didactic[35] – Rhys's early novels explore her characters' sense of performing mechanical routines as though they were in a dream, seemingly without the ability to do anything else. Julia's fatalistic 'sometimes one just has to do things' also holds true for her lover who visits her, talks to and sleeps with her, all as though he were an automaton performing an expected set of actions. And yet the dream-like setting of Julia's lodgings is also a place of reckoning for Horsfield, where his life itself is revealed to be meaningless, like an empty dream – this is where things put on, for his benefit, their 'true – surrealist – face', to borrow Walter Benjamin's much-quoted phrase.[36] Leaving Julia's lodgings, Horsfield has several unsettling encounters. Coming down the same stairs he had ascended the night before, 'in the dimness of the hall a white face glimmered at him. He stared, and braced himself for an encounter. Then, relieved, he saw it was a bust of the Duke of Wellington.' On the surface this is a comical encounter, a consequence of Horsfield's fear of being caught by a stern landlady. But it leads to involuntary, only partially understood, realisations. Outside, passing a policeman, Horsfield exclaims, despite himself, '"This is grotesque" . . . He did not know whether he meant the policeman, or his excess of caution, or the Duke of Wellington, or the night he had just spent.'[37] Kenneth Burke wrote that the grotesque signals 'the perception of discordances . . . without smile of laughter';[38] Horsfield's exclamation in the dark reads like an involuntary admission of the deep discordances that define his life.

The figures Horsfield meets guard, as it were, the deep secret of his life, a life in which dummies have replaced people and emotion. Lying next to Julia in her room, he touches her hair – 'it was incredibly soft, like the feathers of a bird, and touching it gave him extraordinary pleasure', but the sensation simultaneously makes 'something sensitive in him . . . puzzled and vaguely unhappy'.[39] Nothing obvious is ever suggested about this man – he is not quite a cad, like Julia's ex-husband, or indeed most men in Rhys's fiction, nor is he a desensitised urban type whose only thoughts are about respectability and money, like Julia's uncle Griffith. The relentless hatred of London for which Rhys is known here gives way to a subtler reading of the city. The nocturnal London in *After Leaving Mr Mackenzie* is a city which, in Sanford Sternlicht's words, 'gargoyles roam'.[40] Characters who are awake in this dark London are bound to have encounters that remind them, above all other things, of the tragic elements in their lives.

In the nocturnal setting of the dark lodging-house room, Horsfield's thoughts take unfamiliar shapes. Lying in bed with Julia, he thinks 'all manner of things, disconnectedly and discontentedly', and indeed his unexpected warmth towards Julia seems like an out-of-body experience, disconnected from himself, and quickly forgotten. In this section of the novel, Rhys approaches closer than ever a Surrealist aesthetic that is seemingly at odds with the Naturalistic content of the novel. Julia's shabby lodging house ought to be a setting for a tale of unromantic sex and inevitable deception, but instead it accommodates encounters of a more complex kind. In fact, the sordidness of the surroundings becomes a necessary component in the construction of the dreamscapes that the characters inhabit. The dubiousness of Rhys's interiors enables them to become gateways into the deep reserves of her characters' minds. Perhaps the best description of the permeability of such places was provided by Louis Aragon in his Surrealist meditation on urban experience in *Paris Peasant* (1926):

The whole fauna of human fantasies, their marine vegetation, drifts and luxuriates in the dimly lit zones of human activity, as though plaiting thick tresses in darkness. Here, too, appear the great lighthouses of the mind, with their outward resemblance to less pure symbols. The gateway to mystery swings open at the touch of human weakness and we have entered the realm of darkness. One false step, one slurred syllable together reveals a man's thoughts. The disquieting atmosphere of places contains similar locks that cannot be bolted fast against infinity. Wherever the living pursue particularly ambiguous activities, the inanimate may sometimes assume the reflection of their most secret motives: and thus our cities are peopled with unrecognised sphinxes which will never stop the passing dreamer and ask him mortal questions unless he first projects his meditation, his absence of mind, towards them.[41]

Aragon makes 'human weakness' central to revelatory or mystical experiences; vulnerability and error are the keys to the aquatic dream-zone where human secrets are on display. Rhys's novel shares with Aragon's probing of the city this belief in the centrality of human frailty – the false step or slip-up – but Rhys's interpretation of her characters' encounters with the mysterious is unrelentingly pessimistic. To Mr Horsfield, Julia's lodging house is yet another place of illicit sexual encounter, exactly like the many others he has undoubtedly visited. And yet the illusory solidity of this house conceals much more than clandestine sex; it becomes a 'dim zone' of the city where, similarly to *Paris Peasant*, the characters' hidden inner lives are involuntarily exposed. In Julia's room, Horsfield confronts the empty core of his own life. It is a life in which all that is hollow and false – his financial security of which the expensive flat is a manifestation; his 'business like' affairs with women – takes priority over everything that is genuine, like his tender feeling for Julia and his memory of war trauma. Greg Dart has written that 'the Surrealists hoped that a liberation of the unconscious would help post-war Europe out of its contemporary *impasse*', via a 'total immersion in the psychopathology of urban life'.[42] In order to awake from the nightmare of bourgeois life, one must enter another, more profound, dream.

Rhys's novels feature a mirror-like reversal of values where genuine emotion is assigned the status of irrational dream, of temporary 'insanity',[43] while the ruthless 'business instinct' of self-preservation which allows people to make decisions that have a terrible effect on others, assumes the role of lucidity and sensibility. The casual cruelty with which people treat each other is sanctioned by their strangely unreal perceptions of reality. Julia visits first her wealthy uncle, and then an even wealthier ex-lover, Mr James, who professes to be her 'friend for life'; for both, she is a slightly unreal figure. To Mr James, she is a 'tactless' 'resurrection of the past', and her troubles are an inconvenient draught from the outside world by which he does not wish to be 'harrowed'. Like most men in this novel, he is happy only to talk about himself and his home, and his painting. In a poignant closure of the scene, Mr James accompanies Julia to the front door, and she experiences 'a lump in her throat – she had hoped that he would say something or look something that would make her feel less lonely'. Rhys once more translates her characters' emotional turmoil into acts of intense looking. In order not to cry, Julia fixes her gaze on a vase of tulips in the hallway – 'some thrust their heads forward like snakes, and some were very erect, stiff, virginal, rather prim. Some were dying, with curved grace in their death.'[44] As elsewhere in her fiction, drooping flowers symbolise women's lives, but in this novel, it seems, men are, too, implied in this image. Their emotional stiffness, a kind of sterility, is caused at least in part by the recent trauma of the Great War. Mr James briefly mentions it to Julia, casually referring to the many 'mad' friends he has now. And Mr Horsfield is irritated when Julia suggests that he does not know what she means by saying that people 'crack up' – 'perhaps I know something about cracking up too. I went through the war, you know'.[45]

The impasse of Rhys's characters' lives is at least partly caused by the effects of the war, and, although the men in her novels have no crippling wounds to show, as they do in Jameson's, there is a sense in which they 'cracked up' long before they met her female characters. And it is in the lodging house that the humourless incongruity of material solidity preserved from the pre-war years and the surreal, immaterial quality of present-day life becomes apparent. The dark, sleeping houses of London, with their unwieldy furniture that has seen generations of lodgers, accommodate Mr Horsfield's increasing sensation that 'everything solid melts into air'. Marshall Berman, in his book-length meditation on Marx's statement, wrote that 'every table and chair in a bourgeois interior resembled a monument', but 'everything that bourgeois society builds is built to be torn down'.[46] Mr Horsfield, upon entering the familiar territory of a stuffy London interior which he seems to know without having seen, experiences a further paradox: he is surrounded by interiors crammed with *things* that were built to last, but have come to symbolise a phantom life. For Rhys's women, the rooms were never solid – their lives had been just as transitory and uncertain before the war as they are after. It is the men who increasingly retreat into interiors that wrap them in an illusion of solidity.

Women like Julia always leave London in the end, for places where they do not have to live within oppressive and squalid imitations of the solid life. In *Good Morning, Midnight*, Paris is the alternative, a city where rooms are airier, and where the privations Sasha Jansen suffers are somehow borne more easily, without a sense of shame. Paris is referred to affectionately, as a lover: 'my beautiful, my darling, and oh what a bitch you can be! But you didn't kill me after all, did you?'[47]

Moving back to Paris is an almost automatic choice for the Rhys woman, in the same way that a move to the suburbs is for Hoult's characters, or even Storm Jameson's. When Hervey Russell gets fed up with her bedsit life in *Company Parade*, she moves out to a suburban home and fills it with antique furniture. This is never an option for Rhys's characters who, above everything else, cannot hold down a job, and would not stand even a day of the suburban commute (it is somehow impossible to imagine any of Rhys's characters strap-hanging on their way into the office). The bohemian model of metropolitan living they adopt depends on the spatial milieus of leisure – the café, the bar and the bedsit – rather than the garden, the kitchen and the train.

The intense and bitter disappointment with London that defines Rhys's work seems to result partly from a fundamental expectation about city life that is not, cannot be met in London, although it can be, tentatively, in Paris. Rhys's women attempt to navigate London as though it were a metropolitan city, but even 'urban' London is, in fact, deeply suburban, its typical home 'the semi-detached or terraced suburban house'.[48] Rhys's heroines provide a pertinent counterpoint to the many character in 1930s fiction who, even as they profess to hold radical social and political views and bohemian aspirations, ultimately navigate central London as though it was another suburb, just one that is sympathetic towards single rather than family life. Andrew Thacker has observed that 'the typical Rhys heroine never really occupies anywhere, never "dwells"'.[49] But the truth is that she does not really want to 'dwell'. All the cravings in her fiction for rooms – 'A nice room . . . A beautiful room with bath'[50] – do not amount to a desire to belong. London is presented in Rhys's fiction as a city that will not give her shelter or comfort, mocking her lack of money; but, on the other hand, what it does have her heroines do not want: the pleasures of this city have almost everything to do with structured routines – with the tapping of tired feet to radio tunes, as in Macaulay's *Keeping Up Appearances*. Rhys's women are the only ones to resist this tamed way of being to the bitter end. Olivia in Lehmann's *The Weather in the Streets* can righteously think of the 'us' in bedsits and the 'them' in country mansions, but the novel's anger is really about not being fully accepted by 'them'. Rhys's women, by contrast, have nothing to lose, status-wise, and they seek the metropolis proper, with a spatial culture uncompromised by unholy alliances between city and suburb.

It simply would not occur to a Rhysian heroine to live in the outer suburbs; the women in her novels are depressed enough in Notting Hill and Camden – as far from Bloomsbury and Mayfair as they will stray. The omission of the outer suburbs from Rhys's work is a significant one; the idea that London still equated the West End was increasingly a fantasy; by the late 1930s London had become a city where the suburbs increasingly held their own. In a sense, Rhys was a writer with pre-1918 sensibilities who wrote during the 1930s, and she stopped writing about London altogether after 1938. Her affinities were with Zola, Colette and perhaps even Dorothy Richardson, rather than with the writers who came of age during the 1930s and carried on writing during the 1940s and beyond. For that type of continuity one has to look to writing that made the most of London as a suburban city. Stevie Smith is exemplary of this tendency to embrace the suburbs in mid-century writing (a term one struggles to apply with confidence to Rhys). Her darkly comical and acerbic poems about the suburbs combine a disdain for the social conformity they foster with a relish of the privacy and opportunities for meditation they offer; the suburb is both dreary and a setting in which desire or melancholy pleasure may blossom unexpectedly. In 'Freddy' (1937), Smith's sardonic narrator complains that she doesn't 'care much for his meelyoo', 'the ha-ha suburban scene' to which her lover belongs. At the same time, she desires this suburban young man – 'there was never a boy like Freddy / For a haystack's ivory tower of bliss'.[51]

Smith made a clear distinction between the inner and the outer suburbs – in her 1949 essay 'A London Suburb', the inner suburbs are defined as belonging to London proper, or 'captured' by it;[52] instead, she outlines a preference for the outer sprawl of London, the self-contained replicas of cities with their own pubs, cinemas and complex social scenes. Even if these places are sometimes 'intolerable', Smith prefers writing about them to describing metropolitan London. In Louis MacNeice's *Autumn Journal*, there is a similar sense in which one must now go to the outer suburbs to observe London:

Surbiton, and a woman gets in, painted
   With dyed hair but a ladder in her stockings and eyes
Patient beneath the calculated lashes,
   Inured for ever to surprise;
And the train's rhythm becomes the ad nauseam repetition
   Of every tired aubade and maudlin madrigal,
The faded airs of sexual attraction
   Wandering like dead leaves along a warehouse wall . . .[53]

Here the familiar tale of sexual weariness and socio-economic discomfort has moved out of central London; paradoxically, MacNeice is able to see this familiar image of urban weariness – the woman with a ladder in her stocking – in a fresh way, his vision framed by the suburban train carriage. MacNeice's is an example of a 1930s text that manages to make this scene of weariness exciting, even sensual. This is a not so much a commentary on suburban alienation, as a demonstration of the writer's precise attentiveness.

## Notes

1. On twentieth-century suburban fictions, see Kristin Bluemel, *George Orwell and the Radical Eccentrics: Intermodernism in Literary London* (New York: Palgrave Macmillan, 2004); Faye Hammill, 'Stella Gibbons, Ex-centricity and the Suburb', in *Intermodernism: Literary Culture in Mid-Twentieth-Century Britain*, ed. Kristin Bluemel (Edinburgh: Edinburgh University Press, 2009), pp. 75–92; Todd Kuchta, *Semi-detached Empire: Suburbia and the Colonization of Britain, 1880 to the Present* (Charlottesville: University of Virginia Press, 2010); Judy Giles, *The Parlour and the Suburb: Domestic Identities, Class, Femininity and Modernity* (Oxford: Berg, 2004).
2. George Moore, *Confessions of a Young Man* (London: William Heinemann, 1937), p. 143.
3. Mary Hepworth Dixon, *The Story of a Modern Woman* (London: Merlin Press, 1990), p. 85.
4. Dorothy Richardson, 'The Tunnel', in *Pilgrimage*, vol. 2 (London: Dent, 1938), p. 17.

5.  Jean Rhys, *Voyage in the Dark* (London: Vintage, 2000), p. 41.
6.  Rhys, *Voyage*, pp. 8, 16.
7.  Franco Moretti, *The Way of the World: The* Bildungsroman *in European Culture* (London: Verso, 1989), p. 204.
8.  Andre Breton, *Manifesto of Surrealism*, trans. Richard Seaver (Ann Arbor: The University of Michigan Press, 1969), pp. 7–8.
9.  Virginia Woolf, *Mr Bennett and Mrs Brown* (London: Hogarth Press, 1924), p. 15.
10. Woolf, 'Mr Bennett and Mrs Brown', p. 16.
11. Woolf, 'Mr Bennett and Mrs Brown', p. 4.
12. Woolf, *Mrs Dalloway* (London: Vintage, 2004), p. 24.
13. Rosamond Lehmann, *The Weather in the Streets* (London: Virago, 2006), p. 206.
14. Lehmann, *The Weather in the Streets*, p. 174.
15. Lehmann, *The Weather in the Streets*, pp. 189–90.
16. Lehmann, The *Weather in the Streets*, pp. 203–4.
17. MacNeice, *Autumn Journal*, pp. 134–5.
18. Lehmann, *The Weather in the Streets*, p. 147.
19. Rose Macaulay, *Keeping Up Appearances* (London: Collins, 1928), p. 28.
20. Macaulay, *Keeping Up Appearances*, p. 64.
21. Norah Hoult, *Four Women Grow Up* (London: William Heinemann, 1940), pp. 40–1.
22. Jameson, *Journey from the North* (London: Collins & Harvill, 1969), vol. 1, p. 30.
23. George Orwell, Letter to Brenda Salkield, in *The Complete Works of George Orwell*, ed. Peter Davison (London: Secker & Warburg, 1998), vol. 10, p. 374.
24. Hoult, *Four Women*, p. 187.
25. Hoult, *Four Women*, p. 201.
26. Hamilton, *The Midnight Bell*, in *Twenty Thousand Streets under the Sky* (London: Vintage, 2001), p. 170.
27. Hoult, *Four Women*, pp. 206–7.
28. Orwell, *Down and Out in Paris and London*, p. 95.
29. Storm Jameson, *Here Comes a Candle* (London: Cassell, 1938), p. 115.
30. Jameson, *Candle*, p. 116.

31. Jameson, *Candle*, pp. 27, 28.
32. Jameson, *Candle*, p. 117.
33. Jean Rhys, *After Leaving Mr Mackenzie* (London: Penguin, 2000), p. 112.
34. Rhys, *After Leaving*, p. 109.
35. For instance, Marya Zelli listens to Miss De Solla's denouncement of 'English people', delivered 'in a dogmatic voice', in *Quartet* (London: Penguin, 2000), p. 9.
36. Walter Benjamin, 'On the Theory of Knowledge, Theory of Progress', in *The Arcades Project*, trans. Howard Eiland and Kevin McLaughlin (Cambridge, MA: The Belknap Press, 1999), p. 464.
37. Rhys, *After Leaving*, p. 113.
38. Kenneth Burke, *Permanence and Change: An Anatomy of Purpose* (New York: New Republic, 1935), pp. 145–6.
39. Rhys, *After Leaving*, p. 110.
40. Sanford V. Sternlicht, *Jean Rhys* (New York: Prentice Hall, 1997), p. 46.
41. Louis Aragon, 'Passage de l'Opéra', in *Paris Peasant*, trans. Simon Watson Taylor (Boston: Exact Change, 1994), p. 13.
42. Greg Dart, 'Daydreaming', in *Restless Cities*, ed. Matthew Beaumont (London: Verso, 2010), p. 88.
43. Rhys, *After Leaving*, p. 19.
44. Rhys, *After Leaving*, pp. 79, 82, 84.
45. Rhys, *After Leaving*, p. 111. Janet Montefiore has written that 'to read at all deeply in the literature of the interwar years is to realize that collective and individual memories of the First World War continued to be important, living issues in politics and literature right up to 1939 and beyond' (*Men and Women Writers of the 1930s: The Dangerous Flood of History* (London: Routledge, 1996), p. 120).
46. Mashall Berman, *All That Is Solid Melts into Air: The Experience of Modernity* (New York: Penguin, 1988), p. 99.
47. Rhys, *Good Morning*, p. 15.
48. Matthew Taunton, *Fictions of the City: Class, Culture and Mass Housing in London and Paris* (London: Palgrave Macmillan, 2009), p. 49.
49. Andrew Thacker, *Moving through Modernity* (Manchester: Manchester University Press, 2003), p. 193.

50. Rhys, *Good Morning, Midnight*, p. 29.
51. Stevie Smith, 'Freddie', in *The Collected Poems of Stevie Smith* (Harmondsworth: Penguin, 1985), p. 65.
52. Stevie Smith, 'A London Suburb', in *Me Again: Uncollected Writings of Stevie Smith* (London: Virago, 1981), p. 103.
53. MacNeice, 'Autumn Journal', in *Collected Poems, 1925–1948* (London: Faber & Faber, 1949), p. 103.

# Conclusion

Writing about 1930s writers he referred to as 'the stark realists', V. S. Pritchett commented on what he believed to be the habitual and unwelcome intrusion of sentimentality into modern novels:

> If only the hard-headed were not so soft-hearted, if only the new story camera man could resist self-improvement under the guise of a little tinkering in the evening with colour photography – those sugared almond pinks, those cachou mauves! But then stark realists are all the same. They give you two hundred pages of their best, and then slip in 50 pages of their worst because some reviewer has warned them not to forget 'humanity'.[1]

The confidence with which Pritchett wields the multiple photographic metaphors used to describe both the strengths and the flaws of modern fiction suggests an intimacy between the two modes – even if only in terms of goals rather than technique – that was ubiquitous and would have been immediately understood by his readers. The equation of the novelist to 'the new story camera man' is striking, but by the mid-1930s there was nothing unusual about such a comparison; it was commonly assumed that what modern novelists were producing, especially when they were writing about cities, was equivalent to modern photography. The aim of the present book has been to elucidate what this proximity between fiction and photography meant in practice, beyond the generalised comparisons. On the one hand, if 'photography' is mainly a metaphor for a literary mode, then what kind of a literary lineage can be said to have influenced it? And on the other, what were the affinities between the two art forms, and, crucially, what kind of photography can the period's urban fiction be said to have resembled or imitated?

The equation between the photographic and the effortlessly (or lazily, depending on a critic's perspective) mimetic has a long history, going back to nineteenth-century fiction and the considerable hostility towards the instantaneous reproducibility of the real that greeted the emergence of photography.[2] In this sense, comparisons between 'the stark realists' and camera men were meant as straightforward gestures of disapproval; as John Taylor points out, '[a] relative innocence in the 1930s about the conditions of mediation and the currency of imagery meant that both film and photography were still believed to be the source of raw, unmediated sights'.[3] References to 'photographic' fiction in the period's literary reviews exhibit this innocence, but they also unwittingly point to a much more complex relationship between the fictional and the photographic, and towards representations in both literary and photographic forms that were increasingly aware of the fact that photography is much more than uncomplicated realism, and of the increasing overlapping in concerns and subject matter between photography and fiction. The fact that both 1930s novelists and photographers were frequently drawn to urban, lower-middle-class milieus is directly related to the fascination of the 'stark realists' with the possibilities offered by anti-realist, highly stylised and even Surrealist modes. Such modes hardly required a complete abandonment of everyday settings or conventional narrative structures; tripping into the fantastical, the surreal or the compulsively aesthetic was easily achievable within such narratives, if they allowed for moments of discomfort, anxiety or intense frustration. The lower-middle-class Londoners' irresolvable insecurities, to do with the city's social hierarchies, small income, and perennially unfulfilled dreams and desires, provided the ideal gateway into such experimentation with non- or anti-realist points of view.

Photography itself was not the model for the 1930s London novel, but photography shared thematic and aesthetic concerns with a cluster of representational modes that did give the impetus to the surge of interest in lower-middle-class urban lives during the 1930s. Naturalism, especially its French strand, inspired many urban writers of the 1930s; choosing to write about the seedy spaces and inhabitants of Soho and the West End meant, to a large extent, choosing to write like Zola, though opting to focus on the petite bourgeoisie rather than the milieus of the *Lumpenproletariat* more typical of Naturalist fiction meant that it was still possible to spare one's characters the relentlessly grim fates that awaited Zola's Parisians.

Naturalism was not a merely less forgiving realism, which has been pointed out by several scholars who have emphasised the Symbolist, Impressionist and Surrealist aspects of Zola's work in recent decades. Zola's interest in photography, which peaked later in his life, suggests that he was hardly naive to possibilities photography offered for modifying and expanding reality: 'In my opinion, you cannot say you have thoroughly seen anything until you have a photograph of it, revealing a lot of points which otherwise would be unnoticed, and which in most cases could not be distinguished.'4 This is quite a departure from Zola's earlier confident claim, in 'Le Roman experimental', that the novelist 'ought to be the photographer of phenomena', though perhaps the photograph could accommodate both the impulse to record reality objectively and the unexpected effects that can de-familiarise reality. This was the kind of duality of purpose that, I would argue, informed 1930s urban fiction: novels that began as sociological investigations often strayed into modes that investigated states and experiences irrelevant to the requirements of lucid reportage. And the kind of urban photograph to which such unexpected alterations of course were analogous – and which has a deeper, longer affinity with literary versions of the city – is not straightforwardly documentary.

The photographers whose work this book has examined alongside London writing pushed their explorations of London milieus beyond the search for stark evidence of social divisions to which documentary photography was committed. Sometimes the same photographer could take different approaches, a flexibility exemplified by Brandt, who tried on, as it were, both the documentary mode, with his 'side by side' images of East End poverty and West End wealth, and the subtler mode of street photography, in which he toyed with the possibilities of staging and social ambiguity. Some of his best photographs were, in fact, of family members posing as Londoners whose class status it is almost impossible to identify.

It is difficult to overstate the importance of *Picture Post* in the growth in popularity of such photographs in 1930s Britain, and this periodical ensured the continued flourishing of the urban photograph well into the 1950s. Photographers such as Thurston Hopkins, Grace Robertson and Bert Hardy built their careers on the work commissioned by *Picture Post* from the late 1940s onwards. They are both often referred to as photojournalists, and some of their photo-essays did use photographs simply as building blocks of self-contained narratives, most notably Robertson's controversial photographic account of a woman giving birth. The photographs there were mainly of interest for the shocking novelty of the previously neglected subject matter. Others are more difficult to classify as journalistic or documentary, because what they are documenting does not fit in the easily demarcated socio-cultural categories essential to documentary work. For unambiguous versions of such categories, one may look to the numerous West End/East End comparisons that really were social commentaries on the English class divisions, by Brandt, Edith Tudor-Hart or Robert Frank.

Robertson's 1948 photograph of a mannequin in Regent Street (Fig. 5.1), for example, is hardly a documentary image. It is not a commentary on the rise of consumer culture in post-war Britain, as one would expect from the work of a documentary photographer or photojournalist. Rather, its luminous intensity seems to express a fascination with how preternaturally realistic this mannequin is; like its literary counterparts in Rhys's fiction of the late 1930s, the mannequin seems more real than the West End passers-by. But it is also – like the heroines in novels by Rhys and other authors discussed in this book – a pensive figure; Robertson's framing, combined with the way that the shop window's lights fall on the mannequin's face, and the pose

Figure 5.1  Grace Robertson, 'Christmas on Regent Street, 1949'.

– almost a stoop – make for a scene that radiates melancholy. What is so fascinating about 'her', after all, is that she is all too like the many women walking past her on the other side of the glass. The photograph was taken in the late 1940s, but it could have been taken at any point between the mid-1920 and the late 1950s. I would argue that what makes it of this wider period, rather than of the 1940s alone, is the way in which the mood it projects is inseparable from the urban *mise en scène*.

Gill Plain has suggested that '[f]or understanding the shaping forces of culture in the mid-century, 1933–45, for example, might be seen to form a more coherent period, or 1939–56'.[5] The continuity of photographic subject matter, at least, supports this possibility for expanding the temporal frame of 'the 1930s'. Literature, too, continued to explore the aesthetic potentialities of London milieus well into the 1940s. Patrick Hamilton put a Claridge's Hotel bathroom to spectacular use at the end of *The Slaves of Solitude* (1947). Miss Roach escapes her dreary life in a boarding house in a small Thames-side town called Thames Lockdon, by unexpectedly coming into a small fortune – a benign plot twist denied to Ella in *Twenty Thousand Streets*. Miss Roach's long bathing session has a direct continuity with numerous scenes in 1930s novels; the dazzling interiors of interwar London still have the power to synthesise a peculiar mode of dreaminess with the full awareness of the outside world's harshness: 'As she went into the bathroom, and tried to find out how to work all its wonderful gadgets . . . it struck her that it would be funny if the sirens suddenly went and the blitz came back to London the night she returned to it.'[6] The glamour and the tension are inseparable; indeed, the setting only amplifies the anxiety. This was also the case in Elizabeth Bowen's novel of wartime London, *The Heat of the Day* (1948), in which two young working-class Londoners, Louie and Connie, have a tense exchange in the bathroom of a West End café. The two women are friends and temporary flatmates, and now Louie is pregnant – by a man who is not her conscript husband:

> Louie flinched at once. She set and unset her lips; she held on to the edge of the marble slab – meaninglessly, unless this were for support. Between her reflection, and Connie's, and Connie's actual face, no one of them longer to be confronted, she simply physically did not seem to know which way to turn. 'Don't you be angry: you're the first I've told! . . .'[7]

This scene is one of the last in mid-twentieth-century London fiction to use a character's milieu to such an intense effect. The priorities of the London novel shifted in the 1950s; the potential of city spaces is of less interest than the reinventions of voice available to the young – the first teenagers of Colin MacInnes's *Absolute Beginners* and *City of Spades*. In many ways, MacInnes's Absolute Beginner inhabits the same city as that portrayed in fiction of the 1930s; he drinks coffee in the same Soho coffee bars and walk streets that have hardly changed much since he was born 'one night during the Blitz'; but, crucially, it is the idea of this continuity that depresses him and that he vehemently rejects; this observer consciously and assiduously edits out the London of his parents – the 1930s appear to him almost as remote in this novel as the Victorian era. London is reassembled to become a city that someone like this teenager will want to inhabit – a city he chooses to share with African and Caribbean immigrants rather than with his dysfunctional family. They are the people who are the future and transform a London that is otherwise bankrupt, a place that makes MacInnes's character howl with despair: 'My God, my Lord, how horrible this country is.'[8] And although this young man is a photographer, and he mingles in many of the spaces familiar from the fiction and photography of the 1930s and 1940s, his camera work is directed at people who, like himself, are trying to reinvent these settings. The photographic here functions not as a vehicle for detailed description, but as a way into the many extended dialogues during which MacInnes's characters describe and explain themselves.

Nineteen-thirties London writing did form continuities both with earlier urban writing and the versions of London that continued to revisit the spaces examined in this book throughout the 1940s and 1950s. But the decade did produce an extraordinary flowering of London fiction that traced an intense mode of sensory engagement with the city that was available almost exclusively to characters whose life in the city was defined by insecurity, rootlessness, and continuous physical and emotional strain. This type of character, caught between daydreams of glamour and the monotonous reality of reduced (though not quite desperate) circumstances, is replaced by other representative urban types. Her peculiar expressions of anxiety through compulsive visual framing of urban life are superseded by other forms of anxiety. The end of the 1930s marks an end not to writers' interest in London spaces, but to the practice of externalising lower-middle-class nervousness and making it legible in the configurations of the city's spaces. There are exceptions to this trend – Elizabeth Bowen the most prominent among them, though one could also consider Inez Holden's experimental wartime narratives *Night Shift* (1941) and *There's No Story There* (1944). Generally, however, settings in London fiction after the 1930s tend to reassume their position as the backdrop or *context* to the perennial negotiations of class and gender, and the emerging ones of nationality and race.

What made London fiction of the 1930s distinct was, broadly speaking, an interest in, and sometimes a feeling of solidarity with, a way of living in the city to which a sense of belonging was antithetical, and in which what replaced it was what might be best described as a state of tense alertness. The chapters of this book have traced a way of inhabiting London spaces that cannot be summarised simply as pleasure; rather, the subject of its discussions has been a combination of a bitter awareness of marginality and a stubborn attentiveness to the dense networks of gestures, material details and spatial arrangements that contributed to London's atmosphere of vexed restlessness during the decade.

## Notes

1. V. S. Pritchett, in *New Statesman*, 24 June 1933, p. 850.
2. On nineteenth-century responses to photography and realism, see Nancy Armstrong, *Fiction in The Age of Photography: The Legacy of British Realism* (Cambridge, MA: Harvard University Press, 1999).
3. John Taylor, *A Dream of England: Landscape, Photography and the Tourist's Imagination* (Manchester: Manchester University Press, 1994), p. 156.
4. Emile Zola, quote in Leo Braudy, *Native Informant: Essays on Film, Fiction, and Popular Culture* (New York: Oxford University Press, 1991), p. 98.
5. Gill Plain, 'Introduction', in *Literature of the 1940s: War, Postwar and 'Peace'* (Edinburgh: Edinburgh University Press, 2013), pp. 1–2.
6. Patrick Hamilton, *The Slaves of Solitude* (London: Constable, 2006), pp. 325–6.
7. Elizabeth Bowen, *The Heat of the Day* (London: Vintage, 1998), p. 324.
8. Colin MacInnes, *Absolute Beginners* (London: Macgibbon & Kee, 1959), p. 31.

# Index